One
Nation
Under
Which God?

Serious Questions For The Serious Christian

RL Wentling

authorHOUSE®

AuthorHouse™
1663 Liberty Drive
Bloomington, IN 47403
www.authorhouse.com
Phone: 1-800-839-8640

First published by AuthorHouse   07/09/2011

ISBN: 978-1-4634-2590-6 (sc)
ISBN: 978-1-4634-2589-0 (ebk)

Library of Congress Control Number: 2011911094

Printed in the United States of America

Any people depicted in stock imagery provided by Thinkstock are models, and such images are being used for illustrative purposes only.
Certain stock imagery © Thinkstock.

This book is printed on acid-free paper.

*Dedicated
to those
blessed with
a love of the
Truth.
May
Almighty God
add wisdom and
understanding to that love.*

Preface

n Matthew 10:24 Christ says, "'*Do not think that I came to bring peace on earth. I did not come to bring peace but a sword.*'" Sometimes I get the feeling that the Lord gave me a "stick" with instructions to insert it into the nearest hornets' nest and stir vigorously. I've done my best. Although controversy per se was not my intention, it also proved unavoidable. What I really intend to do is to rouse the reader from a comfortable and potentially deadly complacency, but in order to do that it has proven necessary to seriously challenge some of Western Civilization's most cherished ideals both ecclesiastical and political. As we'll see, the two concepts have much more in common than most of us realize. Hence, this work's title.

A good many years ago, a roommate labeled himself a "social Christian." I didn't pay much attention at the time, but that phrase stuck in the back of my head. Only now, many years later, have I come to realize the importance of what those two simple words convey. We may *profess* Christianity, and may seem Christian to each other, but we could also apply a variation on that description to the Pharisees, well known for their hypocrisy. We must seriously ask ourselves a far more difficult question: *are we Christian?* To that we can readily add another question: just what does that mean? Hence, this work's sub-title. Although it poses many questions, it essentially means to address two: What do we believe, and why do we believe it? We could re-phrase the latter question as, "Who says so?" That too is a more important question than most of us acknowledge. In our quest for social acceptability and political correctness, we have long since forgotten that "God" is not a name but a title, and is therefore an imprecise means of identification. We have likewise forgotten that another spiritual entity—a "higher power" if you will—also covets that title. Even more importantly, we've forgotten that, in spite of the self-evident plethora of options, we actually have but two—and a great many of us have made the wrong choice. Far from the depictions we commonly see in art and film, that other power guises himself as an *angel of light,* and his primary weapon is deception. Seeing is believing, defined as physical perception and our most universally accepted criterion for truth, will not penetrate those deceptions. Thus, the time has come for us to employ a more appropriate form of perception in order to make sure our relationship to the divine.

You will soon notice that we use the first person plural—the "we" form—with very rare exceptions throughout this work. There are two reasons for that. Firstly, I use it to imply that I in no way intend or attempt to put myself above anyone else in what is described in the coming pages. Trust me, I'm a sinner, and can make absolutely no claim otherwise. Neither can I claim to know the "Gospel truth" of Christ's religion, and have no desire to set anyone straight on their theology. I intend this not as a book of answers, but as a book of *questions.* I neither want nor expect anyone to accept the proposed answers at face value, and I certainly don't want anyone to follow me just because my name is attached to a smart-sounding book. What I really want to do is to motivate the readers to seek the Truth for themselves, for that is what Christ means for us to do. I've done that most of my life, and have been blessed by it in a very specific way. Although I've since learned that many refer to it as the "discerning spirit," for years I referred to it as a "spiritual filter." Whatever the label, it comes down to an automatic tendency to see things in their spiritual context. I must emphasize that *I can take no credit for it.* That does, however, help to explain the more important reason for using the third person.

One may legitimately ask what qualifies a guy like me to question some of history's greatest theological, political, and philosophical minds. Where do I get the gall to contradict some of Western society's most cherished and long-held truisms? How can I expect anyone to take seriously my challenges to the accumulated ecclesiastical wisdom of nearly two millennia? I am not a priest or a minister; I don't even have a college degree. So how can I consider myself qualified to write this? Some years ago a long forgotten pundit observed, *"God doesn't choose the equipped, He equips the chosen."* Never has that proven more true than in my case. I believe that I have been guided by the Holy Spirit of God Almighty throughout the writing of this manuscript and, for reasons which the manuscript will make clear, would not have published it had I even a serious doubt to the contrary.

To understand that, perhaps a brief history of this work's evolution might be in order. I'd pretty much always known that I wanted to be a writer, and made a conscious decision to that end at the age of eighteen. Only four years earlier I had seriously considered the Lutheran ministry, and yet by the time I graduated high school I had left the Church entirely. Coming of age in the '60s, I was what you might call an "intellectual hippie." Although it seems terribly sophomoric in retrospect, I posed the question, "What is Truth?", not realizing that it would guide the rest of my life. Seeking the answer to that question took me very far afield, and I read everyone from Ayn Rand to Garner Ted Armstrong. In an almost Saul/Paul kind of dichotomy, at one point I went so far as to call myself "an agnostic with atheistic leanings." Yet the tiny seed of faith planted in my youth survived. I cannot say that I maintained it, but glory be to God, I *retained* it; it too was a gift. No matter where my studies led me, I kept returning to the Scriptures.

1992. I was forty-two years old, divorced and working in a dead-end job. I'd tried my hand at writing short fiction, and even a novel or two, but had failed miserably. Even so, I finally decided that if I were going to write I'd better get on with it, and decided to forgo fiction for non-fiction. To that end, I made up a list of proposed subjects, and began pursuing them one after another. The one with the most apparent promise was titled, *The Bottom Line: Why America Can't Compete.* You may recall that books comparing American industry and business to the Japanese were quite fashionable for a time. But every line of reasoning I took led back to the same premise: *"For the love of money is the root of all evil"*—I Timothy 6:10. Bear in mind that I did not consider myself particularly religious at this time and, more importantly, I had absolutely no intention of writing anything even remotely resembling a religious tract. Be that as it may, the *very second* I changed the title from its current form to

The Bottom Line: Re-defining the Good Life, a miracle happened. Indeed, I consider that the moment of my re-birth.

In that very instant, it was as if someone had flicked a light switch. Suddenly inspiration came so fast that I couldn't scribble quickly enough to keep up with it. For a long while I made lists of subject headings on a separate piece of paper to pursue later because I had hardly begun to explore what had come previously. I wrote the entire first version in a matter of days, and promptly began a second. I very quickly gained every intention of writing a religious tract, but I also very quickly realized that this work was not mine. Accordingly, I soon initiated a small ritual. Before each writing session I would silently pray for guidance. On a few occasions I forgot that prayer, and found myself blankly staring at the sheet of paper (or computer screen) bewildered, wondering what I was doing, having no clue as to what to write next. Upon remembering and praying, the inspiration came right back again. Of particular pertinence to anyone who has written extensively, I should note that *not once* in the eighteen years I worked on this did I ever experience "writer's block," although I experienced it plenty of times before.

Clearly *Re-defining the Good Life* is far too broad a subject, and it took a very long time to narrow it down. I can now see it as a learning experience. I spent many years writing and re-writing the manuscript without being able to find a cohesive center for it that would limit the subject matter to an acceptable extent, but at the same time constantly refining and deepening my understanding of what had been revealed to me. I realize how melodramatic and even self-important that phrase seems, and I do not use it lightly. Nevertheless, that very concept plays an enormous role in what you're about to read. As we'll see, there is a huge difference between excogitated doctrine and that which is divinely revealed to the true believer. Integral to that revelation, not until the Pope's death in early 2006 did the final element fall into place; only then did I realize that our governmental system is our religion enacted. Even at that, it took more than four additional years to complete.

Please don't misinterpret my intention in writing this. I'm not looking for converts, nor do I desire to establish a new religion or religious doctrine. Indeed, I don't want you to follow me at all; I want you to follow Christ and therefore do what He said to do: *worship God in Truth and in Spirit.* Christ Himself is the Truth in question, while the Holy Ghost is the Spirit in question."*Whosoever denieth the Son, the same hath not the Father: he that acknowledgeth the Son hath the Father also. Let that therefore abide in you, which ye have heard from the beginning. If that which ye have heard from the beginning shall remain in you, ye shall continue in the Son and in the Father"*—I John 2:23-24. Religious freedom, founded on the human rather than on the Holy spirit, has led us to grant equal legitimacy to all definitions of the Almighty, and that is about as far from the Truth as one can get.

Yet we find that freedom at the heart of the United States of America as an integral part of our own self-assessed "greatness" and an essential reason for going to war. One nation under *which* God? As that implies, what you're about to read will question some of the Free World's most cherished and widely accepted religious and political beliefs. Please bear in mind that people often react to challenges of their most deeply-held beliefs as if they were threats to their lives, and for good reason: they constitute a kind of death threat in that they threaten the most fundamental aspects of our identity. By the same token, we quite frequently react the most strongly when we suspect at least some truth to the challenge, and don't wish to acknowledge it.

As something of a disclaimer, I intend this for the relatively mature Christian, as a means of facilitating spiritual growth. One can find many evangelical works on the market; if that is what you seek, I suggest that you look elsewhere. Rather, I aim this at those who have been called, and who may have been deluded by an increasingly apostate mainstream Christian religion. I greatly fear that many who think they follow Christ, like my social Christian roommate, will find themselves cruelly deceived come Judgment Day. Unless we accept the God described in the Bible, the God and Father of the Lamb who gave His life so we can preserve ours, then by definition we worship and serve some other god—and, despite the apparently bewildering array of options, there's only *one* other choice. But still more importantly, *lukewarmness*, (see Revelations 3:16), is epidemic in our world. Yet it is not a casual "faith in God" that saves us, nor will a halfhearted love of Him do the trick. Christ tells us that *we must love Him with all our beings,* and a great many earthly forces militate against that, patriotism and love of country chief among them. If that statement piques your interest, I invite you to read on. Please bear in mind that I do not wish to intentionally offend anyone; I don't mean this as an indictment of any group or individual but as a *warning* aimed at *every* group and individual. I also strongly recommend that you do as I did: before reading this, pray to God for guidance and understanding. Let us begin our journey.

P.S., for the sake of reference, I have used the King James Version (KJV) almost exclusively, with an occasional allusion to the *Amplified Bible*. I've also utilized a rather old convention: I have capitalized all divine pronouns as a matter of respect.

Chapter One

n April 2, 2005, Pope John Paul II died, ending one of the lengthiest and most popular Papal reigns in modern history. While both Popes and the Catholic Church in general often generate a good deal of interest among Protestants, that holds particularly true for this one, partly because of the overall time frame of his death. A growing number of Christians are convinced that the End Days have come, that the Messiah will soon return, and eagerly look for portents described in the Scriptures. According to many, the head of the Universal Church will play a vital role in the scenario of those days, some going so far as to call a future Pope the Antichrist. Those End Days are to be preceded by a "falling away," a departure from the faith, often called *the Great Apostasy*. With that in mind, if we broaden "Antichrist" from an individual to a movement, we can find much to concern us not only within the Universal Church, but within most of mainstream Christianity as well.

The influence of Antichrist goes well beyond religion, however. For that reason we find the Pope's death especially important largely due to the amount of interest it generated in political circles and what others, notably President Bush, had to say about him. We find it quite revealing to find our President saluting the autocrat of a literal church-state in spite of arbitrarily trying to separate church and state at home. After all, the Leader of the Free World largely defines itself in terms of freedom from absolute authority both political and ecclesiastical. Ironically, the office of Pope, who leads both the Church and the independent state of Vatican City, epitomizes the futility of such an arbitrary separation, while embodying a truth central to this work: our political system is our religion enacted. It must be, for our government and our relationship to it reflect what we hold as our ultimate authority, both collectively and individually. What we take as the source of that authority exercises paramount influence over that relationship and, by definition, a god exercises such influence over its followers. Thus, that which exerts that influence is what we truly take as our deity, in spite of what we may tell others or even ourselves. That makes idolatry far, far more common than we would dare to imagine. Indeed, we can take the growing appeal of self-government as an intrinsic part of the Great Apostasy defined as a major falling away from the true Faith. Think about it: what does our governmental form as our religion enacted suggest about a governmental form dedicated to the idea that political power properly derives from the people? That holds especially true when contrasted to the idea that political powers rightfully derive their authority from God. Don't such opposing views constitute battle lines between Biblical Truth and self-evident truth? While that holds true of any government, it holds particularly so for the United States. No other country on earth, not even the open theocracies, not even Vatican City, has dared call itself *one nation under God*, and this work delves into the implications of our doing so. Far from a contemporary phenomenon, that sentiment reflects the myth of America's "special destiny" lying at the heart of our national foundation and very largely guiding our Manifest Destiny. Moreover, it guides this nation's course, most especially in terms of foreign policy, even today. As the title suggests, we must consider under *which* god we call ourselves one nation and, more importantly, under which god we truly *are* one nation.[1]

We can begin to answer that question simply by posing another: what single word best summarizes our actual relationship to the divine? Duplicity! America calls itself one nation under God, while advocating a doctrine of religious freedom which necessarily maintains all *gods* as equally valid. If our governmental form is our religion enacted, then that poses a very important question: upon what authority do we make that declaration? More pertinently, upon *whose* authority do we make it? It's not the God of the Bible, nor the God associated with the Messiah commonly called Jesus Christ. Quite the contrary, that God is quite specifically (and emphatically) defined as

---

[1]   Bear in mind that we speak in generalities and in terms of official national policy.

"Jealous" (See Exodus 20:5 among many others.) Even so, we like to maintain that "we all worship the same god," which may well prove tragically, terrifyingly true—but *which* god? Unless we worship and serve the God described and delineated in the Bible, then by definition we serve some other god. At least by a Biblical definition, which the Christian must accept, that means that we serve a false god and all false gods share the same name: *Satan!* As Christians, we must decide whether we believe that or not, for there is no middle ground. Yet, the vast majority of us try to occupy that middle ground and, as a result, try to serve two masters.

The nature of that service goes well beyond physical acts, and deals instead with *motivation.* That brings up a theme we'll encounter often as we proceed. Although most of us equate them, there is a significant difference between goodness and righteousness. Goodness stresses what we obey, leaving the door open for many paths to the divine while ultimately providing Satan with endless means of deception. Righteousness, on the other hand, stresses not what but *whom* we obey, thereby linking it directly to divine Truth. As a simple example, let us assume that changing a light bulb is a good thing to do. If you do so because I tell you to, you've done a good deed; if you do so because Christ tells you to, you've done a *righteous* deed. That in turn brings up another subject we'll touch on many times in the coming pages. There are two Basic Questions that responsible adults must consciously ask themselves: *What is my purpose in life?* and *Who do I serve?* The first has been debated by philosophers for centuries, yet we can answer it in four simple words: *to proclaim God's glory.* That's the whole purpose of existence as we understand it, and that includes what little we can infer about how the Heavenly Host spends its time. The other question is a bit more complex and we'll deal with it presently. For now simply note that unless we make a conscious decision and put forth consistent and deliberate effort to serve God Almighty, unless we *"earnestly contend for the faith which was once delivered unto the saints"* (Jude 1:3), we serve His would-be usurper by default. Satan, of course, goes to very great lengths to mask that Truth, and his favorite tactic is to substitute self-determination for service to him. That's quite consistent considering that Satan's primary weapon is deception. Deception implies perception. There's a very valid reason why Paul says, *"For we walk by faith, not by sight"* in II Corinthians 5:7. So long as we depend exclusively on physical perception we cannot avoid misjudging reality. Given that, what can we learn from President Bush's adulation of the late Pope?

Although they seem quite different, the two actually have a good deal in common. Consider: the Mother Church on several occasions declared that no one could be saved outside its influence. In short, it built an entire empire on the fear of damnation by arrogating unto itself all the elements necessary to avoid it. In other words, it founded its empire on fear. As we'll explore more fully as we proceed, secular governments, especially the United States, more and more lean on fear to maintain and expand their political control. To that end, they create an endless array of bugbears to constantly generate the requisite apprehension. But, consider a much more fundamental and vastly more important commonality. In spite of all the rituals and rites and incomprehensible incantations the Church deems necessary to that end, we nevertheless eventually save ourselves by embracing all that nonsense *of our own volition!* That ultimately comes down to my will be done—the foundation of this country! We are saved if we join the Church, and are damned if we do not, but either way, it's up to us! Reduced to its most elementary concept, the Church, including the vast majority of the mainstream Christian religion, and the world's democracies, beginning with the United States, hold *self-determination* as their holy of holies. That casts the essence of democracy as the essence of salvation: no wonder we take it as an unqualified good. There's only one slight problem: *my will be done* is at diametric odds with *Thy will be done* which entirely characterized Christ's earthly sojourn, the example He set for us to follow, and which He Himself defines as the essence of righteousness. We thus find the essence of *unrighteousness* at the core of both the world's most highly acclaimed political system and the most popular Christian denominations. No wonder President Bush could so readily laud the late Pope. *"Enter ye in at the strait gate: for wide is the gate and broad is the way that leadeth to destruction, and many there be which go in thereat:'"*—Matthew 7:13. We'll return to that idea often as we proceed.

That broad way is largely characterized by a broadening of the definition of God. Just as the United States not only accepts but actively *encourages* religious egalitarianism not only domestically but as part of its foreign policy and basic definition of freedom, we likewise find a good part of mainstream Christianity, including the Mother Church, involved in various "inter-faith" functions designed to bring the world together under the most expansive possible definition of the Almighty. That is, of course, diametrically opposed to what Christ and His representatives said: as were the Jews, Christians are called to remain excluded from the world (more about that as we proceed). As we might expect, that leads to idolatry. As an especially dramatic and fairly recent example, we can look to South America, where we find Catholicism and paganism intimately interwound. In 1991, Pope John Paul II visited the *Aparecida* Cathedral in Brazil to honor the "Black Virgin", a small statue pulled from a nearby lake that reputedly performed miracles. He then led the congregation in prayers and songs to the idol, asking it for forgiveness and dedicating their lives to it. This is the same Pope who would a little later maintain that there are "many paths to God." Apparently he meant that. Also in 1991, he began a letter to *"my beloved Muslim brothers and sisters"* where he concluded that, *"We believe in and confess one God, admittedly in a different way, and daily praise and venerate him, the creator of the world and the ruler of this world."* Perhaps we do all worship the "ruler of this world", but is that necessarily a good thing? *"And you He hath quickened, who were dead in trespasses and sin; wherein in time past ye walked according to the course of this world, according to the prince of power of the air, the spirit that now worketh in the children of disobedience"*—Ephesians 1:1-2. Christ Himself makes it still clearer in John 14:30: *"'Hereafter I will not talk much with you; for the Prince of the World cometh, and hath nothing in Me'"*. A supernatural prince of the world clearly combines religion with politics. *Satan promised the kingdoms of the world to Christ in return for an act of worship,* and He refused. Apparently he found some other takers.

God is a title, not a name, and so an imprecise means of identification. That holds equally true for His Son and, consistently enough, we also find a great many *false messiahs* throughout history, prophecy, and contemporary times, all united in the concept of *Antichrist.* How can we tell the difference? Christians are considered the "children of God"; whom did Christ define as His brothers and sisters? *"'Whosoever shall do the will of my Father which is in heaven, the same is My brother, and sister, and mother'"*—Matthew 12:50. Is it God's will that we accept many paths to God? *"Be it known unto you all, and to all the people of Israel, that by the name of Jesus Christ of Nazareth, whom ye crucified, whom God raised from the dead, even by Him doth this man stand here before you whole. This is the stone which was set at nought of your builders, which is become the head of the corner. Neither is there salvation in any other: for there is none other name under heaven given among men whereby we must be saved"*—Acts 4:10-12. Perhaps we do all worship the same god—but *which* god? As we'll see a bit later, virtually all of mankind unites under one very specific deity.

President Bush commonly justified our "holy war" with Islamic extremists with the idea that they "hate us because of our freedom." Yet, as we found with the Papacy, while on the surface we seem quite different, if we dig a little deeper, we find that we have a good deal in common with them as well. Consider: the radicals apparently seek nothing less than the ultimate imposition of a world-wide Islamic theocracy—global dominion under their religious rules very similar to what the Mother Church spent centuries trying to implement. Yet we seek to do the same thing with democracy, and the prohibition of such rules. Superficially they seem diametrically opposed, but if we dare to look a bit more closely we find that both share as their ultimate goal a rebellion against the true God as the sole authority. Think about it. If we assume Islam a false religion, which we must if we call ourselves Christian, then both the terrorists by way of religious exclusivity and the United States by way of religious egalitarianism share the same ultimate objective and the same common adversary: the Truth as expressed and embodied in the Christ, the Son of God. This illuminates a much larger issue which we'll repeatedly encounter as we proceed. If Christ is *"the Truth"* (see John 14:6,) then Anti-Christ is "Anti-Truth"—i.e., doctrine both diametrically opposed to and actively militating against that Truth. Whether it comes about as a matter of the imposition of a single false religion or by way of the proliferation of many false religions, the end is the same. We "free" ourselves from God Almighty, and more importantly, from our relationship to Him as defined and espoused by the Truth incarnate. In other words, while we may mouth platitudes about God, we eliminate His Son as our sole intermediary, making Him an option rather than a necessity, while making the absolute Truth He embodies a matter of opinion. The means may differ but the end is the same. That's what religious freedom, despite its lofty sounding rhetoric, is all about, and that in itself hints at its likely originator. Given the United States as perhaps the world's most prominent champion of religious freedom, that likewise hints at the answer to our title question.

Religious freedom founds on the most basic freedom of them all: the freedom to believe what we want. It also shares a very great deal in common with *teaching the commandments of men as doctrine* (see Matthew 15:9)—which, we hasten to add, Christ cites as futile. But once we accept one interpretation of God's word as valid, we inevitably must declare all of them equally valid and, again we encounter the issue of authority. If religion is a human construct that cannot be proven or even logically demonstrated, then no individual has the right to promote one at the expense of the others. As a result, we carp and rail about one group imposing its vision of the Almighty, and then use that as a validation of countless other visions. Consider the irony: Satan has literally turned the Truth upon itself, using it to drive away many more than it attracts.

But that simply reflects a much larger and far more serious problem. As we'll see in the coming pages, the most basic and all but universally accepted doctrine essential to that insidious work is the idea that we "come to Christ" to find salvation which is, of course, partly true. It's really quite ironic: the salvation of humanity is intended as a free gift—but it must be accepted as such, and there's where we go astray. The very idea of a gift implies a Giver. Moreover, it implies a very specific relationship between that Giver and the recipient. If we change that relationship we create a concatenation of consequences. As but a single example, as soon as we take self-determination as the road to salvation—which we do when we in any way believe that we can save ourselves—then we must reach one of two conclusions. Either, as the Mother Church long maintained, there is but one way that can and should be imposed on everyone, or that it ultimately doesn't really matter what spiritual truths we accept because "good people go to heaven." Both are wrong. But both illustrate an image we'll encounter a number of times as we proceed: a *strait and narrow way* between those extremes.

Ironically, in a sense contention is a cardinal characteristic of the Christian character, though not in the conventional sense. Our current Holy War fought against Islamic terrorists, as with all conflicts fought with guns and bombs, is but a smokescreen obscuring the far deeper issues, and far more subtle *Spirit War* that has engulfed humanity since the Fall of Man. That war is fought with thoughts and ideas, with the heart and mind the battleground, the soul the ultimate prize. *"For we do not wrestle against flesh and blood, but against principalities, against powers, against the rulers of the darkness of this age, against spiritual hosts of wickedness in the heavenly places"*—Ephesians 6:12. The weapons are myriad and subtle, and often not recognizable as weapons at all. Nearly all of them share deceit in common, with evil appearing as righteousness, vice as virtue, just as we might expect from an evil *"angel of light"* (II Corinthians 11:13-14.) The battlefield is an endless labyrinth of deception and misdirection, most closely resembling a house of mirrors. But perhaps most of all, we must bear in mind that the deceived is unaware of the deception and, in fact, takes the deception as the truth. That gives us a clue as to both the scale and the nature of this conflict. Christ did say that the way to *destruction is broad and that many are finding it*. Tragically, many who have found it do not realize it and probably won't until it's too late. Such of course, is Satan's intention.

How can we recognize those deceptions? We take one concept often repeated in this work from Matthew 7:20: *"By their fruits ye shall know them."* We derive our virtues from our values, and what we most highly value exercises paramount, deital-like influence over us. Thus, what we count as virtues has much to say about what we revere as our god regardless of labels we may attach to it or even what we may believe about ourselves. If, for example, we consider that the entire world holds the same essential virtues, then we can surmise that it holds essentially the same values in spite of sometimes radically different superficial appearances. That implies that the whole world venerates the same ultimate moral and ethical authority, and we find the first major suggestion of a universal influence. We can fairly say that the vast, vast majority of humanity is united in their reverence of and service to a single deity: *the God Life.* Here too we find a mirror-image: we take life as our god rather than God as our life. If we take life as our highest good, what virtues should we expect to derive? Sure enough, the entire world also shares a common set of virtues at sharp odds to those professed by the Prince of Peace which, consistently enough, inevitably leads to conflict.

The God Life exerts its influence in a huge number of ways, but nowhere do we find that influence more pronounced than in a single mirror-image underlying virtually every conflict from world wars to personal disputes. Matthew 10:28 says, *"'And do not fear those who kill the body but cannot kill the soul. But rather fear Him who is able to destroy both soul and body in hell.'"* Just as political correctness has us pleasing ourselves rather than God, so our conflicts have us fearing each other rather than God. That is not coincidental. Fear and love are the two most powerful motivators in the human experience, and in many ways are flip sides of each other. But that masks a far deeper and more fundamental problem. We have long since elevated faith above love, making faith not love that which fulfills God's Law. This has yielded the common, but incorrect, apprehension that a simple "faith in God"—or, increasingly common in today's climate, a belief in a "higher power"—will save us. As that implies, religious freedom allows us to believe what we want to believe which means we can have faith in whatever we want. Casting faith—or, more specifically, our beliefs (see below)—as what save us then casts our own desires as what save us, and we can begin to see the link between such beliefs and self-deification. In our unchanged state—before the change of nature central to the Christian experience—we have no natural love of things divine, most assuredly including divine Truth. Not until the end will we see how genuinely wrong taking faith as what saves us really is, and how tragically deluded many of us have been for, in the end, only God and His love will remain. That means that only those who love Him will remain. Thus we encounter a very fundamental question: as a nation, which more commonly exerts paramount influence over us, love of God or love of money? As we'll see later, religious trappings notwithstanding, this country was founded on Love of Money (LOM).

LOM is another example of the aforementioned universal influence. Emblematic of that influence, we find *economy* at the root of our major conflicts, first with the Communists, and now with the terrorists. Indeed, regardless of the specific enemy, in hot spot after hot spot around the world, we remain ever ready to engage those who oppose our economic interests. In that same vein, America's thirst for Middle Eastern oil is perhaps the world's worst kept secret. However, *economy* has a seldom-heard tertiary definition also at the root of many of our conflicts: *the divine plan for humanity, from creation through redemption to final beatitude* (Dictionary.com). If God has such an economy based on eschewing the things of the earth, and with *Thy will be done* as its foundation, should it surprise us to find His would-be usurper with an economy of his own in diametric opposition to it? More specifically, should it surprise us to find conventional economics, which deal entirely with the physical, as Satan's means of interacting with and ruling the world? Should it surprise us to find that economy based on the things of the earth which *Christ cites as choking the word?* (See Matthew 13:22)? Should it surprise us to find it inspiring aggression and defensiveness characteristic of the Old Covenant instead of the love and forgiveness central to the New Covenant? Should it surprise us to find the vast majority accepting that aggression and defensiveness as virtues, usually guised as patriotism and love of country? Here we find evidence of the aforementioned Great Apostasy, and another example of religion and politics inevitably blending. We once fought in defense of "the Faith;" we now fight to defend our way of life. There is no difference. Just as our political system is our religion enacted, our way of life is our faith enacted. No wonder self-evident truth holds such an appeal. More pertinently, no wonder it proved so essential to the formation of this country.

The classic Biblical dichotomy *between the things of the earth and the things above* (see Colossians 3:2,) both requires and squires virtues and values at diametric odds with each other. That difference extends all the way to the most basic considerations underlying those values, including life itself, and this can prove difficult to accept. Here we find the most fundamental juncture of religion and politics where we must avow our allegiance to one deity or the other. Please note the operative term: we *must* so avow, for that avowal reflects in our every thought and action. One way or the other, we serve either The Father or His usurper, in each case adopting the appropriate value systems as our guiding principles. Consider what this means. Plain and simple, it's quite doubtful whether a physical, political entity could survive by adhering to the teachings and examples of Christ. Religion and politics merge still again, for that means that from the very beginning we must choose whether we serve the cause of physical life or eternal life. Consider a very well-known passage from Revelations 13:10: " . . . *he that killeth by the sword must be killed by the sword. Here is the patience and the faith of the saints."* We commonly forget that this is prefaced in verse seven with: *"And it was given to him* [the Beast] *to make war with the saints and to overcome them."* The Beast obeys the law of the jungle: kill or be killed, thereby taking violent aggression in the name of survival as a prime virtue. We Christians do not: *"And behold, one of them that were with Jesus stretched out his hand, and drew his sword, and struck a servant of the high priest's, and smote off his ear. Then Jesus said unto him, 'Put up again thy sword into his place: for all they that take the sword shall perish with the sword'"*—Matthew 26:51-52. There's a very valid reason for that: love, not faith fulfills the Law. *"And though I have the gift of prophecy, and understand all mysteries, and all knowledge, and though I have all faith, so that I could remove mountains, and have not charity, I am nothing"*—I Corinthians 13:2. Love is not love without trust. Hence, the intimate connection between faith and love.

If a political entity couldn't survive by adhering to Christ's teachings and examples, we should expect much the same from Christ Himself. Sure enough, when we read the Gospels, we run across numerous instances when His enemies should have been able to take Him, and would have except for the Father's intervention. They literally could not do so, and always for the same reason: *for His time had not yet come.* In spite of their desire to do so, they could not defy God's will. That says much about the illusion of self-determination as applied to life itself. By that same intervention alone could such a nation hope to survive, and by that means so survive the individual members of His kingdom now. *"Therefore take no thought, saying, What shall we eat? or, What shall we drink? or, wherewithal shall we be clothed? (For after all these things do the Gentiles seek:) for your heavenly Father knoweth that ye have need of all these things"*—Matthew 6:31-32. A bit of cross-referencing defines *Gentiles* as more than simply non-Jews, but as *pagans.* Given that, notice that He defines all of those earthly pursuits as appropriate to pagans, while at the same time defining the problem not with the things themselves but with our relationship to them. As we'll see, that proves a very important distinction.

Since Christ's *kingdom is not of this earth,* (see John 18:36) His subjects are not of this earth either—we live *in* the world but not *as part of it.* That reflects our relationship to the earth in general. *"Love not the world, neither the things that are in the world. If any man love the world, the love of the Father is not in him. For all that is in the world, the lust of the flesh, and the lust of the eyes, and the pride of life is not of the Father, but is of the world"*—I John 2:15-16. If our political system is our religion enacted, what must we conclude about our national religion when we find that political system obsessively devoted to and dependent upon the rabid pursuit of just such things, not to mention the pride associated with them? Again we find a mirror-image: the more obsessed we are as a nation with the things of the earth, the healthier our national economy grows. Given that as a pagan pursuit, can we take it as coincidental that so much pagan imagery has found its way into our national iconography on federal, state, and even local levels? Doesn't that imply our form of government itself as pagan? Think about it. Democracy and religious freedom, two of our most revered and cherished ideals, share in common my will be done which is the most basic concept the righteous reject. More than that, the righteous reject the aforementioned world *system*, which comes down to the values and resultant virtues shared by most of the world based on life and associated concerns. That includes intangibles such as freedom, human rights and pride in favor of meekness, forbearance and forgiveness. Hence, our title question.

Consider how the idea of worship per se has changed since the days of the Old Covenant. Although the Jews had their fabulous Jerusalem temple, and considered it alone the proper place to worship God, the early post-apostolic congregations met at people's individual homes, thereby making these literal "houses of worship" invisible to physical perception quite consistent to worshiping God in *Spirit and in Truth.* By contrast, some formal houses of worship now rank among the most recognizable structures in the world. Please notice that this not only amounts to a difference, but a *diametric* difference, similar to that between light and darkness. More importantly by far, a great many still believe these structures to be the proper (and perhaps only) place to worship the Almighty. Consistently enough, while the Jewish means of religion emphasized physical rites and rituals, Christ said, *"But the hour is coming, and now is when the true worshipers will worship the Father in spirit and truth; for the Father is seeking such to worship Him. God is Spirit, and those who worship him must worship in spirit and truth'"*—John 4:23-24.

There's more to that little exchange, however. Christ begins by telling the Samaritan woman that, although her people worship God, they don't understand what they're doing nor whom they're worshipping, for salvation comes of the Jews. The woman responds by saying that she knows that a Messiah, an

Anointed One, will come and explain all these things to them, at which Christ announces, *"'I that speak unto thee am He'"*—John 4: 26. Consider what that means. Without Christ, we have no knowledge of whom we worship nor of how to do so. That's the "Truth" part of how we properly worship Him. Indeed, He just answered both of those questions, telling her both who and what God was and how to properly worship Him. That's the major difference between the two Covenants, for if we must worship God in Truth, and if Christ is the Truth, then that means that we must worship God *in Christ*.

This illustrates one of the greatest fallacies running through many a Christian doctrine that is at least indirectly responsible for its sanguinary history and blemished reputation. As was true of the Chosen People, those early congregations consisted of groups who had been called to salvation, united by the Holy Spirit, and those not falling into that category were generally excluded (see II Corinthians 6:14.) We find much the same attitude in Jewish ceremonies, and for a very similar reason: both Jews and Christians are *God's chosen people* (see Romans 11:12-24.) Consistent with the mirror-image motif, we now see those houses of worship as places to go to *be* saved, resulting in an "everybody's welcome" attitude and, far more seriously, a unity based not on the Holy but on the human spirit. Note how that proves very consistent with man-derived doctrine and self-determination. In essence, we save ourselves by choosing to go to church. In many ways self-determination has made Christianity a mirror-image of what it should be.

We find that reflected most dramatically in another of the biggest fallacies in all of Christendom: the idea that we can and must "save souls." As with all of Satan's deceptions, we find a lie concealed in a truth. God's word is in fact to be spread to every corner of the earth, so the *intention* is both correct and justifiable. *"And some have compassion, making a difference: and others save with fear, pulling them out of the fire; hating even the garment spotted by the flesh"*—Jude 1:22-23. The problems begin when we take the credit unto ourselves for those who heed that Word—i.e., the misguided belief that *we* save souls. That fallacy alone accounts for more of Christianity's compromises with paganism than all other issues combined. In truth, we cast forth the seeds, but what happens to those seeds is quite literally out of our hands. *"I have planted, Apollos watered; but God gave the increase. So neither is he that planteth any thing, neither he that watereth; but God that giveth the increase"*—I Corinthians 3:6-7. Consider John 1:12-13:*"But as many as received Him, to them He gave the right to become children of God, even to those who believe in His name: who were born, not of blood, nor of the will of the flesh, nor of the will of man, but of God."* In John 6:44, Christ Himself is even more explicit: *"No one can come to Me unless the Father who sent Me draws* him; *and I will raise him up at the last day."* Consider that very carefully. Obviously saving ourselves by "coming to Christ," or saving others by bringing them to Him amounts to the exact opposite. Think about what this means. Best of intentions notwithstanding, that makes our salvation a matter of *my* will be done—the essence of *unrighteousness!* Again we make ourselves (or each other) God's Chosen People. Good appearances notwithstanding, doesn't that put us in God's place? Hasn't that been Satan's objective all along? Isn't self-determination the foundation for this one nation under God as well as this spiritual belief? Doesn't that suggest the answer to our title question?

Our governmental system is our religion enacted. If we save ourselves from eternal evil as a matter of human will and volition, it follows naturally that we should do likewise with mundane evils. As a result, we see *my* will be done as divinely sanctioned and so, by extension, see democracy as divinely sanctioned. We therefore also see it as our divine duty to spread it to the world as our Manifest Destiny. No wonder evangelical and Fundamentalist Christians have grown into such powerful political entities in this country. Just as God's word must be preached in every corner of the world before the End of Time, so we find the same thing happening with democracy. The one stresses *Thy* will be done, the other *my* will be done. Doesn't that sound a bit like establishing battle lines? Doesn't that sound frighteningly like a contest between Christ and Antichrist—and so, of Truth vs. Anti-Truth? Can we not at least seriously entertain that concept as one of the *"damnable heresies"* Peter mentions in

II Peter 2:1? On which side does that cast this one nation under God with, we must sadly add, the blessings and complicity of many mainstream churches? What, or more specifically *whom,* do we therefore hold as holy? Just as self-determination maintains that governmental power rightfully derives from the governed, so religious freedom maintains the same: a deity presides over us only by our consent. We make ourselves the children of whatever god we chose in complete compliance with that most basic of rights: the right to believe whatever we want. That is the freedom doctrine the United States of America evangelically spreads to the rest of the world, and one of the major reasons we like to fancy ourselves a great nation. Sadly, we all too often fail to ask, great in *whose* eyes? After all, Babylon is also called "great." Babylon is also notorious for its idolatry which is a pretty good definition of believing what we want to believe.

Ironically, we find perhaps the most subtle, but also most damaging manifestation of that in one of the cruelest mirror-images of them all. Specific doctrinal differences notwithstanding, nearly every mainstream Christian religion promotes *personal salvation* as the primary if not sole reason for worshiping God. Well, after all, isn't that what Christianity is all about? Isn't damnation vs. salvation the core of the Christian religion? Based on good vs. evil, we have no choice but to believe that. Yet, think about it. If we find salvation by worshiping God, then we find salvation by *choosing* to worship God, which means worshiping God by our own volition. Typical of the mirror-imagery we've already seen, that brings us right back to self-determination again which brings us back to the essence of *unrighteousness* again. The mirror-imagery continues from there. We make ourselves the children of God, and do so not as a result of divine love but of the human fear of perdition! Thus, we end up with the essence of unrighteousness as the essence of salvation, with fear rather than love that which fulfills the Law. Doesn't that sound like a pretty accurate definition of Anti-Truth? Self-evident truth and self-excogitated doctrine have so much in common as to be virtually synonymous, and again we find religion and politics merging. Just as evangelicals seek to save the world from sin, so democracy seeks to save it from the evils of authoritarianism—and both teach essentially the same doctrine: the divine efficacy of the human will. Without this fundamental belief, the Mother Church could never have gained its global dominance, bullying royalty and commoner alike into doing its bidding. Without that similar belief, America would not have attained its global prominence, often due to similar bullying. Both have *fear* in common. Fear of myriad foes, ranging from Communists to terrorists lies at the heart of American power and its dreams of global hegemony. Fear of damnation lies at the heart of most of mainstream Christianity, beginning with the Mother Church but including most of her protesting offspring. Both share the same fallacious mirror-image: *fear does not fulfill the Law!* Quite the contrary, fear implies punishment and that which we seek to avoid; love implies mercy, that which we seek to attain. If we are to consider ourselves forgiven, *then we must also be without fear* (see I John 4:18 among others.). If we remove fear, we remove one of Satan's most effective means of manipulation, not to mention a major part of *conforming to the world* (see Romans 12:2). Simply put, if we make Thy will be done our guiding principle, then we quite literally have nothing to worry about and nothing to fear. That, in turn, yields the internal peace that Christ promises in John 14:27. As we'll explore a bit later, seeking external peace is a waste of time unless we first seek that internal peace.

For those not called to redemption by the Holy Spirit, those attempting to save them must rely on the human spirit instead. Thus, rather than worshipping God in *Truth and in Spirit*, they must attempt to worship Him in the flesh. In fact, *no power on earth can give us the right or the ability to worship God*. At the same time, no amount of worshipping God in the flesh propitiates Him in the slightest! *"It is the Spirit that quickeneth; the flesh profiteth nothing: the words that I speak unto you, they are Spirit and they are life'"*—John 6:63. Although it has nothing to do with actually worshiping the Father, the emphasis on rites and rituals, on costumes and sets, on rote prayers that border on magical incantations rife within the mainstream Christian religion serves an indispensable purpose. Since for the most part, those churches have replaced a unity based on the Holy Spirit with that based on the human spirit, they need physical manifestations to act as a cohesive focal point to hold the congregation together in the same way that doctrine—what we believe—holds it together intellectually. Just as we do not become the children of God of our own wills, and by the power of the human spirit, neither do we worship Him of our own volition or by that spirit. Given that, then our worship under those circumstances comes down to idol worship.

Casting salvation as Christianity's centerpiece perverts that which is holy into that which is terribly, horribly profane. Think about the fundamental good salvation represents. Now consider: crossing every line imaginable, from racial to ethnic to economic to political to religious, virtually everyone on earth holds one supreme good in common: *survival.* That one characteristic is shared not only by every government from the most ultra-modern to the tribal, but by every living creature on earth as well. Biologists almost unanimously rank the *survival imperative* (self preservation) as nature's number one instinct, and *instinct* means a pattern of automatic behavior, and associated responses. In other words, survival is the most basic truth in the natural animate world, both faunal and floral. In more immediately pertinent terms, physical survival is the most basic concern of the earth—and *Christ and His representatives repeatedly exhort us to eschew the things of the earth*—but is just what we would logically expect from a veneration of the God Life. If we take survival as our guiding principle, we must apply it not only to our lives but to everything we associate with them. That means that we share exactly the virtues and values as would animals were they capable of it. Does that not cast us in the *image of the beast,* just as we might reasonably expect from Christ's mirror-image? Furthermore, consider: a *mark* can mean "*a distinguishing characteristic*" with *survival* just that characteristic shared by every living thing. That makes the survival imperative the dreaded *mark of the beast* at least in a metaphorical sense. It is, after all, the philosophical basis for accepting the literal mark as described in Revelations 13:15-17 where people take the it *in order to avoid death.* Taking personal salvation as our life's purpose simply translates that same imperative into spiritual terms. What seems a self-evident good is in fact unrighteous and therefore Antichrist.

Consistent with fear as our motivation, we spend so much time focused on from what Christ's sacrifice saves us—perdition, the Lake of Fire and so on—that we spend very little time pondering *for* what He did so. He does so for the same reason He does everything else: to manifest His glory! *"'I have glorified Thee on earth: I have finished the work which Thou gavest Me to do'"*—John 17:4. By making salvation Christianity's focal point, we do the exact opposite; we over-sanctify that most precious gift by putting the Gift ahead of the Giver and, by doing so, putting the recipient above the Giver. Thus, we end up seeking our own glory rather than God's. Think about it. Those of us who are saved will be greatly glorified. *"When Christ, who is our life, shall appear, then shall ye also appear with Him in glory"*—Colossians 3:4. Thus, to seek that salvation as its own end is to seek that glorification as its own end: we seek our own glory rather than God's, quite consistent with self-deification. What appears to be righteous transforms into the essence of unrighteousness. Unless we accept Christ as our cynosure, we cannot claim to have been saved. That means that unless we take *Thy will be done* as our guiding principle we cannot claim to have been saved, for that is the most basic of the Truths which Christ embodies. More immediately pertinent, it summarizes the essence of salvation. A point which we'll reemphasize a number of times as we proceed, we are saved by God's mercy, *and that alone!*

We can neither attain that mercy nor make Thy will be done our guiding principle as a result of our own wills, but must allow God to do so. That's why we see so many exhortations to humble ourselves before God and, in terms more immediately pertinent to our discussion, to submit to His authority. *"'No man can serve two masters: for either he will hate the one and love the other; or else he will hold to the one and despise the other. Ye cannot serve God and mammon'"*—Luke 16:13. Easily lost in that is the fact that, while we cannot serve two masters, neither can we avoid service to one or the other. As implied by service to Mammon, a personification of money, the difference is that we must serve God by conscious choice and on-going effort. If we don't, we serve

Mammon by default. In the end that service largely comes down to valuing the things of heaven, God's glory above all else, more than the things of the earth. While that service rests squarely on LOM, it isn't limited to greed or wealth; after all, we can love money as passionately as paupers as we can as fat cats. Don't get us wrong, LOM in its conventional guise can cause problems aplenty. Christ does warn against the *"deceivableness of riches,"* after all, (see Matthew 13:22) and material riches inevitably constitute the major reason for our conflicts and intrigues. Still, Paul calls the love of money the *root* of all evil which poses an obvious question: where do you find a "root?" Beneath the surface. Once we begin to dig beneath the surface, we begin to realize that LOM entails that oft-mentioned "world system" in ways that frequently have no relationship at all to money in the conventional sense, but have a paramount relationship to what we value and love.

In order to understand that, we must understand the basis of money. Simply (and admittedly, simplistically) put, whether we deal in beads 'n' clam shells, or dollars and cents, our currency ultimately has only the value its users agree to assess to it, and that amounts to an agreement on the value of what underlies it. We call this phenomenon "value addition" and, rather than limited to pecuniary concerns, it applies to virtually everything in our lives on an individual as well as collective basis. Take something as innocent as a rain shower for example. The picnickers might well curse it for spoiling their day in the country, while the farmer less than a mile away might rejoice over the desperately needed water for his crops. As that implies, in every instance, we measure the relative value of a thing, event, condition, idea or person in terms of how it relates to us. That not only explains why a $20 bill is an enormous Godsend for that street person and but a trifle to the wealthy businesswoman, but also explains why we prefer certain people over others—family and friends over strangers, for example.

We also find debits and credits in the unconventional sense. Consider: we most commonly define our relationships in terms of one of two questions: what can you do *for* me? or what can you do *to* me—i.e., how can you profit me, or what can you cost me?

That which we find beneficial, we call good; that which we deem as threatening or unbeneficial, we deem evil, and that which elicits neither response we usually ignore, but "me" always remains as the fundamental criterion against which all else is measured. In essence then, we can expand *money* and the love thereof to include all the different manifestations money can take both tangible and intangible, all of which share that basic judgmental value addition in common. In what possible context could the questions *what can you do to me* and *what can you do for me* apply more profoundly than in the issue of perdition vs. salvation?

Consistent with economy's tertiary definition, people often go shopping for religion with the same questions in mind: *what can you do for me* and *what's it going to cost me?* If we combine that with the fact that at least some religions have become big business, it shouldn't surprise us to find the same value addition, the same root of all evil, lying at the foundation of Christianity's fragmentation. Think about it. We look at the Bible (or other "spiritual" works,) add value to what we like, and take value away from what we don't like until we find or create a blend that suits us. We thereby follow the basic market axiom of giving the customers what they want, while pandering to our cherished freedom to believe what we wish. The parallels to democracy and self-evident truth are almost too obvious to point out: as soon as a sufficient number of people accept a sufficient number of common spiritual truths a religion is born—a god of the people, by the people and for the people, acting in concert with the consent of the governed. Our governmental form is our religion enacted.

Economic, political and religious freedoms now sweep the world as a kind of secular trinity, with the United States the chief advocate and primary motivator. If the *whole world is under the sway of the Evil One,* (see I John 5:19,) then what can we infer from the fruits these freedoms manifest? Let us consider economic freedom for example. Satan is characterized as a liar, while Christ is called *the Truth.* We refer to our economic system as the *free market economy,* while nothing in it is actually free, most assuredly including the participants—all have at least some regulations imposed on them. But far more revealing, rather than free, the whole point is to make a profit, and the bigger the profit the better. If it's big enough, we can even claim to have *"made a killing!"* Does that term make you a little uncomfortable? *"He was a murderer from the beginning..."*"How many lives have we collectively taken in the name of the material things represented by that economy? In Mark 8: 36-7, Christ poses two of the most famous questions in the Bible. *"For what shall it profit a man, if he shall gain the whole world, and lose his own soul? Or what shall a man give in exchange for his soul?"* Our entire social structure rests firmly on the *Profit Motive*. Once we begin down that path it can prove very, very difficult to change, and we began that path at our very inception. Power never voluntarily relinquishes itself, but always seeks to enhance itself instead. Money is power, and it follows the same pattern. Thus, no amount of profit is ever enough, and those making the biggest profits wield the greatest power. Thus, we increasingly find corporate power leaking into the halls of government and many speculate that what we see—chiefly lobbyists and other power brokers—represent but a very small fraction of the Corporate America's true influence. But in a more immediate sense, consider what has happened over the past century or so. Our capitalist economy has transmogrified into a *consumerist* economy. Rather than quality in workmanship or fulfilling a legitimate need or even an existing desire, now it's all about the sale and the profit to be made from it, with needs and desires expertly and deliberately manufactured right along with the product. Now consider the philosophical connection between politics and that pursuit of profit and power. *"Life, liberty and the pursuit of happiness"* are the most commonly acknowledged of the self-evident truths at our national foundation. Consider how they fit together, and then ask yourself, who do we serve by taking them as our guiding principle? What love then motivates us? What fear motivates us? What do we seek to gain, and what price are we willing to pay for it? What do we fear to lose, and at what cost will we prevent that loss? Historically, we have answered those questions with countless millions of deaths and destruction on a cataclysmic scale. Does that sound like a logical end resulting from following *"the Life"?* If Christ is *the Life*, then what must we call His mirror-image, and what fruit would we expect following him to yield?

That poses a somewhat larger question. What does our way of life suggest about the faith of which it is a reflection? As holds true for nearly every aspect of our modern world, it isn't what it says it is. No wonder paltering politicians have become the norm! Which of the two cited spiritual leaders does that describe? No wonder we so frequently find deception necessary to maintain our national security, which always comes down to the fiscal security of one of America's corporate giants. (We once officially embraced the motto, "What's good for GM is good for the country"). At the same time, the primary advocate of that free market economy and the self-proclaimed "leader of the Free World" has imposed more laws—and so, more restrictions—on its citizens than any nation in history. Is that the kind of economy and resulting government we would expect to find based on the Truth? Isn't that frighteningly reminiscent of Christ's criticism of the Pharisees. Have we not seen countless instances where the government considers itself above its own law while at the same time proclaiming this as a nation of law, seeking not vengeance but justice on our terrorist adversaries? Have those innumerable laws brought us any closer to righteousness? Consider a chilling linguistic curiosity: we call ourselves a nation of law and we also call ourselves one nation under God. If we combine the two, we find ourselves one nation under God's Law—i.e., the *Synagogue of Satan: those who are not Jews but who call themselves Jews!* (See Revelations 2:9 and 3:9.) Can we take it as coincidental that Zionist Israel exerts a profound influence over United States foreign policy?

Consider another disturbing piece of evidence that finds ever-growing pertinence in this "green" world of ours. The world's economy, led by the United States, rests on *consumption*. Consumerism, much more than simply an economic principle, maintains that we can attain happiness and contentment by the acquisition and consumption of stuff—the more stuff the better, the more frequently replaced the better. Indeed, that has been a matter of national policy long before the term made its way into the popular lexicon. George Kennan, Director of State Department Policy Planning staff of the Truman Administration, wrote: *"We have about 50% of the world's wealth but only 6.3% of its' population. This disparity is particularly great as between ourselves and the peoples of Asia. In this situation, we cannot fail to be the object of envy and resentment. Our real task in the coming period is to devise a pattern of relationships which will permit us to maintain this position of disparity".* Document PPS23, 24th February 1948. Ironically, the most harmful of all those products—military weaponry—accounts for a huge percentage of our annual expenditures—and an equally huge percentage of annual profits—which we have found necessary to the end of maintaining our that position of disparity. Doesn't that rather smack of armed robbery? Even more cruelly, while millions live lives of conspicuous consumption—there are more billionaires in the world now than at any time in history—other billions literally consume dirt just to have something in their stomachs. Yet, that same report went on to say, *"We need not deceive ourselves that we can afford today the luxury of altruism and world benefaction. We should cease to talk about such vague and unreal objectives as human rights, the raising of living standards and democratization. The day is not far off when we are going to have to deal in straight power concepts. The less we are then hampered by idealistic slogans, the better."* Now consider Mark 12: 30-31: *"And thou shalt love the Lord thy God with all thy heart, and with all thy soul, and with all thy mind, and with all thy strength: this is the first commandment. And the second is like, namely this, Thou shalt love thy neighbor as thyself. There is none other commandment greater than these.'"* To which god does this nation devote itself as a matter of official policy? A "healthy economy" by the consumerist definition rests entirely on covetousness and discontent, both of which the Scriptures proscribe, but both of which we must assiduously and deliberately foster. That means that we actively promote Biblically defined vice and call it virtue because we find it essential to our economic survival! What sort of relationship to money does that suggest? Whose economy does that reflect? Look again at I John 2:15: *"Do not love the world or the things in the world. If anyone loves the world, the love of the*

Father is not in him." If the love of the Father is not in us, what love takes its place? What love acts as our primary motivator? If the *whole world is under the sway of the evil one,* what does that suggest about America's global leadership role? Those economic principles motivate every national action of this land of the free. We fairly commonly pose the question, *freedom from what,* and answer with freedom from absolute authority. We all too seldom ask, freedom *for* what? This issue makes it clear: we demand the freedom to sin!

Neither is "demand" an ill-chosen term. *"The meek may inherit the earth,"* John Paul Getty observed, *"but not its mineral rights."* That little statement reveals a mirror-image common to most of the world. The vast majority of humanity highly values qualities such as standing up for ourselves, fighting for what we believe in, demanding our rights and all the other stuff we learn in self assertiveness classes, all of which stand in diametric opposition to that Christ-like virtue. *The desires of our father, the devil, we want to do* (John 8:44). Ironically, Revelations 21:8 lists *"the fearful"* first among the list of those who will find their share in the Lake of Fire but, superficial similarities notwithstanding, meekness doesn't have anything to do with cowardice. On the contrary, it takes great deal courage to be genuinely meek, just as it takes great strength to be genuinely gentle. Satan, in diametric opposition to Christ, attracts and develops followers who manifest strength, aggression, assertiveness, and defensiveness as their primary virtues and greatest goods—and does so with fear as the motivation. Then, much as governments often do with false flag operations, he creates an endless array of evils for the good to overcome by way of those virtues, making them seem indispensable. That acts both to justify those virtues and to obfuscate the real issue of Truth vs. Anti-Truth. How important an issue is this? Think about it. If Christ, the Truth, is also *the Life,* then His mirror-image, Anti-Truth, is *the Death.* More specifically, if Christ is *eternal* Life, then His mirror-image is *eternal Death.* Also consider that one normally *inherits* something from those who are dead—and in this case, we refer to the *Second Death,* more commonly known as perdition. What does that suggest about the un-meek who love the world, and the things in it while adopting the appropriate value system? Taking life and what we associate with it as our highest values means that we take the world system as our value system, and live by the appropriate virtues. If we do that, then we make ourselves *friends of the earth* which means that we make ourselves the *enemies of God* (see James 4:4). Paul agrees:*"For to be carnally minded is death, but to be spiritually minded is life and peace. Because the carnal mind is enmity against God; for it is not subject to the law of God, nor indeed can be"*—Romans 8:6-7.

Trying to serve two masters—trying to worship and please God in the flesh—is probably the most common manifestation of that *carnal mind*. True Christianity amounts to considerably more than attending Church services and occasional good deeds, and it certainly amounts to much more than a simple belief in God. Ironically it does amount to a way of life that needs defending, but not in the sense that we normally think. Indeed, rather than self-defense, it is the self from which we need defense. Those of the *carnal mind* can look at Christ's exhortations to peaceful meekness, to *"turn the other cheek"* for example, and maybe even applaud them as abstracts, but find themselves unable to integrate them into their reality when doing so poses a great enough threat. That epitomizes a larger lesson directly related to self-determination and the issue of empowerment. Trying to deliver ourselves from evil delivers us to evil instead. Why? *"'I will put My laws in their mind and write them on their hearts; and I will be their God and they shall be My people.'"*—Hebrews 8:10. That passage makes us the passive recipients of those Laws. Also note how it implies our deital definition as that which exercises paramount influence over us. But in a more subtle sense, here we find the essential difference between unity based on the human spirit, and that based on the Holy Spirit, between the physical Church and what is sometimes called the *Invisible Church*. The former founds on what we know, making it a matter of mind and human will. We write those Laws on our own hearts thereby making ourselves our own gods—self-determination amounts to self-deification. The latter founds on what has been *revealed to us,* and, more importantly in this context, what has been implanted in us by that same Holy Spirit. That makes a world of difference, for we can *know* the Commandments but we cannot *live* them without divine empowerment! The *natural man* and the *carnal mind* cannot see that and, as a result, remain vulnerable to the deceptive equation of goodness and righteousness. Yet consider the ultimate consequences of the physical church in its endeavors to deliver itself from evil. In order to believe that it delivers itself to salvation, it must believe, acknowledged or not, that by doing so it thereby delivers itself to righteousness. That not only makes my will be done the essence of righteousness, it makes it the ultimate *source* of righteousness! How great an example of self-deification do we need? Any doctrine, any belief that in any way maintains that we can save ourselves has that deadly fallacy at its root, and its adherents will share a similar fate. *"Every plant which My Heavenly Father hath not planted shall be rooted up'"*—Matthew 15:13.

We can't have God without Christ, but neither can we have Christ without God. Consider John 5:21-24: *"For as the Father raiseth up the dead and quickeneth them; even so the Son quickeneth whom He will. For the Father judgeth no man but hath committed all judgment unto the Son: that all men should honor the Son even as they honor the Father. He that honoreth not the Son honoreth not the Father which hath sent Him. Verily, verily, I say unto you, he that heareth My word, and believeth on Him that sent Me, hath everlasting life, and shall not come into condemnation; but is passed from death unto life."* In other words, we pass from *carnal mindedness*, which Paul likens unto death, to a *renewal of our minds* (see Romans 12:2) which gives us the desire to please God and, still more importantly, *enables* us to do so. Otherwise, we must found our decisions on worldly wisdom, and that wisdom will inevitably compel us to act in accordance with the nature we see all about us, best summarized in *Nature's God,* this country's official deity. Those decisions will be chiefly characterized by the survival imperative applied to life and all the beastly concerns that we associate with it. Thus, most of us adopt the law of the jungle—kill or be killed—as our first commandment, and again we find ourselves cast in the *image of the beast* while thinking, even truly believing, that we serve God. Since we take life as our highest good (which is appropriate to the beasts,) we therefore take what we associate with it as commensurate goods, and the same imperative applies to them. Thus, we cannot separate our way of life from our faith, which means that we cannot separate our relationship to the world in general from what we really hold as true regardless of what we officially profess or may believe about ourselves.

A unity based on the human spirit featuring man-derived doctrine must reach one of two conclusions: we must either deem the means to salvation exclusive, as the Catholic Church did for centuries (and, to an extent, still does), or allow for variations, which inevitably lead to the fragmentation that characterizes the contemporary Christian religion. One way or the other, we also find a motif used successfully by the Roman Empire for centuries: *divide and conquer*. Rather than maintaining a holy brotherhood, founded on love of God and a quest for the Truth embodied in His Son, we established a hierarchy founded on fear and maintained by a coerced conformity to arbitrary dogma and rote ritual! More subtly, salvation per se superseded our true spiritual function: *to grow!* With their power, prestige and privilege vested in dogma, those preaching it find it very, very tempting not to question nor stray from established truths lest they relinquish their positions, and that attitude frequently get passed along to the congregation.[2] But such a fear merely hints at a far deeper problem. If we look a bit deeper, we can begin to see the more important, and much more pragmatic difference between a motivation based on fear and that based on love.

Coerced love is a contradiction in terms, whether the coercion originates from within or from without. Fear, on the other hand, can be imposed quite effectively, and deliberately. Fear explains our thirst for power, modest or profound, and that certainly applies to the clergy that exists in a hierarchical structure when they fear a loss of prestige. Again religion and politics merge on a very fundamental level. Think about it. In order to control our destinies, which includes ensuring our survival, we must be able to control our environments and everything in them. A

---

[2]   Again, with apologies to the sincere theologians who may be innocently implicated in the generalities necessary to make a point.

unity, political or ecclesiastical, based on the human spirit can be accomplished and maintained only by way of force or fear, and usually by a combination of both. While the Reformation seemed to have eliminated that from the ecclesiastical scene, if we look a bit more deeply we find that untrue. The elevation of personal salvation to Christianity's centerpiece served just that purpose and, as we'll see later, that purpose was firmly rooted in the things of the earth, quite consistent with worshipping God in the flesh. As a result, fear of our spiritual survival rather than love of God (and of His Truth) drove us to accept whatever snake oil a given group had to peddle. Now we are free, and to an extent even encouraged to shop around until we find the blend of the spiritual and the secular guaranteed to assure us of eternal life that meets with our approval. Again we find two extremes with the Truth a narrow strait between them.

We can summarize the theological application of the divide and conquer phenomenon in the clergy/laity distinction. While it's clear that a hierarchical structure exists in God's heavenly kingdom, and so we could expect it to be reflected on earth, we have distorted the basic idea. As an aside, that illustrates an important point. Satan can't actually create anything, not even an original lie. All he can do is to twist and distort God's preexistent Truth, but he is very, *very* adept at that. As a result of that distortion, we began to believe that we cannot properly worship God without specific incantation-like prayers and Romanesque rites invoked by what amounts to a Christian shaman. Speaking at the Worldwide Retreat for Priests in Vatican City, October, 1984, the legendary Mother Teresa was quoted as saying, " . . . *only when the priest is there can we have our alter and our tabernacle and our Jesus. Only the priest can put Jesus there for us . . . Jesus wants to go there but we cannot bring Him unless you first give Him to us . . . . this is another reason you are called 'another Christ'."* Let's get this straight: Christ is our *king*, and yet He's not permitted to come to us unless some men perform the appropriate incantations? That's not what the real Christ says, at least not according to Matthew 18:20: *"'For where two or three are gathered together in My name, there am I in the midst of them.'"* He does warn us about "other christs", however: *"'Take heed that ye be not deceived: for many shall come in My name, saying, I am Christ; and the time draweth near: go ye not therefore after them.'"*—Luke 21:8.

Teresa's comment is applicable to more than just Catholics, however. Many Protestants, which likewise invoke the clergy as indispensible to that end, also subconsciously feel that the formal church service is the only proper place for God's worship. If you think about it, that's really quite consistent with those attempting to worship God in the flesh. It's similarly untrue, however, for those worshipping God *in Truth and in Spirit.* By limiting God's worship to specific times, places and circumstances, we marginalize Him virtually out of existence in all other contexts which is, of course, Satan's intention. Do we not therefore follow a false messiah? Isn't such a false messiah, by definition, Antichrist? Doesn't that sound like a part of the Great Apostasy? As we'll see, we follow the Christ we want to follow just as we believe what we want to believe, and that in itself seriously calls into question the issue of coming to Christ of our own wills and of worshipping the Father in the flesh. Think about the resultant fruits. Which Christ *always did what pleased His Father?* (See John 8:29.) To what extent did He marginalize Him out of His daily life? To what extent did He *make* Him His daily life? Wasn't He always *about His Father's business?* (See Luke 2: 43-49.) As part of His body, it sort of follows that we'd at least seek to do the same thing. What we seek, however, reflects what we want to find, and in our unchanged state we have no inherent love of things divine, including divine Truth.

But again we find the deceptiveness inherent in self-determination. We like to think that we believe what we want to believe, but we would be more accurate in saying that, in our natural state, we believe what *Satan* wants us to believe. We Christians are called to serve God's Truth embodied in His Son. It then logically follows that Satan wants us to follow Anti-Truth which he expertly disguises as goodness. As an example, consider what is perhaps the most dramatic difference between the two covenants, and certainly the most difficult to comprehend and integrate. We serve Christ's Truth *by not resisting evil* (see Matthew 5:39.) That defies common sense and our every natural instinct which, ironically enough, adds weight to its credibility. The *natural man* is ruled by instinct, and cannot please God. *"All flesh is not the same flesh: but there is one kind of flesh of men, another flesh of beasts, another of fishes, and an another of birds"*—I Corinthians 15:39. Only the former dies and rises again in an incorruptible form. *"Blessed be the God and Father of our Lord Jesus Christ, which according to His abundant mercy hath begotten us again unto a lively hope by the resurrection of Jesus Christ from the dead, to an inheritance incorruptible, and undefiled, and that fadeth not away, reserved in heaven for you, who are kept by the power of God through faith unto salvation to be revealed in the last time"*—I Peter 1:3-5. We serve God by not resisting evil, including the most self-evident evil of them all: physical death. That is, of course, the diametric opposite of the survival imperative obeyed by all not given to Christ.

Thus we may conclude that God's mercy and the power of Christ's resurrection differs humans from the beasts just as our refusal to take its mark or worship its image implies. Given that, to whatever extent we live as beasts to that same extent we do not live as the children of God. That includes a preoccupation with the things of the earth beginning with our own survival and safety—two of America's major considerations. Critics often point out that the Jews fought evil, and use that as a pretext for doing so ourselves. That smacks of both the survival imperative and the territorial imperative noted in some species, which again casts us in the *image of the beast*, but it goes further than that. It also suggests a connection to the *Synagogue of Satan* in that we again act as Jews (thus *calling ourselves Jews* by our actions) *who are not Jews*. More importantly, we fail to note the significance of the fact that they fought evil as God defined it and, more importantly still, at His explicit command, and under His direct guidance. Indeed, when they failed to heed that guidance, they found themselves in serious trouble.

That portrays a very special relationship between God and His Chosen People which we emulate only at our own risk. The Jews fought evil in physical terms for the same reason that they worshiped God by way of physical rites and rituals: their lives founded on good vs. evil defined by the minutiae of the Law.

That's why their expiation for sin took on its grisly animalistic guises, with the blood of countless beasts used to cleanse them of their imperfections. Such activities have been severely criticized by many animal advocates, but it means to show just how harsh God's ultimate justice can prove for the unbeliever. Just as the Jews could never perfectly keep the Law in the flesh, and just as they could never physically eradicate evil, neither could their animal sacrifices permanently cleanse them. By contrast, the New Covenant stresses that *sin and evil lie not in the flesh but in the heart* (see Matthew 5:28, for example.) As with God's worship, it's a matter of *spirit* rather than flesh, which explains how and why Christ, the perfect sacrificial Lamb, took the place for all of those animals once and for all. Although physical in appearance—and including the physical—it was actually spiritual in nature. If we deny that sacrifice, *there is no other*. If we act as beasts, we deny that sacrifice, and we share a far worse fate.

Yet, if we take good vs. evil as our philosophical foundation, best of intentions and appearances notwithstanding, we do just that, for the eternal contention is not between good and evil but between Truth and Anti-Truth. To accept Christ is to accept the Truth He embodies, and that Truth tells us quite specifically *not to resist evil* and to *love our enemies!* Indeed, Christ makes a point of differing His covenant from the Old (see Matthew 5:43-44). Ironically, that too is a Law of survival. Good vs. evil and self-determination go hand-in-hand. Self-determination demands that we deliver ourselves from evil, for it cannot allow for any other authority above itself. Consider where this has led us. What chiefly empowers our illusion of self-determination? Can we call it coincidental that our current Holy War finds its genesis in the destruction of the world's most prominent symbols of LOM and of our illusory military might? Consider that the way of life based on LOM which we stand so ready to defend by way of that might, usually with the full support of most Christian denominations, is not the *"way"* that Christ embodies. If that's the case, then whose "way" is it? If Christ's way is the way of eternal Life, what might we logically expect of the way of life offered by His mirror-image? A master of deception, Satan's temptations often won't appear as temptations at all, and may even seem righteous. That explains why he's gone to such lengths to equate righteousness with goodness.

As an especially dramatic example, consider the immediate aftermath of 9/11. At our government's official behest, leaders from a number of religions prayed not only for the families and loved ones of the victims, but to beseech God's—or *gods'*—blessings for America as well. While that might seem a good thing to do, we Christians could hardly consider it righteous. On the contrary, we could readily envision a similar scene in a Roman or Babylonian court. Yet, what else could we expect from a government that mandates that all religions be treated as equally valid? That defies one of Christianity's most basic precepts—that salvation and the worship of the true God come *exclusively* by way of His Son! Still more commonly overlooked, they come by way of the true God's Holy Spirit which we have almost universally replaced with the human spirit! America's roots yielded the inevitable fruit: in the name of expediency and tolerance, the self-evident truth of polytheistic idolatry won out over the much harder monotheistic Truth expressed by the Son of God! Like it or not, the God of the Bible is a *jealous God* who will brook no rivals. Yet, we look at an absolute God as an evil, while considering an egalitarianization of all deities a major good. How can the Christian not see that as Antichrist?

There is an element of good in absolutely every event, circumstance or situation and 9/11, for all its tragic components, is no exception. *"And we know that all things work together for the good to them that love God, to them who are the called according to His purpose"*—Romans 8:28. Indeed, 9/11 has proven very illuminating in that it reflects which god we truly serve as a nation and, while that's a good in itself, the news it reveals is not. Justice and revenge stand at the center of the Old Covenant, while mercy and forgiveness are the primary characteristics of the New. Which do we nationally embrace? Shortly after those religious leaders prayed for God's blessings, President Bush's told us: *"Our nation is somewhat sad, but we're angry. There's a certain level of blood lust, but we won't let it drive our reaction. We're steady, clear-eyed and patient, but pretty soon we'll have to start displaying scalps."* The blessings of which god did we request? It's somewhat ironic that, although associated with the Native Americans, scalp hunting actually began with the whites who stole their lands—in the name of God, of course. Moreover, although partially motivated by fear and hatred, it was largely a matter of dollars and cents: each Indian scalp fetched a substantial bounty. It was also President Bush, a self-avowed "born again Christian", who popularized "God bless America" and reintroduced "One Nation Under God." While not meaning to criticize the President, doesn't that sound eerily similar to a wolf in sheep's clothing, or a false prophet?[3] *"'Verily, verily, I say unto you, he that entereth not by the door into the sheepfold, but climbeth up some other way, the same is a thief and an robber'"*—John 10:1. We literally stole this land from its rightful owners whose scalps we later displayed; what other harvest could we expect?

Fruits must follow the pattern of their seed. Given that, and given that Satan's major weapon is deception, consider the fruits coming from this resultant wars in Iraq and Afghanistan. Ostensibly aimed at first ousting Saddam Hussein, and then at bringing Osama bin Laden and friends to "justice," it has featured a number of lies, cover-ups, and illegal activities in both the fomenting and the execution of the conflicts. The *Wikileaks* controversy of mid-2010—where the whistle blowing website released thousands of secret documents concerning the Afghanistan conflict—demonstrated just how commonly our government dedicated to self-evident truth resorts to such measures. The government's frantic response demonstrated how important it considers concealing facts about its actions from the people in whose name it performs them. Which god does that describe? *"'No man, when he hath lighted a candle, covereth it with a vessel, or putteth it under a bed; but sitteth it on a candlestick, that they which enter in may see the light. For nothing is secret, that shall not be made manifest; neither any thing hid, that shall not be known and come abroad'"*—Luke 8:16-17.

---

3   Even more frightening, especially in the case of Mr. Bush, the false prophets very probably don't recognize their fallacy and, so, many can be taken in by their legitimate sincerity even as they are.

If we take this as a confrontation of good vs. evil—as the term "evil doers" clearly implies—how do we define those terms? Consider: bin Laden and his cohorts are wanted for physically killing people and threatening America's security and interests in general. Yet, in John 8:44, Christ clearly links Satan's evil to his lack of Truth—a lack which America demonstrates in abundance. Who do we serve by combating evil, especially when we define the term? The embodiment of the Truth that he lacks also tells us quite specifically *not to fear those who can harm or kill the body,* yet we make war on terror—by definition the fear of those who can harm or kill the body. In addition to the falsehoods we find essential to conducting the war, do we not defy Christ's commandments in the most fundamental sense? Isn't that, by definition, *Antichrist?* The lie of life—survival—as the supreme good begets more lies defined in terms of national security that we hold worthy of preserving regardless of the whatever breeches of God's Word might prove necessary, including the idolatrous display alluded to in the wake of 9/11. As an especially prominent example, again and again we see the CIA's use of illegal interrogation techniques (in addition to other issues) justified as enhancing our ability to combat terrorism and preserve American lives. In a similar fashion, we find even investigations into what they actually do denied with the argument that it would prevent us from working smoothly with other intelligence gathering agencies around the world who presumably do much the same thing. Again we find a universal influence characterized by deception, untruth, and defiance of Christ's commands all based on the *mark of the beast.* That's what happens when we take Life as both our god, and as our unquestionable highest good.

If we take life as our greatest good, we must take all that we associate with it as commensurate goods, but those associations need not remain confined to the tangible. Consider two of our most cherished freedoms. Both the rights of freedom of expression and freedom of religion share speaking of ourselves in common, which means that both have the Devil in common. *"He that speaketh of himself seeketh his own glory: but He that seeketh His glory that sent Him, the same is true, and no unrighteousness is in Him'''*—John 7:18. Fruit must follow the pattern of its seed: we founded this country on the lie of self-determination which amounts to self-deification. How then could we not replace the Word of God with the word of man just as we replaced divine Truth with self-evident truth, and divine wisdom with human wisdom? How could we expect not to manifest the appropriate desires? No wonder we've grown so obsessed with the things of the earth while counting our material affluence as a sure sign of divine approval! We believe what we want to believe, and in our unchanged states, divine Truth has no inherent appeal for us even when it's quite reasonable. Think about it! Does it make sense that God would reward our righteousness with the very things His own Son, speaking on His behalf, tells us to eschew? Given that He did so for His Old Testament favorites, doesn't such a belief at least hint at the *Synagogue of Satan?* Consider the concatenation of mirror-imagery. We exchanged Jehovah God for "Nature's God" as our national deity, self-evident truth for divine Truth as our messiah and, inevitably, the human spirit for the Holy Spirit as what ultimately unites us! For all practical purposes we've replaced God, just as Satan has intended all along! This is but the beginning. As we proceed we'll find example after example of things that we universally hold in high esteem that are actually *abominations to God,* and in diametric opposition to Christ's teachings.

Nowhere in our history can we find a broader or a more consistent campaign of glorifying freedom and democracy than that launched by George W. Bush in the wake of 9/11. Although exaggerated, he nevertheless reflected the general sentiment of the people: the vast majority of us have long taken them as unqualified goods worth both dying and killing to maintain.[4] Largely due to his influence and as a racist reaction to Barak Obama's election in 2008, we now see a most revealing blending of patriotism and religion among the nation's conservatives. Religion implies a deity: which god do we have in mind? These Conservatives, especially the new Tea Party offshoot, apparently appeal to the American God. That seems a curious appeal

---

[4]   Perhaps it's only coincidental, but a recent poll demonstrated that more than 50% of Americans have below average IQs.

to patriotism considering that the Founders emphatically disavowed any divine inspiration and sought to maintain a distinction between church and state. Even they demonstrated the impossibility of doing so. Consider: what American school child has not memorized the famous sentiment, *"Give me liberty, or give me death!"* Consider for a moment the context of that famous phrase: *"Is life so dear, or peace so sweet, as to be purchased at the price of chains and slavery? Forbid it, Almighty God! I know not what course others may take; but as for me, give me liberty, or give me death!"* As with President Bush, Patrick Henry considered himself a Christian. Yet, think about it. Given that God appoints the powers[5] that be, he equates "Almighty God" with freedom from His authority, while equating that legitimate authority with "chains and slavery" that he would willingly sacrifice his life to abandon. Doesn't that sound like Antichrist? Consider what this implies. Death—of self or of adversary—is preferable to absolute authority, yet, it is God's absolute authority—*and that alone*—that saves us from perdition! That is an essential difference between good vs. evil and Truth vs. Anti-Truth. We've held the things of the earth as more valuable than eternal life from our very inception.

Given the mirror-imagery we've already encountered, could it be that, despite what we think, we don't really value life at all? Consider a quote nearly as famous as Henry's. *"And what country can preserve its liberties, if it's rulers are not warned from time to time, that this people preserve the spirit of resistance? Let them take arms. The remedy is to set them right as to the facts, pardon and pacify them. What signify a few lives lost in a century or two? The tree of liberty must be refreshed from time to time, with the blood of patriots and tyrants. It is its natural manure"*—Thomas Jefferson—November 13, 1787. Noted historian Howard Zinn added, *"When people refuse to obey, then democracy comes alive."* By definition, that makes "live" democracy illegal, those embracing it lawbreakers which the Bible defines as *workers of iniquity. "Submit yourselves to every ordinance of man for the Lord's sake: whether it be to the king, as supreme; or unto governors, as unto them that are sent by him for the punishment of evildoers, and*

---

[5]   See Romans 13:1

for the praise of them that do well"—I Peter 2:13-14. Think about it: in a Biblical context, where do we find the *"spirit of resistance"* combined with a refusal to obey except in Satan's heavenly rebellion against God Almighty? In what image does that cast those seeking similar ends?*"Let every soul be subject unto the higher powers. For there is no power but of God: the powers that be are ordained of God. Whosoever therefore resisteth the power, resisteth the ordinance of God: and they that resist shall receive unto themselves damnation"*—Romans 13:1-2. What does that suggest about democracy itself born of violent revolution against just those higher powers? What religious/spiritual foundation does that suggest? To seek freedom from God's authority means that we seek freedom from His mercy—absolutely essential to the idea of self-determination—which means that we seek to make ourselves subject to His justice—quite appropriate to a *"nation of laws and not of men".* That in turn obliges us to keep the *entire* Law which still again returns us to the *Synagogue of Satan!* Yet self-determination drives us to disregard God's Law as well in our quest to replace Him entirely. What do we put in place of it? Our own laws, all of which found on the survival imperative and LOM. Self-determination amounts to self-deification: just as we teach the commandments of men for doctrine ecclesiastically, so we take our own laws, beginning with the law of the jungle as our highest authority, and call keeping it the greatest good. That's how America defines its special destiny. There's also a term in the Bible that could define that destiny: *"THE MOTHER OF HARLOTS AND ABOMINATIONS OF THE EARTH"*—Revelations 17:5.

Again note the very basic deception inherent in the whole issue of self-rule. We cannot free ourselves from authority itself, but only from what we take as its source. Also consider again the Truth found in Matthew 6:24: the idea that, acknowledged or not, *we serve one master or the other.* A master is, by definition, an absolute authority source. To "be in authority," as with a master-servant relationship, implies subordinates, and it is around that issue that most of our common definitions of freedom revolve. Most of us take great umbrage at the very concept of servitude, divinely directed or not. Well we should:

such is our natural state. More pertinently, as the Patrick Henry quote above intimates, we have been systematically *taught* to take umbrage at that concept just as Satan did leading him to his ill-fated rebellion. Again by definition, that means that we have been systematically taught to take umbrage at serving God toward the same end. Far less obvious, someone has put in a great deal of effort to *keep* us in that natural state. Someone guised as Nature's God.

Perhaps we should more carefully examine that state. Not surprisingly, physical growth is a mirror-image of spiritual growth. As we grow physically, we expect to become more and more independent, more and more capable of making our own decisions and, extended to its logical conclusion, more and more capable of guiding our own destinies. By contrast, as we grow spiritually we more and more realize how utterly dependent we are upon the Father for absolutely everything—and what a gloriously desirable state that is. Consider the number of times the New Testament refers to us as *"children"* (sometimes *"little children,"*)and the reason for it. In Matthew 18: 1-4, Christ's disciples ask Him, *"Who is the greatest in the kingdom of heaven?"* He responded by calling a little child to Him and setting him in their midst. *"'Verily, I say unto you, except ye be converted, and become as little children, ye shall not enter into the kingdom of heaven. Whosoever therefore shall humble himself as this little child, the same is greatest in the kingdom of heaven.'"* That naturally poses the question of from what He means for us to convert. Given the context, we can assume that He refers to illusions of maturity defined as self-determination, controlling our own destinies and so on. It also brings up the oft-cited difference between the concepts of childlike and *childish*. Here, Christ refers to children who are humble, trusting, loving, and most pertinent to our current discussion, are subject to parental authority. Indeed, such a child will often conclude that something is true simply because "My father (Father) says so."

More pertinently still, such a child will emulate his Father in every way possible (Matthew, chapter six). As such a child grows, those emulations will revolve more and more around spiritual concerns. On the other hand, children have a natural and excusable affinity for the physical—the state Nature's God teaches us to retain. More tragic still, most of us consider remaining in that stage desirable—"forever young" has become a virtual obsession, and a very great deal of our economy revolves around it. Well, why not? After all, our favorite fairy tales always end with the protagonists living happily ever after. We now take consumerism as our guiding principle in the belief that stuff—the specifics don't really matter—will yield the same end, but only if we continue to perpetually replenish it in a childish quest to accumulate the most toys. We have spread that doctrine to the world, which implies that the whole world shares the same fairy tale.

That in itself implies a disturbing Truth. We also like to believe that "we're all God's children," but it just isn't so, at least assuming that we speak of Biblical God. If we consider ourselves Christian, then clearly we also consider ourselves the children of Biblical God, but given our obsession with the things of the earth as our way to happiness, and with that happiness one of our founding principles, where are our works that manifest that belief? If we express characteristics diametrically opposed to those expressed by the Son of God, what conclusion must we reach? If we not only manifest but laud characteristics in diametric opposition to those Christ exemplified, how can we not be considered hypocritical at the least, Antichrist at the worst? If we assume that we mature, then we must be able to "take care of ourselves," and that includes (and to a large extent is defined by) self-defense. Yet, neither Christ nor His Apostles made any effort to defend themselves, Peter in Gethsemane notwithstanding (more about that later). Thus, we find delivering ourselves from evil a major component of that delusion which, to reiterate, we find as a common thread through every pagan population on earth. Ideas do not and cannot remain confined to their initial context, but spread out to attract similar ideas. No wonder we take it as a virtue to remain ever vigilant, ever ready to defend our homeland, our rights, and our freedom against all aggressors when Christ tells us that *His kingdom is not of this earth* and so, *neither are His subjects*. Where does Christ or any of His apostles justify resorting to violence in defense of self or others—or in defense of *any* consideration for that matter?[6]

"'Ye are My friends if ye do whatsoever I command you'"—John 15:14. If we don't act in accordance with Christ's commands, whose commands do we obey? If we must serve one master or the other, then we must obey one or the other. Who tries to deny that in favor of self-determination? Look at Jeremiah 10:23: *"Oh Lord, I know that the way of man is not in himself: it is not in man that walketh to direct his own steps."* Suddenly, the lie of self-determination gains far greater importance, for it reveals whom we thereby actually serve. Again, consider the deception involved. If we take man as the source of political power, collectively directing our own steps, then our rebellions remain against our own kind. But if *God* is that power behind the throne, and the one who rightfully guides those steps, then our rebellions against those powers constitute rebellions against Him! Plain and simple, *we cannot simultaneously accept the ideas of self-determination and the idea of service to one master or the other for they are clearly self-contradictory.* Thus, if we accept the doctrine of self-determination, we call Christ a liar. That also calls His Father the father of lies which puts God in Satan's place—how's *that* for a mirror-image! Yet that has been his intention ever since the original revolution in the Garden of Eden.

But a simple rebellion against God's authority would not have produced the required results. The serpent didn't beguile Eve into simply taking the *Forbidden Fruit*, but into *wanting* to do so. She therefore expressed a desire to substitute the serpent's judgment for God's, thereby making her an active participant rather than a passive victim. That marks the all important difference between sin and *willful* sin. But more immediately important, here we find a vital though almost entirely overlooked lesson directly related to self-determination. What appeared to be of her own free will actually amounted to *Satan's* will be done! In essence, it made her will and Satan's will one in the same—a phenomenon we'll reencounter as we proceed. Common misconceptions to

---

6   Most critics are quick to point out Christ's encounter with the moneychangers in the Temple; we'll deal with that presently.

the contrary, Original Sin had nothing to do with the taking of the fruit itself, nor of the couple's desire for knowledge—that was its form but not its essence. Original Sin amounted to a *willful rebellion against and rejection of God's authority* very similar in nature to Satan's rebellion in heaven—and to our political rebellion against Great Britain! Consider that very carefully: we can define the illusion of self-determination, the foundation of this one nation under God, as the essence not only of Original Sin, but of all sin. That makes such a rebellion the essence of lawlessness which the Bible defines as *iniquity*. No wonder we pay so little heed to the law be it God's, that of the international community, or even our own! Religion and politics blend on a level so fundamental that it's impossible to separate them. That means that the same rebellion against His authority largely characterizes man's fall from Grace which, in turn, is the reason for Christ's earthly manifestation, and the essence of the New Covenant. No wonder we call ourselves one nation under God, but don't dare claim ourselves one nation under Christ! No wonder we found it necessary to substitute self-evident truth for divine Truth, Nature's God for the true God, and the human spirit for the Holy Spirit! No wonder we find so many of our actions motivated by love of and desire for those things of the earth that that *choke the word* (Matthew 13:22,) and no wonder we find those desires at the very core of our entire social structure. The *whole world is under the sway of the evil one.* Who leads the way toward promoting those earthly values as the essential goal of life? Who has turned my will be done into the world's most popular political doctrine? Under whose authority does this government function? One nation under *which* God?

Contrast that rebellion against God's authority, and the whole issue of self-sovereignty to Christ's encounter with the Roman Centurion in Luke 7:2-9. The Roman plead with the Jews to intercede for him, and to bring Christ to his house to heal his beloved servant. As He approached the house, however, he sent forth his friends to tell Christ, *"'Lord, do not trouble Yourself, for I am not worthy that You should enter under my roof. Therefore I did not even think myself worthy to come to You. But say the word, and my servant will be healed.'"*—Luke 7:6-7. Think about it. Are *any* of us worthy to come unto the Lord? After all, Christ said of John the Baptist: *"For I say unto you, among those that are born of women there is not a greater prophet than John the Baptist: but he that is least in the kingdom of God is greater than he'"*—Luke 7:28. John himself agreed, and considered himself *unworthy to so much as unlatch Christ's sandal* (see John 1:27.) Fittingly, Christ came to John rather than the other way around. But, more immediately pertinent, this encounter strikes at the intimate relationship between God's authority and true faith. The centurion went to explain that he too was a man under authority, and that he understood that when one of his servants or underlings obeyed his commands, it wasn't his authority they obeyed but that of the emperor and so, of the Empire itself and, ultimately, of God. In other words, he realized that he had no authority at all in and of himself, but only that imparted to him by his superiors, which ultimately meant God. Most significantly of all, he recognized the same phenomenon in Christ, that He too did not perform His works of His own but by the authority of His Father. In essence, he saw the Father in the Son, for it is in that sense that they are One. At this insight Christ was amazed and exclaimed, *"Assuredly, I say to you, I have not found such great faith, not even in Israel!"* Consider carefully what this means. If Christ has no authority of His own except that given by the Father, how can we Christians expect to have any? Far more importantly, how can we *desire* any? How can we justify a desire for freedom from God's authority, which we do by embracing democracy, and still claim ourselves part of Christ's body?

In the end, we call evil those leaders whom God has ordained because we do not approve of them. Doesn't that smack of the good and evil legacy of Original Sin? It's no coincidence that the knowledge of good and evil lies at the heart of Original Sin, for it proves to be the very essence of self-deification. *"For God doth know that in the day ye eat thereof, then your eyes shall be opened, and ye shall be as gods, knowing good and evil"*—Genesis 3:5. As perhaps the most deceptive legacy of that day, most of us take Satan (or his equivalent) as evil's originator. Ironically, doing so constitutes one of his major successes as suggested by the judgment inherent in that conviction. If we characterize

Satan as the one who originates evil, we must pose a very basic question: is he then the one who condemns us to the ultimate evil of perdition? Is he the one that we are to fear? If that's the case, then we cast him as the ultimate judge and, again, we put him in God's place. Even more absurd, if we make that assumption, then we must assume that the evils befalling Christ, including His crucifixion, also originated with Satan which ends up casting *Satan as our savior*. How Antichrist can you get? Thoughts and ideas cannot and do not remain confined to their initial context. If we acknowledge perdition as the ultimate evil, and if we seek to deliver ourselves from it, we actually seek to deliver ourselves from God, for He is the One able to *"destroy body and soul in hell"*. Bear in mind that nothing inspires His wrath more than a devotion to a false god, and that false worship need not be formalized—and in fact, usually is not. *Thou shalt have no other gods besides Me* [7] is about as absolute as a statement can get. But we do just that by calling Satan evil's originator which casts him as a secondary sovereign which, by definition, makes God less than an absolute sovereign. Consider the subtle twist involved. We then justify God's lack of absolute authority by undermining His absolute *jurisdiction*, and do so most commonly by judging good and evil for ourselves. Yet the Freedom God could not reign over us without the basic belief in good vs. evil fueled by that judgment, with physical life and death the ultimate definitions of both. If we believe that evil originates with Satan, we can believe that evil-doers serve Satan, and can therefore assume that we serve God by combating them. The trouble is, both parties in any given conflict consider themselves the good, their adversaries the evil—allowing both to share the common sentiment that "God is on our side." That's quite probably true—but which god? Which god told us to combat evil doers regardless of how we define them? Which God told us to love our enemies? Which God told us that those *who live by the sword must die by it?* Which god motivates us to place our national security above all other considerations just as the Antichrist will with the literal *mark of the beast?*

---

[7]   The KJV translates it as *"before Me"* but the Amplified Bible adds *"or besides Me"*

Again we touch on that essential dichotomy and the accompanying decision each of us must make: do we set our minds on the things of the earth or on the things of heaven? Each entails a diametrically different definition of Truth, and each leads us in a diametrically different direction to a diametrically different destination—just as we might expect from a contest between light and darkness. We can define that destination as what we take as our source of ultimate authority. Freedom from God's authority, which includes the freedom to confront and battle evil, is one of the major cornerstones of our entire political and social structure, taken by virtually all of its adherents as an absolute good. Yet, consider: no one but a radical anarchist would argue than *totally* unrestricted freedom would yield anything but chaos, and ultimate destruction. *"As soon as liberty is complete,"* observed noted historian Will Durant, *"it dies in anarchy."* We therefore hold as our ideal that which would destroy us were we ever to attain it. Does that seem a likely path for the *"Truth, the Life and the Way"* to advocate? Abandoning the ideal, (along with most other absolutes,) we acknowledge that we must somehow limit our freedom, and the more people we have, the more individual freedoms we must abnegate. We must now resolve the question of who has the authority to determine what freedoms must go and who must surrender them. We cannot escape our need for authority but can only change what we take as its source. Think about what this means: we put ourselves in God's place by taking that authority from Him and bestowing it upon ourselves. Dictionary.com defines blasphemy as *"The crime of assuming to oneself the rights or qualities of God."* Merriam-Webster agrees: *"The act of claiming the attributes of a deity."* Self-determination amounts to self-deification. Consider the irony: the Jews labeled Christ a blasphemer: *"The Jews answered him* [Pilate], *'We have a law, and by our law He ought to die, because He made Himself the Son of God'"*—John 19:7. Don't we do the same thing when we come unto Christ of our own wills as holds true of virtually the entirety of the mainstream Christian religion? Given that *"'No man can come to Me, except the Father which hath sent Me draw him'"* (John 6:44), clearly making it a matter of God's will be done rather than our own, doesn't that constitute blasphemy?

Do we honestly expect to inherit the Kingdom of God by this means? Yet, isn't that the core of our governmental system? Our governmental system is our religion enacted.

President Bush also praised the late Pontiff as a champion of human rights and dignity, while linking that championing to his duty to God. Most of us in the "Free World", including many who would like to become a part of it, take such considerations as unqualified goods. Yet, such concepts prove difficult to even find much less justify in the Bible. Indeed, quite the contrary holds true. Why do you suppose every one of God's messengers, from the prophets to the Apostles, experienced very difficult times at the hands of those they'd come to serve? Why did they put up with such blatant injustices and violations of their civil and human rights without protest? Why do we find the same true of the later Christian martyrs? For what cause did they give their lives? *"Blessed are they which are persecuted for righteousness' sake: for theirs is the kingdom of heaven. Blessed are ye, when men shall revile you, and persecute you, and say all manner of evil against you falsely, for My sake. Rejoice and be exceedingly glad: for great is your reward in heaven: for so persecuted they the prophets which were before you"*—Matthew 5:10-12. If the battle were truly between good and evil, especially if we take life and what we associate with it, including such intangibles as human rights and dignity, as the greatest good, you'd expect God's official spokesmen to sound the clarion, and to issue the call to arms. In fact, that's pretty much what the Jews had expected from their Messiah (more about that later.) Instead we find the exact opposite. The *meek* shall inherit the earth, and the meek do not act as firebrands.

But it goes further than that. Consider, too, that we refer to these concepts as *human* rights, and here we find good vs. evil in one of its most deceptive guises. In spite of overt appearances, the things of man are at sharp odds with Godly things regardless of how good they may appear. Consider Matthew 16, where Christ tells His disciples of His pending torment and death. Peter responds indignantly with, *"Far be it from You, Lord; this shall not happen to You!"* We would normally applaud that an expression of courage and affection in defense of Christ's human rights and dignity (not to mention His life and wellbeing.) Yet, Christ retorts with one of the sharpest rebukes in the entire Bible. *"'Get behind Me, Satan! You are an offense to Me, for you are not mindful of the things of God, but the things of men.'"* (16:23.) That directly links the things of men in general, beginning with physical survival even of an innocent loved one directly to Satan. As part of Christ's body—and so, as part of God's divine plan—the same holds true for us. *"Who shall separate us from the love of Christ? Shall tribulation, or distress or persecution, or famine, or nakedness, or peril, or sword? As it is written: 'For Your sake we are killed all day long; we are accounted as sheep for the slaughter.'"*—Romans 8:35-36. That doesn't sound much like an advocacy of human rights, does it. It doesn't say much about human dignity either, but then the humility and meekness we find so commonly extolled in the New Testament stand in rather sharp contrast to that basic idea as well. No wonder we so often replace them with pride and assertiveness and, in an ironic twist, refer to them as "rights." No wonder too that we so commonly overlook the virtues of patience and forbearance, not to mention longsuffering and forgiveness. Taken as a whole, this places human judgment and wisdom—the way of the world, aka, self-evident truth—at diametric odds with God's, and links them directly to Satan's judgment and wisdom—just as we saw above in the Garden of Eden. One way or the other, we do serve, and service implies obedience. One way or the other, by our very lives, we promote the agenda contained in Christ's Truth—or in Satan's Anti-Truth. The simple state of existing demands it; we cannot escape that service. At the same time, it places all of the above at the heart of the world system with the United States of America its primary advocate, the late Pope not far behind.

Take that point to heart, for it reveals the true nature of our rebellion against God's authority, and defines it as both political and ecclesiastical. Consider Revelations 17:1-2: *"And there came of the seven angels which had the seven vials, and talked with me, saying unto me, Come hither; I will shew unto thee the judgment of the great whore that sitteth upon many waters: with whom the kings of the earth have committed fornication, and the inhabitants of the earth have been made drunk with the wine of her fornication."*

The United States has a military presence in every one of the seven seas, and in the vast majority of the world's nations. We quite literally sit upon many waters and deal with most of the earth's kings. We must bear in mind that "fornication" refers to idolatry, and that we can define idolatry as any devotion taken as more central than devotion to God. Given that harlotry also refers to idolatry, it also means abandonment of the true faith in favor of idol worship—the Almighty Dollar, for example. Ask yourself, as a nation, to what extent do we take a devotion to that dollar—the Profit Motive—as more central to our lives than our devotion to God? What accounts for our ubiquitous presence in all those seas and in all those nations? A harlot is a prostitute—i.e., a woman who indiscriminately fornicates with anyone willing to adequately pay her. Her political counterpart will commit idolatry whenever it sufficiently benefits her financially. Given our global advocacy of that doctrine, we could make a very strong case for this one nation under God qualifying as having made the world's nations *drunk on the wine of that fornication*—and playing a key role in the Great Apostasy at the same time.

Religion and politics merge again: virtually every protestant denomination likewise supports that governmental form in its present manifestation, and most imbibe their fair share of fornicational wine as well. As but a single, albeit perhaps the greatest example, consider that most of mainstream Christianity embraces faiths having no affiliation with Christ at all in the name of *tolerance.* We exchange a brotherhood of Christ for a brotherhood of man and consider that embrace an essential element of the freedom we feel so strongly obliged to defend. Here again we find a mirror-image. We generally call it "fairness" which means, *"not exhibiting any bias, and therefore reasonable and impartial"* (Encarta dictionary.) True Christianity is *extremely* biased: we believe that the Son of the Living God is the only way to redemption—period! Historically, this has caused many problems, but the command is clear:*"Be ye not unequally yoked together with unbelievers: for what fellowship hath righteousness with unrighteousness? And what communion hath light with darkness? And what concord hath Christ with Belial? Or what part hath he that believeth with an infidel? And what agreement hath the temple of God with idols? For ye are the temple of the living God: as God hath said, I will dwell in them and walk in them; and I will be their God, and they shall be My people"*—II Corinthians 6:14-16.

That, too, has a political application. Religious freedom allows us to chose the church that will save us, adding still another dimension of blasphemy. Not only are we saved by our own efforts, we are saved in the manner that we choose, (and, one could argue, by the deity we chose!) Since all but the true God are figments of our imagination (at best), can we not see that as saving ourselves, right in line with the overall concept of self-determination? How clear a picture of self-deification do we need? If we take that a step further and ask, how clear a picture of self-delusion do we need, all of a sudden the mask of the one behind that deception begins to slip. If our governmental system is indeed our religion enacted, and this characterizes religious freedom in the United States, then how must we answer our title question? We have spread both democracy and religious freedom, as well as their attendant beliefs, to the world as a global ideal, all in the name of God! How better could we describe *the abominations of the earth?* How better could we define *wine of fornication?* Consider the irony: we've essentially equated God with freedom from His authority. Where do we find even a hint of Christ or His followers advocating that? If we can't find it, then on whose authority do we do so? Again, must we not consider such an authority *Antichrist?* Consider the insidious deception involved. As a result, as a matter of increasingly rabid desire, the world eagerly surges toward this freedom concept while surging away from God in equal proportions. Doesn't that accurately describe the Great Apostasy? Who plays a leading role in that apostasy? One nation under *which* God?

While it's easy and even somewhat appropriate to blame "materialism" for this, as holds true for LOM, we can find materialism in an unconventional form as well. For example, we also find it in the very widespread dissemination of physical "truths" such as evolution and modern cosmology. Consciously or not, those beliefs color virtually every aspect of contemporary life, and that is a far more important issue than most of us realize. *"For though we walk in the flesh, we do not war after the flesh: (for the weapons of our warfare are not carnal, but mighty through God to the pulling down of strongholds;) casting down imaginations and every high thing that exalteth itself against the knowledge of God, and bringing into captivity every thought to the obedience of Christ . . ."*—II Corinthians 10:3-5. There's a very important reason for that. Whether we ever give it any thought or not, in a very fundamental sense, we are all philosophers in that we all have a metaphysic which we can define as a basic view of the universe and our relationship to it. Most of us don't give even the existence of such a thing, much less its content, any thought at all. Most of us would rather simply absorb the prevalent ideas expressed by our society in general, and our significant others in particular and let it go at that. Hence the danger of the pervading influence of modern scientific thought which we could rightfully liken unto propaganda. This brings up a question we'll deal with more extensively later: *who's really in charge here?* Consider: aside from Charles Darwin, how many "evolutionists" can you name? Yet evolutionary theory pervades every part of our society. In a similar sense, aside from Albert Einstein and perhaps Stephen Hawking, how many cosmologists can you name? Yet modern cosmology also permeates every part of society. Someone is making a very concerted effort to make us believe the Anti-Truths put forth by contemporary science while remaining safely anonymous. Perhaps more telling, that entity is making a concerted effort to make us *want* to believe those truths as we can readily see in their prominent presence in many of our entertainments. Seemingly innocuous, that serves a very potent purpose. After all, we can't fully accept the doctrine of self-determination if we believe ourselves to be divine creations. The desires of our father the devil we want to do.

If we break the word down, we find "de" meaning *of the* or *derived from*, while "sire" can refer to both a king and a father. Our deepest, most heartfelt desires both determine and reflect who and what we are. They likewise act as the most powerful motivators in our lives—i.e., whom we take as our Father (and whose characteristics we therefore seek to emulate,) and who exercises kingly influence over us—i.e., whom we ultimately serve. They color everything we see and hear, and again we encounter that dichotomy between the things of the earth and the things of heaven. As the biggest case in point, when Christ tells us to *"Seek and ye shall find"* (Matthew 7:7,) that exhortation depends on what we *want* to find. What we desire is what we call good, so from those broad categories we derive our entire view of existence and our proper place in it, including our values, virtues, vices and, most important of all, what we are *able* to hold as true and good. So long as we limit ourselves to the *carnal mind,* we can never really accept spiritual Truths in any more than an abstract sense, and certainly not as a value adequate to act as an overall guiding principle.

In actuality, Christ's religion has virtually nothing to do with reason or intelligence (more about that later,) but that doesn't mean it has nothing to do with the mind. Intelligent or not, the mind remains an extremely important portal through which ideas flow, and we need to pay *at least* as much attention to what we feed it as to what we feed our bodies. Not wishing to overdo a point, yet reluctant to allow the significance of such a statement to pass, that means that we need to bring our every thought into accordance with God's Truth—that essentially defines *piety*, which the Bible often translates as *"godliness"*. Needless to say, that seldom proves the case, and it gets harder to do by the day. As we grow older and burden ourselves with increased responsibilities such as family and career, we can easily find ourselves so inundated, so swamped with the attendant details that we have little time or energy left over for what's truly important. That's part of the appeal of the religious service where we pigeonhole God's worship into a neatly prescribed slot that meets our convenience while allowing someone else to tend to the necessary details. It's also not hard to see how those responsibilities and details reflect what Christ said about the *"'. . .care of this world, and the deceitfulness of riches . . .'"* in Matthew 13:22. We then add to this the fatigue and stress often associated with dealing with modern life and, much as merchandisers do with their products, we find ever-increasing diversions a panacea sure to relieve the stress and help us to relax. Soft, gaudy, and attractive packaging defuses the threat, lowering both our defenses and our standards, tempting us with pleasant pursuits that require little effort, and even less thought. In the meantime, in virtually all of those thought-numbing pursuits we find, if we choose to look, a subtle undercurrent of Anti-Truth, quietly eroding our basic beliefs in every manner possible.

Why we should guard our minds and how propaganda works have a very great deal in common. Propaganda cannot create entirely new attitudes, at least not all at once. Instead, it changes existing attitudes a little bit at a time in an insidious process similar to erosion which is cleverly and effectively disguised both by appeals to expertise and by a wide variety of pleasures. Of the two, perhaps the pleasure is the more important, for what we find pleasurable is generally what we find desirable. Thus, we come to take the effects of the propagandistic erosion as a matter of desire. Bear in mind that Paul warned that the End Days would be characterized by " . . .*lovers of pleasures more than lovers of God . . .*"—II Timothy 3:4. Whatever the motive, when we compromise the Truth, we eventually come to take that compromise as the Truth, and so as the baseline for the next compromise. In that manner, incremental step by incremental step, we are led further and further from divine Truth without even noticing it.

This also has a cumulative effect. Ideas cannot and do not remain isolated to their initial context. Instead, they strongly tend to gather into groups of similar ideas which systematically reject dissimilar ones. These thought groups in turn cluster together into *constellations of beliefs.* Taken together, these constellations of ideas along with their emotional responses, create our "introcosms," that private little universe we all carry around inside consisting of all that we hold as reality. That accounts for the long noted fact that no two people perceive the external universe in exactly the same way. That internal reality, where we find the aforementioned heartfelt desires, comes complete with its own set of natural laws, and we can no more consistently defy them than we can their cosmological counterparts. Thus, we must have those laws re-written. Again consider Hebrews

8:10:*"'I will put My laws in their mind and write them on their hearts; and I will be their God and they shall be My people.'"* This removes service and obedience to God from the realm of compulsion or obligation and moves it into the realm of desire. More importantly, we don't obey God in order to be saved but *because we have been saved,* not due to our own efforts but due to God's empowerment, motivated not by fear but by the desire to please Him whom we love.

"'Blessed are they who hunger and thirst for righteousness: for they shall be filled'"—Matthew 5:6. That hunger and thirst does not come naturally. Indeed, as that phrase implies, that hunger and thirst constitutes a blessing that we receive from the Lord. That stands in diametric opposition to the very concept of ecclesiastical self-determination. Think about it: to control our own destinies, to make our own decisions, to be our own person largely define our concept of maturation. One could even make the case that a government built on self-determination is the logical outgrowth of humanity's racial maturation. If we believe that, then we must take a return to an authoritarianism—such as a kingdom, for example—as a retrogression. But again we find a mirror-image, for fear motivates us far more readily than love. Try as we will, we can't outgrow that pesky posthumous risk of hell and damnation, and many of us seek to hedge our bets a bit. Ironically, more Americans now than any time in recent history believe in God, due in large part to that consideration.

But here self-determination does its insidious work, and religion and politics merge still another time. The recent advent of the "Tea Party" in America has spurred a movement to "return to God" for political reasons not far different from what we found in Constantine's Rome in what we could call the hijacking of Christianity (more about that later). This epitomizes America's duplicity concerning religion, for, instead of turning to the true God, we turn to ourselves by way of endless interpretations of the Scriptures. *"And account that the longsuffering of our Lord is salvation; even as our beloved brother Paul also according to the wisdom given unto him hath written unto you; as also in all his epistles speaking in them of those things; in which are some things hard to be understood, which they that are unlearned and unstable wrest, as they do also the other Scriptures, unto their own destruction. Ye therefore, beloved, seeing ye know these things before, beware, lest ye also being led away with the error of the wicked, fall from your own steadfastness"*—II Peter 3:15-17. Note that "wrest" means to *"twist or turn from the proper meaning"* (Dictionary.com.) Notice, too, how he essentially equates that perversion of Truth with wickedness, which likewise tends to equate evil with Anti-Truth. But more pertinent by far, he is warning us not to divorce ourselves from the Truth, and remain steadfast in that which has been *divinely revealed to us.* That steadfastness, which we can essentially equate with faithfulness, is an integral element of the righteousness for which the blessed hunger and thirst. *"Wherefore laying aside all malice, and all guile, and envies, and evil speaking, as newborn babes, desire the sincere milk of the word, that ye may grow thereby: if so be ye have tasted that the Lord is gracious"*—I Peter 2:1-3. Where do we find room for combating evil if we put off the essential warrior attitudes of malice, evil speaking and guile? What motivates us to do so if we put away envy? According to those verses, how can we define growth as self-defense or as concerns over national security? We cannot attain righteousness by our own efforts regardless of what fear might motivate us, so what do we strive to attain instead? As with everything else, our salvation is a matter of *Thy will be done.* Yet a great, great many of us, in ways both blatant and subtle, have perverted that into a grotesque and deadly mirror-image. Nothing engenders God's wrath so fiercely as a devotion to a false deity, yet devotion to any god lacking Christ amounts to just that, and violating that Truth in the name of equality and fairness is largely what this one nation under God promotes! It's one thing to tolerate it within our own borders, but we champion the same cause around the world. That moves the issue from a matter of necessity to a matter of preference and open advocacy! It's no coincidence that the same nation spreads the doctrines of political and religious freedom to the world as the ideal. The whole world is under the sway of the Evil One, and his evangelists have busily wrested God's Truth for centuries, doing all they can to make religion appealing to the *natural man* and the *carnal mind.* The United States is merely the logical result. We mentioned that Satan's temptations won't always seem evil and will sometimes even seem righteous; this makes an excellent case in point. Satan will lure some away from even a semblance of faith, while at the same time leading others along the far more righteous appearing path of false religion. Indeed, he may well even encourage us to worship God—so long as we don't do so in *Truth and in Spirit.* We cannot worship God in the flesh any more than we can follow Christ in the flesh, for the flesh and the Spirit are antagonistic toward each other. *"For the flesh lusteth against the Spirit, and the Spirit against the flesh: and these are contrary the one to the other: so that ye cannot do the things that ye would"*—Galatians 5:24. In verse 24, Paul makes the issue still clearer: *"And they that are Christ's have crucified the flesh with the affections and lusts."* Still again we find two extremes with the proper path a narrow strait between them. A strait that few are finding. It is for those seeking that path that we've written this.

As we might expect from Satan's ministers, they have also long utilized the survival imperative in their Scriptural wresting. As a result, in a well-intentioned bid to save souls, the vast bulk of mainstream Christianity has made doctrine the essence of salvation. Since true faith must come from God (see below), that actually means that we've made the content of our beliefs the essence of salvation which ultimately comes down to believing in ourselves—another form of self-deification, and another form of blasphemy. Much as we find in the difference between righteousness and goodness, no matter how hard we may try, we cannot divorce the content of our faith from the means by which we attain it. No matter how we may argue to the contrary, self-excogitated doctrine which we learn amounts to salvation by way of the human spirit and as a result of my will be done. It is to this righteous looking but impious end that Satan in his guise as the Angel of Light, and his legions of "ministers of righteousness" lead the unwary. Notice a curiosity: the idea of learned doctrine parallels the evolutionary thesis that our intellects—our capacity to learn—saved proto-humanity from extinction. In other words, we racially delivered ourselves from the greatest, most cataclysmic evil we could face, to our current status as masters of the earth. Doesn't that sound like something that would appeal to the *natural man?* Doesn't that sound like a logical doctrine of the *Prince of the World?* Doesn't it seem appropriate to Nature's God—this nation's official deity? Notice too how we find that mirrored in today's belief in education as the panacea sure to cure all of our social ills. In theory, that opens the Pearly Gates to anyone accepting man's words as the truth: self-determination taken to its logical conclusion.

In a subtle example of the two economies merging, and epitomizing the ascendancy of Satan's spiritual economy, doctrinaires, eager to give the consumer what they want toward the self-evident good of saving their souls, custom design, modify and update their deities to make them more palatable, in essence fusing the Constitutional link between self-expression and freedom of religion into an unholy whole. It would seem that self-evident truth antedates the United States by many centuries, and that America merely formalized it. Again meaning no disrespect, and certainly not wishing to advocate iconoclasm as an ideal, we must bear in mind that Christ warns against that sort of thing quite specifically in Matthew15:8-9 while upbraiding the Jewish priests. *"'These people draw near to Me with their mouth, and honor Me with their lips, but their heart is far from Me. And in vain they worship Me, teaching as doctrines, the commandments of men.'"* Bear in mind that He's not castigating the overtly unrighteous here, but those generally considered among the most pious in the Jewish community. Notice too that He says that they worship Him *in vain* which the dictionary defines as "fruitlessly" and which the Amplified Bible translates as "uselessly". It also breaks the Second Commandment in a very specific manner: unless we worship *God in Truth and in Spirit*, which means in the Truth that Christ embodies and enabled by the Holy Spirit we don't worship Him at all, and so have taken His name in vain! That defines a social Christian.

No one has perfect understanding, yet good vs. evil with the faith-obedience combination as the essence of salvation makes just such an understanding indispensable, which likewise makes teachers indispensable. Indeed, if we intend to "save the world" then the more teachers the better! If salvation depends on us knowing the Truth and acting accordingly, which the emphasis on doctrine must assume to make any sense, then salvation comes down to obedience, with the love of the Truth not an end in itself but a means to the end of that obedience. Thus our salvation ultimately rests on our actions, and we're right back to saving ourselves again, with those directing and chastening us fulfilling vital roles to that end.[8] Just as Christ is our personal Savior, so we have a personal relationship with Him. Accordingly, *"'Seek and ye shall find'"* is not intended as a one-time event as casting personal salvation as Christianity's centerpiece implies, but as a lifestyle dedicated to spiritual growth. Consistent with the mirror-imagery we've found, that makes salvation not the end we seek, but the *beginning*, just as "rebirth" implies, and as all the allusions to growth we see throughout the New Testament suggest. If we take obedience as the Law's fulfillment, and take acting in accordance with the tenets of our faith as the definition of that obedience, then, once we figure we've proven ourselves good enough we can feel free to let our guards down and go back to our routine lives. That helps to explain why, for example, people who supposedly believe that *the meek shall inherit the earth* can still proclaim themselves "Proud to be an American," apparently having no problem with the obvious contradiction. It explains why people calling themselves Christian can react like frightened animals to every stock market fluctuation or world event, and in general show so little love to their neighbors. It explains why Presidents who proclaim themselves born-again Christians and invoke God's blessings for our nation can go to war over economic interests and visions of an international terrorist conspiracy determined to destroy us. *We cannot love God and fear man.* To do so, we end up with trying to *serve two masters,* both God and Mammon and, as we'll see shortly, that cannot be.

---

[8]   The proper role of church elders doing just that takes us too far afield from our current subject matter.

Chapter Two

lthough Christ cited God and Mammon, a personification of money, as the only masters we can serve, that service goes well beyond money per se in much the same way that LOM has both a conventional and unconventional application. That service not only relates to pecuniary matters, but to the value system underlying the desire for them. Reduced to its fundamentals, that strikes at our most basic definitions of good and evil and, as we might expect, defines them in earthly vs. spiritual terms. That follows, for nowhere do we find the dichotomy between good and evil more dramatically portrayed than in God vs. Satan.

Given that Satan's chief evil is his lack of Truth, and that his primary weapon is deception, it shouldn't surprise us to find a great many misconceptions surrounding these terms. Yet, how we define them very greatly determines which master we serve, for we cannot serve the true God without His Truth as our foundation, and all of Satan's machinations are geared toward keeping us away from that vital knowledge. *"My doctrine is not Mine, but His that sent Me. If any man will do His will, he shall know of the doctrine, whether it be of God, or whether I speak of Myself"*—John 7:16-17. That doctrine is the *"way"* which Christ embodies. Nowhere do we see that way more clearly illustrated than in the issue of judgment, perhaps the most essential requirement of the good vs. evil mindset. Those of the *carnal mind*, limited to physical perception, cannot do other than define good and evil in physical, chiefly behavioral terms. Yet Christ says, *"Judge not according to appearances, but judge righteous judgment"*—John 7:24. Notice how that strongly implies judging by physical appearances as inherently unrighteous. By extension, that makes physical perception itself inherently unrighteous, or at the least, deceptive. For the most part, we prejudge what we call good and evil, and then attribute the appropriate labels to that which produces the appropriate results.

That helps to explain why so many of us have long taken our prosperity—consisting of the very things of the world that Christ tells us to eschew—as a sign of God's approval. If we do that, then it seems quite reasonable to defend those riches against those who would take them from us. That applies as much domestically as internationally, as much individually as collectively as we see in frequent court battles and law suits.[9] It seems equally legitimate to defend ourselves from those who would threaten what we take as our moral source of that prosperity, and again the two definitions of economy blend, this time with significant political overtones. This has led to what's sometimes called "American exceptionalism," the belief in the unique and utter goodness of the American soul, and the irredeemable, evil of those who oppose our self-evident righteousness. (More about that later.) That's not what Christ says, and again we can see the sharp distinction between good vs. evil and Truth vs. Anti-truth. He tells us: *"And unto him that smiteth thee on the one cheek, offer also the other; and him that taketh away thy cloak, forbid not to take thy coat also'"*—Luke 6:29. Doesn't sound much like standing up for your rights, does it? But then, where does Christ tell us to do that? What we take as our fundamental truth—by definition, our fundamental authority—determines how we define good and evil. That verse, as with many others, reflects an utter divorce from and distain for the things of the earth, both tangible and intangible, both their acquisition and their loss of no importance: the cloak and the coat share an equal lack of value. Even more, Christ tells us not only to accept a slap on the cheek, but *to offer ourselves up for another.* Why? Christ explains: *"'For if you love them which love you, what thank have ye? For sinners also love those that love them. And if ye do good to them which do good to you, what thank have ye? For sinners also do even the same. And if you lend to them of whom ye hope to receive, what thank have ye? For sinners also*

---

9   In that regard, note a widely acknowledged trend. These days the idea isn't so much to serve the truth as to win the case, often due to the strategies of clever and *expensive* lawyers.

lend to sinners to receive as much again. But love ye your enemies, and do good, and lend, hoping for nothing again; and your reward shall be great, and ye shall be children of the Highest: for He is kind to the unthankful and the evil. Be ye therefore merciful, as your Father also is merciful'"—Luke 6:32-36.

How can good *vs.* evil—by definition, resisting evil and seeking to overcome it—fail to contradict that command? Notice how He equates being merciful with doing good (not to mention acting in accordance with God's will). Paul agrees. *"Be not overcome of evil, but overcome evil with good"*—Romans 12:21. We overcome evil with mercy just as our Heavenly Father has, which means that we don't get sucked into evil as our response! By contrast, we generally overcome evil with evil and call doing so good. *"If it be possible, as much as lieth in you, live peaceably with all men. Dearly beloved, avenge not yourselves, but rather give place unto wrath: for it is written, Vengeance is Mine; I will repay saith the Lord.* [Deuteronomy 32:35]. *Therefore if thine enemy hunger, feed him; if he thirst, give him drink: for in so doing thou shalt heap coals of fire on his head* [Proverbs 25:21-22]"—Romans 12:18-20. If you think about it, that's actually quite logical given the appropriate premise. By our own definitions, we generally take death as the greatest evil, yet we frequently use that evil in the service of our self-defined greatest good. If fruit must follow the pattern of its seeds, what does that suggest about that which we seek to defend? Those who walk without Christ are the ambulatory dead, appearances notwithstanding. By definition, a deity exerts paramount influence over its followers. Thus, the influence to which we respond at any given moment acts as our deital influence for that period of time which can make us idolaters for that period of time. Given that, have we ever considered that such a response is Satan's reason for throwing temptations in our path? After all, his overall objective is to put himself on God's throne. Since *the kingdom of God is within* (Luke 17:21), he must do so by putting insinuating his way into our body temples and taking the throne of our hearts! Service to Mammon comes down to facilitating that takeover.

Transcending national borders, traditions, religions or any other consideration, good vs. evil is the most widely accepted truth in the world, which almost by definition makes it part of the *broad and spacious way*. If we look carefully we can find a telltale fingerprint on this issue. Consider: we end up taking good vs. evil as the truth which obviates seeking Christ's Truth. That reveals good vs. evil as evil in the Satanic mode of lacking that divine Truth. If Christ is also the Way and the Life (see John 14:6), and if *"no man cometh unto the Father but by Me"*, then we reveal the real reason for doing so. After all, what better way to convince us not to seek the Truth than to convince us that we've already found it? Consistent with the *natural man* given to physical thoughts and desires, that translates "life" into physical life, and defending that life as the way with both of the above taken as the most fundamental of truths. Doesn't that sound like a false messiah? Coincidentally enough, that's also the essential definition of religious freedom: we believe whatever we want. If we equate goodness with righteousness, and define goodness for ourselves, we therefore also define righteousness for ourselves. That remains perfectly consistent with defining God for ourselves. Given the definition above, does that not constitute blasphemy? Do we not therefore find blasphemy at the root of both our governmental form and the national religion underlying it?

If we must serve one supernatural master or the other, and we do not serve God, then we must serve His usurper instead. That means that by defining goodness for ourselves we actually allow Satan to define it for us just as he did with Eve, and render the appropriate service. Moreover, if we equate goodness with righteousness, we thereby allow Satan to define it for us. Would you consider *that* blasphemy? In the name of good vs. evil, he lures us into combating leaders ordained of God in a matter highly reminiscent of his own heavenly rebellion against the same ultimate authority! All our battles with evil, physical and ideological, are holy wars—or, more specifically, *unholy* wars, fought at the prompting of the one who fomented and orchestrated the original rebellion in heaven. Most of us take the good as that which overcomes evil which, according to our simplistic mindset, means that we take as God that which overcomes the Devil with the servants of each defined accordingly. Do you see the deception involved? That allows the Devil to set himself up as an endless parade of adversaries which we can bowl over in our righteous quest for perfection, overcoming evil and moving further and further from righteousness in the process. Albeit subtly and seldom acknowledged, that makes good vs. evil absolutely essential to the most basic theological constructs underlying the vast, vast majority of the mainstream Christian religion! No wonder it has such a bloody history, and such an evil reputation among many, including our Islamic foes. *"But there were false prophets also among the people, even as there shall be false teachers among you, who privily shall bring in damnable heresies, even denying the Lord that bought them, and bring upon themselves swift destruction. And many shall follow their pernicious ways; by reason of whom the Way of Truth shall be evil spoken of"*—II Peter 2:1-2. The traditional Christian relationship to good vs. evil denies just that.

If we take good vs. evil as the eternal conflict and as the proper relationship of God's servants to the Devil's, we must take an on-going conflict between God and the Devil as a similarly proper relationship. Thus, we encounter a number of centuries old questions about how and why a good and omnipotent God could allow so much evil to exist, and why good has yet to triumph over evil in spite of the countless centuries it has tried. It has even led some to speculate that God *can't* prevent evil which, by definition, makes Him less than All-Powerful! While that's an obvious example, note how this also subtly undermines God's absolute authority in another sense. If we take the conflict as good vs. evil, with God and the Devil cast as the corresponding champions, then God *must* confront the Devil. If He *must* do *anything* we automatically cast Him as less than absolutely sovereign, just as we do when we cast Satan as evil's originator.

Yet, the good vs. evil conflict lies at the heart of our entire social and economic structure, and it demands that we judge everything and everyone with whom we come into contact. Not surprisingly, that's not what Christ tells us: *"Judge not, and ye shall not be judged: condemn not, and ye shall not be condemned: forgive, and ye shall be forgiven: give and it shall be given unto you, good measure, pressed down, and shaken together, and running over shall men give into your bosom. For with the same measure that ye mete withal it shall be measured unto you again'''*—Luke 6:37-38. Freedom from God's authority includes freedom from His judgments and the consequent freedom and obligation to judge for ourselves—again, as a matter of *desire*. Thus, we all commit the essence of Original Sin countless times per day—as a matter of desire. Bear in mind that we've linked the things of man directly to the things of Satan. That means that, rather than our own judgment, we thereby replace God's judgment with the Devil's, which means that we replace God with Satan as our ultimate authority and sovereign. How Antichrist do you want? Good vs. evil provides us with the process by which we most commonly do so while, at the same time, making it an imperative directly linked to survival. Indeed, if we take physical survival as our chief good, it grows more imperative all the time. In order to maintain that good, we must be able to judge what constitutes threats to it—hence the ever increasing emphasis on security with "intelligence" indispensible to that end in international and even domestic affairs. But it goes further than that. Relative good can exist only in contrast to relative evil. Thus, the concepts themselves also follow the survival imperative in that we constantly invent new evils with which to contrast our relative goodness. We see that in the marketplace all the time. Manufacturers constantly must conjure up new evils for their products to address to keep our market healthy while perpetuating our illusions of progress at the same time. It goes much further than that, however.

"*The Soviet Union is no more. Some people think, 'what do we need intelligence for?' My answer to that is we have plenty of enemies. Plenty of enemies abound. Unpredictable leaders willing to export instability or to commit crimes against humanity. Proliferation of weapons of mass destruction, terrorism, narco-trafficking, people killing each other, fundamentalists killing each other in the name of God. These and more. Many more.*"—George Bush. That has become the political reality in the wake of 9/11, which Bush himself said changed the world, and good vs. evil begins to reap its final harvest. At no time in our history has the judgment imperative been in greater and more common force, and we find the survival imperative, which replaces fear of God with the fear of man, at its root. As we'll explore in greater detail a bit later, fear of man rather than of God has grown into an irreplaceable political tool, for without it political power no longer has a foundation. That casts fear of God as a political impediment. That means that, in terms too blatant to any longer ignore, the survival imperative now lies at the foundation of every government on the face of the earth! That suggests a single religion common to the entire earth. Given the broad and spacious way, suddenly the exhortations to divorce ourselves from the things and concerns of this world begin to make a great deal more sense. *"And we know that we are of God, and the whole world lieth in wickedness"*—I John 5:19.

Taking such an inherently adversarial stance automatically implies fear and, since we take *more is better* as a cardinal aspect of our sense of progress, it seems reasonable that we'd invent more to fear. Not surprisingly, very shortly after the fall of the Berlin Wall and the collapse of the "Evil Empire" of the Soviet Union, a new global foe arose to take its place: the Axis of Evil. Now, instead of an international Communist conspiracy, we face an international terrorist conspiracy, and a war that even our leaders acknowledge will not end in our lifetimes. Appropriately enough, "terror" means "Intense, sharp, overmastering fear" (Dictionary.com). We are literally at war with the fear of man in defiance of Christ's commands and so in defiance of a healthy fear of God. Doesn't that seem a likely scenario for the Spirit War engulfing us all? This has some very serious political consequences. As the Cold War was aptly named the "secret war," so our war on terror largely happens beyond the public eye which means without the consent or even the awareness of the electorate. Consider what this means. To whatever extent our government works without the knowledge and consent of the people it represents, or at least to its representatives, to that same extent it cannot be a government of or by the people. Moreover, it casts an unknown Elite in the role of deciding quite arbitrarily what's best for the people. That means that an unseen authority, one for which we did not vote and of which clearly all of us do not approve, makes decisions for us and takes actions in our name over which we have no control, and often no knowledge. Ironically, we long heard that a well informed electorate was absolutely essential to a democracy. As recently as 1963, President Kennedy told his audience at Vanderbilt University that, *"The ignorance of one voter in a democracy impairs the security of all."* We don't hear much about that these days. Quite the contrary, we frequently hear "national security" as an excuse for secrecy which amounts to the ignorance of all the voters, and on an ever increasing scale. On PBS, in March of 2002, the venerable Walter Cronkite observed, *"Not only do we have a right to know, we have a duty to know what our government is doing in our name."* Katherine Graham, owner of the Washington Post and Newsweek Magazine, disagreed: *"We live in a dirty and dangerous world. There are some things the general public does not need to know, and shouldn't. I believe democracy flourishes when the government can take legitimate steps to keep its secrets and when the press can decide whether to print what it knows."* Notice how that differentiates the "government" and even "democracy" from the "general public". Just such a separation accounts for the growing sense of disenfranchisement and apathy, and loss of respect among the general populace.

That in turn poses a question we'll encounter again as we proceed: whose security do we mean? Think about it. That suggests that elements within the government—and even the specific elements are not revealed—and some among the press constitute an Elite empowered by nothing but their own hubris to decide what's best for the country as a whole. Neither is this an accident. Quite the contrary, it is a matter of national policy, and has been for a number of years. In October, 1977, *Rolling Stone* magazine ran an article in which Carl Bernstein (of *All the President's Men* fame) said that more than 400 top American journalists worked for the CIA, and that this arrangement went back at least 25 years. He also cited the *New York Times* as one of the agency's top collaborators. In December of the same year, apparently seeking to spread the blame, the *Times* ran an article revealing that *"more than eight hundred news and public information organizations and individuals"* had participated in the CIA's covert subversion of the media—a subversion known as Operation Blackbird. Considering the amount of clandestine activity deemed necessary to maintain our security, isn't our "free" government actually moving in exactly the same kind of authoritarian direction that we rebelled against in the first place? We are not what we say we are and for a logically inevitable reason: freedom as we define it is not possible. *"While they promise them liberty, they themselves are the servants of corruption: for of whom a man is overcome, of the same is he brought in bondage"*—II Peter 2:19.

Once we accept the government's proper function as our protection, which reflects fear of man of course, it can then do pretty much whatever it chooses in the name of that protection. Once we accept secret activity as necessary to that end, the state needs give us less and less justification or details of its actions. As a result, the ultimate actors are held accountable to no one and have essential *carte blanche* to operate as they will. *"[There] exists a shadowy government with its own Air Force, its own Navy, it own fundraising mechanism, and the ability to pursue its own ideas of the national interest, free from all checks and balances, and free from the law itself"*—Senator Daniel K. Inouye at the Iran-Contra hearings, 1986.[10] In terms of authority, what's the essential difference between that and a dictatorship? Yet, isn't that the logical extension of my will be done, especially when coupled with the Profit Motive? FDR famously observed, *"The real truth of the matter is, as you and I know, that a financial element in the large centers has owned the government of the United States since the days of Andrew Jackson."* Apparently Jackson agreed: *"You are a den of vipers, I intend to rout you out, and by the Eternal God I will rout you out. If the people only understood the rank injustice of our money and banking system, there would be a revolution before morning."*

We define righteousness as doing God's will (see John 7:18,) and this is the Truth that sets us free. Yet, we cannot avoid service to one master or the other, so rather than freeing us from service,

---

10   Taken alone that comment would have little importance. However, as we'll touch on a bit later, that's but one of a great many similar comments coming from people who should be in a position to know.

it binds us to service to God. *"For so is the will of God that with well doing you may put to silence the ignorance of foolish men: as free, and not using your liberty for a cloak of maliciousness, but as the servants of God"*—I Peter 2:16. That would tend to define "foolish men" as those who do not serve God. The dictionary defines *malicious* as "deliberately harmful." The word translated as *cloke* (not cloak) is translated from the Greek word *epikalupto* (Strong's HTML Bible Index) which, figuratively, means "pretext." Thus we are told not to use our freedom from Jewish law as a pretext for doing what is *deliberately harmful.* Combat, be it literal or figurative, *always* entails deliberate harm, and also very frequently entails deception. The fact that deception is Satan's primary weapon poses an intriguing question. *What if the whole issue of good vs. evil itself is a deception?* After all, the very next verse (2:17) begins with, *"Honor all men."* We find that echoed in Philippians 2:3: *"Let each esteem other better than themselves."* Perhaps we should inquire about the nature of the deception.

We almost universally attribute evil to Satan or his equivalent, but, tellingly enough, we also always define that evil in physical terms. What if such evil has another origin? Perhaps more importantly, what if such evil has a different *purpose?* We can find that suggested by the events surrounding both Christ's birth (wholesale infanticide at the behest of King Herod—see Matthew2:16,) and of course, the evil of His tortured death. If we are to accept God as the universal sovereign, and also as the veritable definition of goodness—part and parcel of accepting the Truth and of being a Christian—then we must likewise accept the proposition that every aspect of His divine plan reflects both that goodness and that sovereignty whether we can understand it or not. *"And we know that all things work together for good to them who are called according to His purpose"*—Romans 8:28. What good does he have in mind? The way we define goodness depends on which we seek, the things of the earth or the things of heaven, which we can likewise define as temporal or eternal. Simply consider the number of conflicts in which we have engaged, and then consider that they inevitably revolve around threats to the very things of the earth that Christ and His apostles exhort us to eschew. Remember, those things include more than materialism and extend to rights, human dignity and so on. We take the evil as the good, just as foretold in Isaiah 5:20: *"Woe unto them that call evil good, and good evil; that put darkness for light, and light for darkness; that put bitter for sweet, and sweet for bitter."* To dare a paraphrase: woe unto them who take the house of mirrors as reality. We take self-evident truth and scientific revelations as "enlightenment" in place of the *Light of the World*; we take physical pleasures and gratifications as what makes life sweet, oblivious to the bitter afterlife that will yield. In short, our way of life is the way of the world, endless variations on the *kingdoms of the earth Satan offered Christ* (see above), and we would be well served indeed to take Christ's answer to heart: *"'Get thee hence, Satan: for it is written, Thou shalt worship the Lord thy God, and Him only shalt thou serve'"*—Matthew 4;10. We love God, or we love the world, just as we serve God or Mammon, and just as we accept either divine Truth or self-evident truth. Moreover, we cannot worship God without serving Him. Both reflect in our values and from them we derive our virtues and vices—i.e., our entire notion of good and evil.

Again we find evidence of that universal influence, and a clear indication of its identity. Consider again I John 5:19: *"And we know we are of God, and the whole world lieth in wickedness."*[11] That would tend to class those abiding by that system as those who have *"gone out from us"* (I John 2:19.) It would also classify friendship with the world as friendship with that wickedness, with service to that wickedness and, so, worship of that wickedness. Idolatry takes on many non-formalized guises. No wonder we take the transcendence of God's laws as moral and social progress, while never bothering to ask toward what end we progress! No wonder we so assiduously strive to maintain a separation of church and state while maintaining the state's security (survival) as our primary concern, with economic concerns—the things of the earth and the love thereof—the essential definition of that security. Consider the consistency involved. Evil as we define it *always* founds on the things of life, of the earth, and the friendship associated with it. If we take Life

---

[11]   So goes the KJV; virtually every other translation has some variation on "under the influence of the evil one."

as our highest good, we must also take what we associate with it as commensurate goods. That which we take as good reflects in that which we fear to lose which in turn reflects in that which we seek to defend. Those who accept the world system as their paradigm unite in their service to the Adversary, *and in their enmity towards God.* How *broad and spacious a way* do we need?

Sin is a matter of heart, not of flesh, but that, of course, makes it far more difficult to judge, and good vs. evil demands that we judge everyone and everything. Just as we must try to worship God in the flesh, so we must judge by the flesh. Do you begin to see a trend here? Shall we call it coincidental that James begins his harangue in Chapter Four about friendship with the earth by addressing his audience as *"adulterers and adulteresses?"* Shall we likewise deem it coincidental that Christ referred to the Jews during His earthly sojourn as *an adulterous generation?* (See Matthew12:39.) While evidence holds that sexual adultery had grown quite pronounced at the time, in a far more serious context, adultery also refers to idolatry, covetousness and apostasy! Christians are likened unto *Christ's brides* (see Matthew25:10 for example.) Thus, idolatry and sexual adultery find their common ground in *unfaithfulness,* the primary component of the Great Apostasy and the one acceptable grounds for divorce (see Matthew 19:9.) Bear in mind that Christ defines adultery as *taking place in the heart* (see Matthew 5:28,) which is also where we worship God—or don't worship Him—regardless of where our bodies are. Bear in mind too that the Pharisees were the most overtly pious members of the Jewish community—and that their doctrine, presumably including those overt shows, were defined by Christ Himself as *hypocrisy.* (See Luke 12:1, for example.) Thus, while that faithfulness will eventually manifest externally in the good works cited above, keeping it true in our hearts is what really matters, for that is what properly motivates those consequent actions in response to our Basic Question. Not coincidentally, our hearts are also where we find those aforementioned heartfelt desires that so dominate us, and that helps to explain the link between adultery and covetousness. If we make *ourselves friends with the earth,* which we can do without realizing it, we likewise make ourselves friends with *the entity ruling it*. We then serve him rather than God, even though he does his best to disguise that service. We do so most fundamentally by adopting his values and the virtues derived from them and by buying into his clever sleight of hand equating goodness with righteousness. Thus, to whatever extent the Church accedes to concessions with that system and those virtues, to that same extent we must define it as apostate.

While those values and virtues cover a wide range, we are here most concerned with the good vs. evil mindset at the foundation of virtually every religion on earth, including most Christian denominations. As we've noted, the vast majority of us take as the good that which overcomes the evil which means that we take a basic Anti-Truth as a major good. Consider Matthew 13:24-30: *"'The kingdom of heaven is likened unto a man which sowed good seed in his field: But while men slept, his enemy came and sowed tares among the wheat, and went his way. But when the blade was sprung up, and brought forth fruit, then appeared the tares also. So the servants of the householder came and said unto him, "Sir, didst thou not sow good seed in Thy field? From whence then has it tares?" And He said unto them, "An enemy hath done this." The servants said unto Him, "Wilt thou then that we go and gather them up?" But He said, "Nay; lest while ye gather up the tares, ye root up also the wheat with them. Let both grow together until the harvest: and in the time of the harvest I will say to the reapers, Gather ye together first the tares, and bind them in bundles to burn them. But gather the wheat into My barn"'*.

Take that lesson to heart: His servants are specifically told *to take no action against the children of His enemy*. Given that, pay particular attention to verse 41: *"'The Son of Man shall send forth His angels, and they shall gather out of His kingdom all things that offend, and them which do iniquity.'"* If we can define iniquity as disobeying God's will, and we can, then *He has just defined those who take action against the tares as workers of iniquity!* Rather than overcoming evil, they are overcome by it! What does that suggest about the very concept of good vs. evil? More pertinently, what does that suggest about defining the good as that which overcomes the evil? Yet, every nation on earth, every moral philosophy, every religion, every casual notion of good and evil all share that as their common definition of goodness! How clear a definition of *the broad and spacious way* do we need? How clear an example of the universal influence do we need? How clear a definition of the identity of that influence do we need?

Perhaps more than anything, this parable implies that Christ genuinely means what He's said, and that we will face dire consequences indeed if we fail to heed His word. We should well remember that I Peter 4:18 says, *"If the righteous scarcely be saved, where shall the ungodly and the sinner appear?"* Please note that "scarcely" means *by a very small margin,* and is very similar in feeling to the "few" Christ says are finding *the strait and narrow gate.* That means that even those who accept Thy will be done as their guiding principle are scarcely saved while defining those who do not accept it as the ungodly and the sinners. If we define righteousness as Thy will be done, that quite literally makes democracy a government based on iniquity, just as our lawless nascence suggests! That makes its adherents workers/children of iniquity. Thus, we can take Christ's words as a dire warning, echoed by Paul: *"Nevertheless the foundation of God standeth sure, having this seal, The Lord knoweth them that are His. And let every one that nameth the name of Christ depart from iniquity"*—II Timothy 2:19. This one nation under God was born of iniquity, of rebellion against God's authority and that rebellion now comes to full fruition, posing our title question with eternal persistence. Not as a mass, nor as a group, but as individuals we must genuinely ask ourselves which deity we seek to serve and how our attitudes, desires and deeds reflect that choice.

Good vs. evil and obedience clearly have much in common yet, ironically, the whole purpose of the Law was not to elicit obedience, but to demonstrate the human spirit's inability to comply. *"There is therefore now no condemnation to them which are in Christ Jesus, who walk not after the flesh, but after the Spirit. For the Law of the Spirit of Life in Christ Jesus hath made me free from the law of sin and death. For what the Law could not do, in that it was weak through the flesh, God sending His Son in the likeness of sinful flesh, and for sin, condemned sin in the flesh. That the righteousness of the Law might be fulfilled in us who walked*

not after the flesh, but after the Spirit"—Romans 8:1-4. Notice
the intimate connection between worshipping God in Spirit
and walking in the Spirit. That defines God's worship not as an
isolated, recurring incident but as a way of life often referred to
as "a walk with God". Notice too that it sharply dichotomizes the
two, quite consistent with the flesh and the Spirit in conflict with
each other. Guess which one Peter referred to as being scarcely
saved—and which he defined as the sinners. Only by walking
in the Spirit can we manifest righteousness. By definition, if we
walk after the flesh we classify ourselves as workers of iniquity.
Not surprisingly, that iniquity can often look good to normal
perception.

Case in point. Given the *"Good Shepherd"* imagery we find in
the New Testament, (see John 10:11, for example,) our walk with
God includes Christ as our leader, and protector. Easily overlooked,
that likewise casts His followers as sheep, another common
metaphor, and an image of one of the world's most inoffensive
creatures, emphatically in need of protection. This poses some
vexing questions. Need we point out that, nationally speaking, we
cast ourselves as a mighty avian predator? Consistently, not only
do we ever stand ready to retaliate against anyone so bold as to
smite our national cheek, the Bush administration inaugurated
a policy of preemptive action aimed at smiting those who *might*
smite our cheek in the future. *"We must take the battle to the
enemy,"* the President told us, *"disrupt his plans, and confront the
worst threats before they emerge."* Does that sound like what the
Good Shepherd described in the Scriptures would advocate? If
not, then how can we not call it Antichrist? How does that relate
to *the tale of the tares* related above? Does that not define us
as a nation of workers of iniquity? How can a Christian in good
conscience actively support such a government?

If we take Life as our foundational good, then we must
take anything we see as threatening it as a commensurate evil
and, as we see all around us, those threats simply continue to
proliferate until they entirely dominate our thinking. We must
then see those posing those threats as evil doers, and see
whatever prevents that evil as a commensurate good: the ends
justify the means. Consider: only one entity in existence can act

independently—God Himself. All else that happens is in reaction to what has come before in thought, condition or deed. Thus, given that a god exerts paramount influence over its followers, that to which we most strongly react at any given moment acts as our deity for that moment. Given that, if we react to evil doers, whom do we cast as our deity? Who do we serve if our actions replace mercy, forgiveness and often even justice with expediency aimed at survival?

As but a single, albeit especially dramatic example, to the end of "national security", and in clear defiance of international law, America has resorted to "enhanced interrogation techniques" of suspects ("enemy combatants") who are denied counsel, many of whom are never formally charged or tried, much less convicted of ill-defined "war crimes" against America. Indeed, in some cases we don't even pretend that the detainees are actually guilty of any specific actions, but hold them because they *might* have information that *might* lead to allowing us to prevent a possible attack by unidentified adversaries at an undetermined location in the undetermined future. Consider the implications. We have violated our own laws, and we have violated international law, but we have saved lives—at least those breaking the laws say we have. But, at what cost have we done so? What comes next? Shall we conclude that we break whatever laws or conventions that suits the moment's expediency so long as we can justify it with survival? This poses a deeper question, involving the quantitative element characteristic of LOM. If the death of a gunman saves the life of an innocent, does that justify the death of the gunman? What about two gunmen? Ten? Fifty? A thousand? A nation full? What if that "innocent" isn't so innocent from the gunman's point of view? Who among us is qualified to cast the first stone? What if that innocent's death serves a higher, a more noble, perhaps even a divine purpose from that point of view? Where do we draw the line, and who has the authority to do so? Again we encounter the fact that we cannot avoid authority, but can only alter its source, and those who walk in the flesh will inevitably take survival as that ultimate source with whatever expedients they find facilitating that survival taken as the good. That means that they take the Beast as that authority. Whether we like it or not, whether we mean to or not, we *must* serve one master or the other.

This poses some very difficult questions we Christians must ask ourselves, for our government acts in our name. If we consider ourselves part of Christ's body while actively supporting that government, then that government nominally acts in *His* name. We have noted that life without Christ is actually a kind of ambulatory death. Thus, walking after the flesh rather than the Spirit is also a kind of death, which means that we Christians must seriously ask ourselves which walk our actions really manifest. Consider I Thessalonians 5:3: *"For when they shall say Peace and safety, then sudden destruction cometh upon them, as travail upon a woman with child; and they shall not escape."* Yet it is to those ends that we sacrifice trillions of dollars, countless lives, and our every sense of morality and decency every year. Good intentions and appearances notwithstanding, do we not at least have reason to question the righteousness of such activities? Consider the foolishness involved. No matter how hard or even successfully we may forestall death, sooner or later it will claim us all. Thus, we must ask ourselves for what values we are willing to lose our lives? Death can beget only death; walking after the flesh is a kind of ambulatory death, yet that walk leads us to preserve our physical lives at any cost. The natural man cannot understand that those efforts to forestall it rob us of eternal life, for *those who would seek to save their lives shall lose them.* Maybe we hold self-destructiveness as an unacknowledged ideal after all.

It's commonly noted that America's international stature has plummeted, and the most common reason given for it is that we have lost the "moral high ground." Much of that has to do with America's international involvements, especially the increasingly revealed unethical aspects. Directly associated with that we see calls for a "return to the values that formed this country", especially from the newly formed Tea Party and other religious conservatives. Superficially it would certainly seem that we have changed. We have gone from George Washington and Thomas Jefferson who warned against standing armies and international entanglements, through Dwight Eisenhower and his famous warning about the "military/industrial complex", to

George Bush, who labeled himself a "war president," and who admitted that he made executive decisions with war on his mind. Rather than no international entanglements, we are rife with them, poking our national nose into the affairs of virtually every nation on earth. Yet, these reflect the spiritual foundation of this country while hinting at the type of government we really have in lieu of democracy. America was founded on greed, more politely known as the Profit Motive, Biblically known as LOM, and we now see the inevitable harvest of those seeds. The same plutocratic forces that drove us to aggrandize a continent now drive us to aggrandize the entire world in what some call "global hegemony," and others call imperialism. Note the operative term: *driven!* We can no more consistently break our introcosmic natural laws than we can their cosmological counterparts. In Christian terms, we cannot bring about the change of nature central to the entire Christian experience, which means that we can in no way, shape, manner or form save ourselves. Taken together, does that not suggest self-determination as an elaborate ruse? Does that not suggest LOM as the engine so driving us? Does that not suggest a plutocracy rather than a democratic republic as our true governmental form?

We like to call ourselves a "nation of law," but we chronically break or at least circumvent the "Law of the Land" whenever expediency so dictates, just as we so break God's Law with the same rationale. In other words, we violate every principle we presumably hold, both politically and ecclesiastically, in the name of survival—which demonstrates what prime value we actually hold, and what law we feel compelled to implement. More importantly, it reveals *whose* prime value we hold in highest regard. It also goes a very long way toward demonstrating our definitions of good and evil. But here too we find a deception, for the prime value we hold isn't necessarily the survival of the country as a whole. Consider, for example, the validity of our war on terror. Al Qaeda or any of its affiliates cannot hope to seriously injure the United States (or any other major power) militarily. Their sole weapon is fear: that's why we call them terrorists. Thus, this "Holy War" is holier than most of us realize, for *we cannot simultaneously love God and fear man.* Neither can we simultaneously love God and love the things of the earth, and without that love, what threat can losing them pose? On the other hand, war is big business—*very* big business. Not only do we spend more on the military than the rest of the world combined, the Pentagon alone has a larger annual budget than all but a small handful of nations. If money is power, then the Pentagon wields an exorbitant amount of influence over this nation's policies. If we expand that beyond the Pentagon per se, and include its adjuncts such as the intelligence apparatus, and munitions makers who grow very, very rich from our international interventionist policies, we begin to develop a picture of the specific Elite class that actually rules the United States and profits from this holy war. Indeed, we can begin to see peace as actually disadvantageous to them, for peace would curtail both their influence and their wealth.

So, the wars go on and on, and spending on "national security" remains absurdly, obscenely high. In his 2010 State of the Union address, President Obama promised to curtail spending and to work to get the economy back on track—while at the same time saying that defense spending and spending on "homeland security" would not be touched. Consider what this means. If we cannot act but can only react, then we must submit that the terrorists have scored a major, and perhaps decisive victory that has seriously harmed and perhaps even crippled the United States economically. Then again, perhaps they are but puppets themselves, albeit unwilling and unwitting ones—they too must serve one master or the other. The Elites—perhaps best exemplified by the bankers receiving enormous dividends from the bailout money provided by Congress against the people's wishes in 2008—keep lining their pockets while the poor get poorer and the middle class virtually evaporates. On July 30, 2010, *Estado Brazil* cited the *Financial Times* as reporting that the incomes of the majority of Americans had risen only 10% over the past 37 years. At the same time, the incomes of the top 1% trebled over the same period. Top executives now receive more than 300 times the median income. Given that our previous international involvements have inevitably revolved around the protection of American corporate interests, who do we have in mind when we invoke national security as a pretext for our actions? Could that help to explain why the government seeks to keep the majority of those actions secret? If *the whole world is under the sway of the evil one*, and if the evil one's method of interacting with the world is economy in the conventional sense, can we not logically expect to find duplicity, deception and murder intimately related to it? Given that the evil one is, by definition, Anti-Truth, should we not expect to find fear of man at the expense of fearing God an integral part of his means of control? Dare we deem it coincidental that both the Evil One and the war merchants both benefit from that fear and death? The Love of money is the root of all evil, and the Profit Motive is nothing but the love of money. If fear of man can prove profitable, can we not logically expect it to be manufactured toward that end?

We've noted that America and its terrorist foes have a great deal in common, with fear of man the most obvious commonality. Consider: in the wake of 9/11 the news media, which many consider little more than a propaganda organ of the Federal Government, sensationalized the event by showing it over, and over again while making inane comments about how "terrified" the rest of the country was. In point of fact, while distraught, saddened, perhaps angered, the rest of the country did not fear a similar attack or any other direct evil. The vast, vast majority of Americans intuitively realized that a terrorist group could not militarily harm the country as a whole. That poses a disturbing question. If the fear was not genuine, but was deliberately manufactured, exacerbated, and manipulated, what purpose did it hope to serve? Perhaps more pertinently, *whose* purpose did it serve? Consider how the subsequent fear of "sleeper cells" and clandestine terrorist activities parallels the similar fears deliberately fomented as a result of the Communist Conspiracy during the 50s and early 60s—resulting in a Cold War that lasted nearly half a century and resulted in billions of dollars worth of weaponry and war related material. Without fear, there can be no war and without war, there can be no war profiteering nor any power mongering. Power brokering, the buying and selling of political favors, has grown into a major and highly lucrative business in itself, but it too depends on fear. Think about it. If fear per se were the terrorists' objective, then they scored a major victory with the active collusion of the major arm of the State's Propaganda Machine. That suggests a common end sought by both. What ends? Bush got the war he wanted; bin Laden got the holy cause for a *jihad* that he wanted, and both consolidated their personal power. Moreover, both did so in the name of God. As it happens, both did so in the name of a false god.

Even as we break our own laws whenever expediency so demands it, so we do likewise with God's Laws. We are to *love our enemies*, yet we pursue them, kill them and seek to defeat them—in the name of God. We incarcerate them, mistreat them, intimidate them, even torture them—in the name of justice. Again, we must pose our title question. Consider how that parallels the difference between Mother Nature (Nature's God) and Father God. Forget about the specific abuses which again conjure up good vs. evil and invite condemnation. Instead, look more deeply with our title question in mind. Any biologist will tell you that Nature is entirely indifferent to the survival of individuals, but is concerned only with the survival of the whole. The survival of the species usually comes down to the survival of the most dominant individuals—i.e., those who can best contribute to that overall survival. Although generally considered a bit out of date and over-simplified, if we take the "survival of the fittest" as that survival's focal point, then we find a distinct parallel to the survival of the Elite described above, even at the expense of sacrificing innumerable commoners.[12] Simply consider the huge number of civilian casualties (some estimates put it as high as one million) in Iraq, and the growing number in Afghanistan taken as "acceptable" in our battles with the Taliban and al Qaeda. That's right in line with Nature's God as our national deity, and Nature as our cynosure, and in direct opposition to our cherished, albeit illusory notion that *"all men are created equal"*. By contrast, Father God intensely cares about us individually. True Christianity involves a very personal relationship with a very personal Savior. How personal? Consider Revelations 21:4:

---

[12]   While that smacks of "Social Darwinism", no one adopts or confers that designation any longer.

"And God shall wipe away all tears from their eyes; and there shall be no more death, neither sorrow, nor crying, neither shall there be any more pain: for the former things are passed away." Consider that carefully: God *Himself* will wipe away the tears from our eyes! How can we return such love and devotion with anything less, especially if we consider ourselves Christian?

Yet we all do, and that includes the most devout among us. We cannot serve two masters any more than we can live by two sets of conflicting introcosmic laws, yet the vast majority of us try to do just that. Here we can see one of the most tangible results. Satan has scored one his most major triumphs in the over-sanctification of physical life, for, in so doing he has also elevated the survival imperative to our first commandment. As we've noted, if we take life as our highest value, we must take all that we associate with it as commensurate values. Thus, he also elevates a devotion to the things of the earth to a prime commandment which automatically breaks God's First Commandment. By threatening these values, he can then readily translate good vs. evil into physical terms comprehendible to anyone, and open to endless manipulation, with fear of man the key manipulative tool. Then he can lead us to believe that we can and must deliver ourselves from evil by our own volition and will. Self-determination—my will be done—lies at the core of his every temptation for, as proved true for Original Sin, all sin is actually the same sin: deliberately substituting Satan's will for God's. No wonder we find the Satanic economy described in Chapter One as the baseline for our every governmental decision both foreign and domestic! No wonder we find the ones most successfully operating within that economy acting as the Elite. No wonder we exchanged divine Truth for self-evident truth. Who do we serve?

Shortly after His baptism with the Holy Spirit, that same Spirit led Christ into the wilderness for the express purpose of being tempted by the Devil. His forty days in the desert mirrored the forty years Moses and the Children spent wandering in the wilderness after their Exodus from Egypt. That sojourn had a very specific purpose: *"And thou shalt remember all the way which the Lord thy God led thee these forty years in the wilderness, to humble thee, and to prove thee, to know what was in thine heart, whether thou would'st keep His commandments or no. And He humbled thee, and suffered thee to hunger, and fed thee with manna, which thou knewest not, neither did thy fathers know; that He might make thee know that man doeth not live by bread only, but by every word that proceedeth out of the mouth of the Lord doth man live"*—Deuteronomy 8:2-3. Appropriately enough, Satan's first cited temptation was for Christ to turn the stones into bread so that He could satisfy a hunger resulting from a long fast. That bread of course would mimic the *manna* God gave His people during their wilderness sojourn—i.e., the manner in which He delivered them from the evil of starvation. In this case, however, Christ would have provided it for Himself. He would have delivered Himself from evil, which was the actual nature of Satan's temptation. We find a very similar incident during His crucifixion. *"Likewise also the chief priests mocking Him, with the scribes and elders, said, 'He saved others; Himself He cannot save. If He e th king of Israel, let Him now come down from the cross, and we will believe Him'"*—Matthew 27:41-42. Of course He couldn't do that because He was the Truth incarnate and the Truth is that we cannot in any way save ourselves. Take that lesson to heart, dear friend: if even the Son of God was subject to God's mercy, how can any of the rest of us think otherwise?

In both instances we find survival at the core of the temptation. Think about it; in spite of the self-evident good of sating a great physical hunger and satisfying a basic physical need, in spite of the self-evident good of delivering Himself from an obvious evil that threatened His survival, whom would Christ serve by so ending the fast, and whom did He serve by continuing it? But there's much more to it than that. The bread also reflected the Living Bread that Christ is—the source of eternal life! But even the Son of God Himself could not provide that for Himself, for His father is the ultimate source, the Son is our means of accessing that source. *"Verily, verily, I say unto you, Moses gave you not that bread from heaven; but My Father giveth you the true bread from heaven. For the bread of God is He which cometh down from heaven, and giveth life unto the world'"*—John 6:32-33.[13] That has a wider application than might initially seem self-evident. Christ's sacrifice secured our salvation, but His sacrifice is utterly worthless in and of itself. *What* He did is irrelevant: many martyrs have died for their causes, many of which had nothing at all to do with God, or even with spiritual matters. What makes His sacrifice adequate to cover our sins is *why He did it.* He continues in John 6:38: *"For I came down from heaven, not to do Mine own will, but the will of Him that sent Me".* The fact that He did so in response to His Father's will, and that alone, makes His sacrifice worthy because that makes Him worthy! Believing that makes us worthy while linking service to God to service to His Son."*And this is the will of Him that sent Me, that every one that seeth the Son, and believeth on Him, may have everlasting life: and I will raise him up at the last day'"*—John 6:40.

Christ was emphatically specific about the nature of that service. In Matthew 4:8-10 the Devil takes Christ to a high mountain and offers Him, *"all the kingdoms of the world, and the glory of them"* in exchange for an act of worship. Just one act. Christ's response was definitive: *"'Get thee hence, Satan: for it is written, thou shalt worship the Lord thy God, and Him only shalt thou serve.'"* Again, also notice how that strongly implies that we unavoidably serve one master or the other, while equating worship with service. If we look at Luke 4:6, we find the same story but with an important addition: *"And the devil said unto Him* [Christ], *all this power* [of the world's kingdoms] *will I give Thee, and the glory of them: for that is delivered unto me; and to whomsoever I will I give it."* That in itself inextricably links religion to politics. Although that has obvious implications for those who actively seek such power, we must always remember that our leaders are ordained of God and, as such, deserve our respect.[14] They also deserve our obedience up to the point where such obedience supersedes our service to God expressed in our devotion to the Truth embodied in and espoused by His

---

[13] That, by the way, is the *"daily bread"* He refers to in the Lord's Prayer.

[14] As with the evils to befall Job, Satan gives that power to whomever he will but only with God's permission.

Son. Modern life makes that ever-more difficult, but all the forces trying to lure us into disservice share good vs. evil as the common denominator, with divine Truth the evil that distorted vision of good seeks to overturn.

Again we can find some telltale fingerprints. Consider the quantitative element involved just as we find in fiduciary concerns, which we have established as Satan's means of interacting with and ruling the world. If the killing one person is a sin, is killing two people twice as sinful? Is it twice the evil? Does it require twice the retribution? Having established that, Satan can simply run up the numbers until he gets the response he desires. He then tempts us to resist him guised as endless "evils" victimizing endless innocents with delivering ourselves or those innocents from those evils the denominator common to them all. Think about it. Satan sets up one external evil after another for us to bowl over in our inexhaustible righteous wrath, while constantly conjuring up still greater evils for us to battle in the future. Can we take the similarity to the expertly and deliberately manufactured fear used by virtually every nation on earth as coincidental? Where does the evil lie if not in our judgments of it? What authority urges us to so judge them? If we so consistently yield to the Devil's influence, who do we take as our ultimate authority, and so our deity? Dare we deem it coincidental that *every one* of those kingdoms under Satan's sway agrees on good vs. evil as the eternal conflict, differing only in how they define the terms, but with each defining the ultimate good as its own survival?

This creates problems directly linked to the Great Apostasy. We seldom notice that religious freedom also falls under the survival imperative's influence. How so? Given the violence religious intolerance has historically caused, we must reasonably take religious freedom as conducive to physical life and the pursuit of happiness, while seeing religious exclusivity as detrimental to those pursuits. As if to make the matter sure, today we have radical Islam as an especially dramatic example. In Christianity's case, that exclusivity is *supposed to* limit those pursuits. We are to pursue the things of heaven instead of the things of the earth, and that frequently includes deferring transient pleasures for the joy that requires no externals. The *natural man* can neither see nor accept that. As such men have infiltrated Christianity, and to an extent come to dominate it, that lack of acceptance has evolved into doctrine and again we find ourselves trying to serve two masters. But notice a telltale and familiar motif. No one attempts to force us into pursuing prosperity and the worldly concerns associated with it. Rather, in countless ways we are lured to *desire* that end in an echo of Original Sin (see above). Again, we thereby move from passive victim—the Devil made me do it!—to active participants. This has seeped into many mainstream doctrines in manners both tangible and intangible, ranging from "Prosperity Christians" to the far more subtle victims lured into equating righteousness with patriotism. The parallel between patriotism and the glory of the earth's kingdoms seems too obvious to point out.

In spite of efforts to equate the two, love of God and love of country are diametric opposites for those of us participating in the New Covenant. Indeed, we merely need note how intimately intertwined the two were in the Old Covenant—the Holy Land established a very special relationship between the Jews and the Lord—to see that such a relationship among the rest of us again aligns us with the *Synagogue of Satan.* Tellingly, shortly after its discovery some began to refer to the New World as the Promised Land, while others called it the New Eden. At the same time, a group of rabbis dubbed it Babylon the Great, and that appellation seems to have proven more true. As an integral part of America's "divine destiny"—again, in spite of separating church and state, and in spite of declaring itself a secular state—we find a number of references to the New World as a Godly gift. Who has the kingdoms of the world to give to whomsoever he wishes? What was the price he demanded? Have we not paid that price many, many times over? Think about it. For the American patriot, love of country subsumes not only taking both physical life and happiness as unqualified goods, but also as unalienable rights granted us by our "creator".[15] We must therefore take what we find conducive to those ends as equally good, equally right, and equally sanctioned by that creator, and that includes the right

---

[15] As per the Declaration of Independence

to worship God as we define Him in pretty much any manner we chose. How can we define that as divine? Notice the subtly involved. We simultaneously take ourselves as one nation under God and under self-evident truth, not under Christ, and so not under divine Truth. That means that we take ourselves as one nation under a self-designed god which sounds like a pretty accurate definition of idolatry. No wonder we conclude that we all worship the same God! Yet this is what the American patriot seeks to defend. Self-determination, self-deification, idolatry, good vs. evil, the pursuit of and devotion to the things of the earth all blend into an unholy whole, all defended unto the death by the sword against enemies our true Lord tells us to love. Doesn't that sound like a pretty good definition of Antichrist? Doing so in the name of God: does that not add the sin of hypocrisy? Do we not *take the Lord's name in vain?*

A major reason for writing this lies in the fact that many "Christians" may likewise be in severe danger of taking the Lord's name in vain. While we normally limit that commandment to the proscription of a handful of select words—admittedly, with some justification—that commandment goes much further than cleaning up our vocabulary. Feminism notwithstanding, a bride takes her husband's name, which means that she takes his father's name as her own. We Christians are likened unto Christ's brides, and we do the same thing. We do so in vain—i.e., fruitlessly—however if we do not remain faithful to our wedding vows, and a major part of keeping those vows resides in proclaiming the fact of our wedlock in words when appropriate, and in demeanor at all times. It is there that a great many putative Christians fall short not so much as a matter of behavior but as a matter of desire, and again we find expediency and the things of the earth at the root. Most of us try to avoid obvious evils—even nominal Christians usually stay away from brothels, try to limit their drinking and so on. But as with more formalized good vs. evil contentions, these things can readily act as a smokescreen obscuring more subtle but more serious problems endemic to this one nation under God.

Not so long ago the United States, as well as most European countries, considered themselves "Christian nations." Did we really mean it, or did we make that claim in vain? Consider: in order to claim that, we must confess that Christ, the Son of the living God, is the *only way* to salvation—doctrinal differences aside, all Christian denominations hold that one belief in common or we cannot consider them Christian. *"And we know that we are of God, and the whole world lieth in wickedness. And we know that the Son of God is come and hath given us an understanding, that we may know Him that is true, and we are in Him that is true, even His Son Jesus Christ. This is the true God, and eternal life"*—I John 5:19-20. Yet, an elected official making such a claim these days would be committing political suicide, and already we see the satanic roots of serving two masters inherent in our political system—our governmental system is our religion enacted. Think about it. A candidate may confess that he believes in Christ as *his* salvation, and it has become somewhat fashionable to do so, especially among Conservatives. Even at that however, a person running for national office could not hope to win an election by categorically stating that no other way to salvation exists, yet just such a confession is germane to being more that a social Christian (see Luke 12:8.) Thus, such candidates run the distinct risk of making themselves hypocrites in the hope of currying favor among those able to further their political ambitions. *"These are murmurers, complainers, walking after their own lusts; and their mouths speaketh great swelling words, having men's persons in admiration because of advantage"*—Jude 1:16. Ironically, such a misrepresentation stems from the very core of most mainstream Christian doctrines: making personal salvation Christianity's focal point which in fact makes *the mark of the beast* Christianity's focal point. Think about it. As with some of the statements in this work, stating that no one not accepting Christ as their Savior is doomed to perdition can be taken as a threat. Yet, while such ultimately will prove the case in general terms, it is not for the Christian to judge in specific terms. Although *every knee shall eventually bow to the living God* (see Romans 14:11,) there is good reason to believe that a passionate pagan will find greater favor with the Father than will a lukewarm Christian. After all, ultimately it is a passionate, all-consuming love for God that actually fulfills the Law, and that excludes social Christians regardless of how devout they may appear. More immediately pertinent, it excludes duplicitous Christians who use shows of their piety to their own advantage and advancement.

Thus we find love of God and love of Truth combined in the person of His Son, and we can't deny the One without denying the Other. Here too we find perhaps an even larger and more important political problem, for no politician would dare claim Christ as the sole embodiment of Truth and still retain any slender hope of victory. Yet that, too, is integral to the Christian experience. Serving two masters applies as much politically as it does spiritually. *"Pilate saith unto Him, 'Art Thou a king, then?' Jesus answered, 'Thou sayest I am a king. To this end was I born, and for this cause came I into the world, that I should bear witness unto the Truth. Everyone that is of the Truth heareth My voice'"*—John 18:36-37. As that implies, not just everyone can hear and understand that voice which goes to reemphasize the observation that *"the whole world lieth in wickedness"*. At the same time, it does imply that those able to hear His voice accept Him as our king not as a future state but as a contemporary reality! Most patriotic Americans, including many who consider themselves Christian, gloss over or ignore that fact. Instead, we patriotically define absolute authority as evil, freedom from it as our greatest good, both politically and spiritually expressed in democracy and religious freedom. Do we not thereby take Christ's name in vain? Do we not thereby define Him as evil? Do we not thereby also define His *position* as evil? Does that not define the One who sent Him, and in whose Name He spoke, evil as well? *"When ye pray, say, Our Father which are in heaven, Hallowed be Thy name. Thy will be done. Thy kingdom come, as in heaven so in earth'"*—Luke 11:2. You doubtlessly recognize *the Lord's Prayer*. Notice that Christ establishes God as a king, as an absolute authority and reconfirms it with *Thy will be done on earth as it is in heaven*. American patriots defend the diametric opposite. How Antichrist do we want?

Religion and politics merge in an extremely fundamental question we Christians must address. When the time comes, our leaders will be judged by standards we cannot comprehend.

Even so, as individuals, we Christians must consider: if our king is not from this world, and if His kingdom is not of this world, how can His followers be of this world? How can we support the concerns and agendas of this world and still claim to be part of His kingdom when we find one exhortation after another to eschew earthly concerns? Note, for example, that Matthew 15:22 lists the *"cares of the world"* along with the *deceitfulness of riches* as what choke the Word and make it unfruitful. It doesn't curtail the Word itself: we can mouth them all we like, but those cares and concerns keep us from actually *enacting* it and bringing forth the fruit of true righteousness. While we are obliged to obey our leaders up to the point where doing so supersedes our service to God, we must ask ourselves how can we in good conscience actively support a governmental form so diametrically opposed to the kingdom of which we are supposedly a part? Especially given that such support inevitably involves the things of the earth, how does such activism differ those "Christians" from other "good" people sharing the same agenda? Note that such agendas inevitably concern things of which we disapprove—just as we found with the *"murmurers and complainers"* in the verse cited above.

What fruit do we realize by trying to blend patriotism with Christianity? We try to serve two masters and, just as Christ warned, we have come to hate the true God—why else would we seek freedom from His authority?—while evermore fully embracing the earthly values of our chosen master. We have tried to separate church and state; all we have accomplished is to separate our state from Christ, just as substituting self-evident truth for His Truth demands. This is far more important than might seem self-evident. Bear in mind that Christ says to *"strive"* to find *the strait and narrow gate*, and *strive* means to put forth a considerable effort. He's not alone in that sentiment. *"Beloved, when I gave all diligence to write unto you of the common salvation, it was needful for me to write unto you, and exhort you that ye should earnestly contend for the faith which was once delivered unto the saints"*—Jude 1:3. If we don't serve God as a matter of conscious choice and deliberate effort then we serve His usurper by default for, again, we cannot avoid service to one or the other.

But even more fundamentally, that service reflects our love for our Lord and, since it is an all-consuming love for Him that fulfills the Law, it follows that our service would likewise absorb us. Most of us have replaced our efforts to please God with commensurate efforts to please ourselves and each other. Sadly, that applies to the mainstream Christian religion as much as anywhere else, for such pleasing lies at the root of many of the compromises and concessions to paganism spotting the religion's history. On a grander scale, in the name of peace, progress, and political survival, nearly every "advanced" nation has tacitly embraced the ideal of religious freedom which, no matter how you slice it, come down *spiritual murder*—or suicide. Just as we fear God or fear man—and cannot do both—so we value physical life or eternal life—and cannot do both. No wonder every nation on earth so commonly uses death in the cause of life, violence in the cause of peace, prevarication and deception in the name of truth, with economics and survival their goals. No wonder we demand "justice" for the evil doers who interrupt our bacchanalian life styles. We fight for the right to sin as freely as we like. *"See then that ye walk circumspectly not as fools but as wise, redeeming the time, because the days are evil. Wherefore be ye not unwise, but understanding what the will of the Lord is. And be not drunk with wine, wherein is excess, but be filled with the Spirit..."*—Ephesians 5:15-18. He refrains the same sentiment in Romans 13:12-14: *"The night is far spent, the day is at hand: let us therefore cast off the works of darkness, and let us put on the armor of light. Let us walk honestly, as in the day; not in rioting and drunkenness, not in chambering and wantonness, not in strife and envying. But put ye on the Lord Jesus Christ, and make not provision for the flesh, to fulfill the lusts thereof."* Fulfilling the lusts of the flesh pretty well summarizes consumerism and, if you think about it, has a very great deal in common with the pursuit of happiness. Most of us equate happiness with pleasure which usually entails some sort of physical gratification. That pretty well summarizes the way of life we defend to the death of self or adversary. Who do we serve?

As a nation, we currently spend multiple billions of dollars per year, and put thousands of lives, military and civilian alike, at risk all in the defense of those pursuits, for they almost entirely define our way of life. Of course we seldom admit that. Instead, we claim to pursue al Qaeda and friends in the name of justice. That follows; pretty much by definition, a nation of law is a nation of justice. Consider a very telling and disturbing irony: the Old Covenant stresses *"an eye for an eye,"* and virtually the entire world takes that as its judicial and political baseline. Yet, that essential element of the Old Covenant, that is of *the Synagogue of Satan* for non-Jews, remains one of the extremely few (perhaps only) religious conventions that we have *not* transcended, nor even challenged in our march of "progress," and that applies to the entire world. Yet we hear no protests about this concept as a matter of undue religious influence over our political processes or as a violation of the separation of church and state. Perhaps still more curious, we continue that tradition in spite of the fact that we have repeatedly found throughout history that punishment, regardless of how severe, does not act as an effective deterrent to crime. By contrast, the New Covenant stresses *mercy and forgiveness,* and virtually no organized entity adopts that as policy. Admittedly, it would *seem* that mercy and justice are diametric opposites, which has caused many to wonder about the "inconsistency" of Biblical God as presented in the two Testaments. That too relates to authority. We must bear in mind that, under the Grace Economy, God's mercy is the definition of justice: *"'I will have mercy on whomever I will have mercy, and I will have compassion on whomever I will have compassion.'"*—Romans 9:15.

Given that, we must pose the question of how we fulfill God's Law, especially if obedience per se does not do it. We commonly hear that love fulfills the Law, but just what does that mean?*"Whosoever believeth that Jesus is the Christ is born of God: and every one that loveth Him that begat loveth Him also that is begotten of Him. By this we know that we love God, and keep His commandments. For this is the love of God, that we keep His commandments: and His commandments are not grievous"*—I John 5:1-3. That directly links loving God (and His Son) to obeying Him, with that divine love as both the reason for and the empowerment of that obedience! In other words, we obey God because we have been saved, not as an effort to gain salvation. Moreover, we do so as a matter of desire rather than obligation, as a manifestation of divine love reflected back as our love for Him. By contrast, in many ways the world has reduced Christ to little more than a moral philosopher whom we are to emulate of our own resources, just as we'd expect from self-determination. A good many doctrines also strongly suggest obedience as the key to salvation—which, of course, again invokes the *Synagogue of Satan.*

Thus, it's not hard to see how this relates to the difference between mercy and justice. Indeed, it makes showing mercy a matter of justice. It's really quite simple: if we hope to attain God's compassion, we'd better *show* that compassion; if we hope to obtain God's mercy, we'd better show it; if we hope to find forgiveness for our sins, we'd better forgive those who offend us. *"For if you forgive men their trespasses, your Heavenly Father will also forgive you. But if you do not forgive men their trespasses, neither will your Father forgive your trespasses.'"*—Matthew 6:14-15. Since we can reasonably take that which fulfills the Law as a valid definition of justice, that makes love and forgiveness the primary if not sole components of justice as reinterpreted by the New Covenant. *"Be ye therefore perfect, even as your Father which is in heaven is perfect'"*—Matthew 5:48. If we do not show that love and forgiveness, we are workers of iniquity and will be turned away from the *strait and narrow gate. "But He shall say, I tell you, I know not whence ye are: depart from Me, all ye workers of iniquity'"*—Luke 13:27. If we contrast that to our nation's policy of preventive actions against our enemies, then we must ask ourselves how we can associate ourselves with that. How can we accept *"turn the other cheek"* individually and not do so collectively, especially when that collective presumably acts in our name? Since we cannot legitimately condemn or even criticize our leaders, our only viable alternative is to withdraw from such affairs altogether and let them run their course. Don't try to fix the system, for it is inherently corrupt. Rather, we should look to our own houses so that we may face the Lord with the confidence of grace. *"According to the eternal purpose which He* [God] *purposed in Christ Jesus, our Lord: in Whom we have boldness and access with confidence by faith in Him"*—Ephesians 3;11-12.

While the New Covenant supersedes the Old for a time, the Old will be reinstated, and the full force of the Law will be brought against those who have not accepted the free gift of Grace embodied in Christ and the temporary re-definition of justice inherent in it.[16] They are then obliged to keep the entire Law, and will find themselves subject to the penalty for not doing so. Again we can see how that free gift which the Truth proclaims, and the concept of good vs. evil, which stresses punishment rather than forgiveness, are diametrically opposed just as are the flesh and the Spirit. How then do we relate to conventional justice? As with many physical gratifications, often including pleasure and happiness, it defers it. *"And when He had opened the Fifth Seal, I saw under the altar the souls of them that were slain for the Word of God, and the testimony which they hold: And they cried with a loud voice, saying, How long, O Lord, holy and true, doest Thou not judge and avenge our blood on them that dwell on the earth? And white robes were given unto every one of them; and it was said unto them, that they should rest yet for a little season, until their fellowservants also and their brethren, that should be killed as they were, should be fulfilled"*—Revelations 6:9-11.

We must always remember that Christ does not condemn anyone (see John 12:47). By contrast, the Devil is cast as *the accuser* (see Revelations 12:10.) What does that suggest about finding ourselves in an accusatory role as a foundation of justice and a nation of laws inevitably demands? If we adopt good vs. evil as our mindset, again especially if we consider ourselves good by overcoming evil, how can we avoid that role? Accusing evil is essential to overcoming it, so we must take judging and condemning as virtues! Think about it. How often do we nationally "condemn" another country's actions or statements? How often do we accuse them of various breaches of international law—or label them evil doers? More pertinent still, especially over the past half century or so, how often do we accuse them of doing what we do ourselves? In more than one opinion, the United

---

[16]   Much too complicated to deal with here, for a fuller explanation of this mystery see Romans, chapter eleven.

States of America is the biggest terrorist state in the world. Doesn't that essentially define hypocrisy? Isn't that the primary adjective Christ applied to the Pharisees? Didn't He warn us *that unless our righteousness exceeded theirs we will not enter the kingdom of heaven?* Then again, since we've rebelled against God and His Son, since we have defied their authority and called it evil, it appears that we have little interest in the kingdom of heaven.

Fittingly, the role of accuser often turns against us and so we find one of the most common shortcomings in contemporary spiritual life: the failure to forgive ourselves. A great many serious Christians have historically flagellated themselves, literally and metaphorically, in misguided efforts to atone for their sins. This often comes about due to two emotions so similar in their primary components that telling one from the other can prove problematic: guilt and contrition. To put it succinctly, we need the latter but do away with the former. Guilt implies punishment, and stems from an accusation rendered not by Christ or His Father but by His usurper, the aforementioned Accuser. *"And there was war in heaven: Michael and his angels fought against the dragon; and the dragon fought and his angels, and prevailed not; neither was their place found any more in heaven. And the Great Dragon was cast out, that old serpent, called the Devil and Satan, which deceiveth the whole world: he was cast out into the earth, and his angels were cast out with him. And I heard a loud voice saying in heaven, Now is come salvation, and strength, and the kingdom of our God, and the power of His Christ: for the accuser of our brethren is cast down, which accused them before our God day and night"*—Revelations 12:7-10. That directly links accusation to deception while linking both to Satan. It likewise links both to the rebellion against God's authority that we find manifested politically in this one nation under God. Dare we take that as a coincidence? By contrast, contrition implies a desire for forgiveness, which in turn implies a desire for God's mercy: the centerpiece of true Christianity. Rather than seeking salvation per se, we seek the divine mercy that makes that salvation possible, thereby glorifying God rather than ourselves. Having received that mercy, we demonstrate our love of and devotion to our Savior by showing that mercy on those who offend us. If we don't accept God's forgiveness, we don't accept His Truth; if we don't accept His Truth, we don't accept Christ; if we don't accept Christ, we don't accept the free gift of salvation; if we don't accept that gift, we find ourselves bound to the Law and right back in the *Synagogue of Satan* again, where accusation and punishment are appropriate.

However, the Accuser has a subtle downside that can mean the downfall for all but the most vigilant: the ever popular "once saved always saved" attitude. Personal salvation is not the end of Christianity, but the *beginning* of a new life. However, many don't seem to realize that, as with physical life, the prime objective of spiritual life is to grow and to mature and, so, to eventually produce the fruit of righteousness. *"But other* [seeds/word of God] *fell into good ground, and brought forth fruit, some an hundredfold, some sixtyfold, some thirtyfold"*—Matthew 13:8. Again we find good vs. evil and personal salvation as Christianity's purpose at the root of the problem. For example, even parents who don't normally go to church themselves will sometimes send little Johnny off to Sunday School or Bible Camp, primarily in order to save his soul. What kind of an adult does this produce? While it's impossible to make even a generalization, we can cite some highly probable pitfalls. As soon as Johnny learns the Christian basics and becomes a "good kid," what further use has he of Bible stuff? That means that we ask, what further spiritual growth does he need? If good people go to heaven, and if Johnny has become a good kid, then he should be saved, right? If personal salvation is the point of worshiping God, and you gain that salvation by being good and worshiping God, then a yearly "booster shot" at Christmas and maybe at Easter combined with a little charity here and there ought to do the job. Now we can get back to the much more important business of daily life and all those concerns and cares associated with it—the ones that the same parable cite as choking the word. Even if we assume Johnny to be a "good kid," and he may well be just that, we must still ask whether Johnny's goodness makes him righteous.

Clearly, we can apply the same question to America. Many like to quote Proverbs 14:34: *"Righteousness exalteth a nation:*

but sin is a reproach to any people." If we equate goodness with righteousness then we define righteousness for ourselves. But, we have established the essence of righteousness as doing God's will and seeking *His* greater glory, while our good country features the exact opposite. Consider that in light of the parable of the *Pharisee and the Tax Collector* found in Luke 18:10-14. With more than ample self-evident justification from his peers, the Pharisee thanked the Lord for making him so superior and righteous in much the same way that we Americans take pride in our prosperity and security as signs of God's approval. Then contrast that to the tax collector. A virtual pariah in the Jewish community, he would not even lift his eyes heavenward, but beat his chest and prayed, *"God be merciful to me a sinner!"* We must bear in mind at all times that we are saved by God's mercy and that alone! Since one cannot simultaneously feel pride and seek another's mercy, we can intuit the point of the parable. *"'Everyone who exalts himself will be abased, and he who humbles himself will be exalted.'"*—Luke 18:14.

Consider that in a political context found in Matthew 20:25-28: *"'Ye know that the princes of the Gentiles exercise dominion over them, and they that are great exercise authority upon them. But it shall not be so among you: but whosoever will be great among you, let him be your minister; and whosoever will be chief among you, let him be your servant: Even as the Son of Man came not be ministered unto, but to minister, and to give His life a ransom for many.'"* Bearing in mind that we can define "Gentile" as "pagan", what does that suggest about our national obsession with being "number one" in virtually every area, not merely as a matter of desire but as a matter of compulsion? We cannot serve two masters, but neither can we avoid service to one or the other. Emblematic of that service, we cannot humble ourselves before God, and consider pride a virtue at the same time, any more than we can embrace self-determination and consider meekness a virtue. Moreover, we find that pride and arrogance directly linked to paganism (the Gentiles) which again questions the religion underlying our national government. Just as pride and contrition cancel each other out, humility and contrition go hand in hand. Many believing themselves to be

"God's chosen ones" in this nation's nascence exhibited just the kind of arrogance Christ refers to, and we can see that legacy lingering in our notion of our national "special destiny". A nation of those proud to be Americans while proclaiming themselves a nation under God demands an answer to our title question.

Pride and self-determination drive us to deliver ourselves from evil in our blind belief that we can define the good as that which overcomes the evil. Yet our efforts to do so deliver us to evil instead. That alone should tell us whom we might logically expect to find urging us to continue doing so. As an ironic example, consider this. We deliberately set out to create a nation of law. Appropriately enough, although we already have more laws than any nation in history, we manufacture more every year, presumably toward the end of creating a just and good society. But rather than creating a lawful society, the more laws we make the more law*breakers* we create. America has by far a higher percentage of its citizens behind bars than any nation on earth, and that includes "repressive" nations such as Cuba and Red China. Recent statistics maintain that one out of every 99.1 adult Americans is behind bars—over 2.3 million total. How can we account for this? *"If you have 10,000 regulations,"* Winston Churchill observed, *"you destroy all respect for the law."* That seems to have happened here, as amply evidenced by any highway in the country. Try driving the speed limit on a major thoroughfare and see how long it takes for traffic to queue up behind you—usually angry, frustrated, impatient traffic.

But that's merely a microcosm of a much larger point. By this time, we can seriously doubt that a single American over the age of accountability has lived without breaking at least one of our laws. Perhaps more importantly, no one really cares. In a kind of mockery to God's Law, rather than meant to be observed, our statutes are intended as a coercive power base. Politics is power and power always seeks to enhance itself. The more laws we have, the more authority those making and enforcing those laws have over us. Doesn't that essentially define a "police state"? Seems an odd end for a nation founded on self-determination, doesn't it? It seems an even stranger end for a nation presumably devoted to freedom. Then again, given that a law, by definition, restricts what we can do, the "land of the free" and a "nation of law" contradict each other. Doesn't that constitute a house divided against itself? Doesn't that reflect the classic strategy of divide and conquer? Doesn't that echo what Christ said He'd come to do in Matthew 10:35? *"Think not that I am come to send peace on earth: I came not to send peace, but a sword'"*. Maybe we fulfill a divine destiny after all. Consider: just as held true with our rebellion against Great Britain, this results in making us a nation of lawbreakers as a matter of conscious choice and active desire—again, just as we found with Eve in the Garden. Perhaps still more pertinently, that choice is not, and does not necessarily reflect the wishes of the people, but rather is made by and reflects the wishes of an increasingly ill-defined Elite. We loosely call it "the government," but more and more we begin to acknowledge it at least in part as those for whom the electorate did not vote and of whose presence we are deliberately and systematically kept unaware. Hence the ever deepening shroud of secrecy surrounding Washington's affairs. That poses a question we'll reencounter a number of times as we proceed: who's really in charge here?

Although that government supposedly acts at the behest of the people, the unpopularity of many of our laws calls that into serious question. Still, fruit must follow the pattern of its seed. Doesn't that reflect our nascence where we acted on a conscious choice to break the law also at the desires of the Elite? We seek goodness by way of the law and, since we equate goodness with righteousness, we therefore seek righteousness by way of the law—our own law rather than God's—yet we found our "greatness" on breaking both. Indeed, transcending "outdated" laws, of both divine and secular origin, is largely how we define social progress. Do we not therefore take iniquity as our claim to righteousness? Self-determination amounts to self-deification, and both amount to idolatry. Pretty much by definition, that casts us as pagans. *"Wherein in time past ye walked according to the course of this world, according to the prince of the power of the air, the spirit that now worketh in the children of disobedience: among whom we also had our conversation in times past in the lusts of our flesh, fulfilling the desires of the flesh and of the mind; and were by nature the children of wrath, even as others"*—Ephesians 2:2-3. What other than "children of wrath" could we logically expect from a society based on war and on competition spurred on by a mindset of good vs. evil? Who does that cast as the children of disobedience? *"Be ye therefore followers of God, as dear children; and walk in love, as Christ hath given Himself for us as an offering and a sacrifice to God for a sweetsmelling savor. But fornication, and all uncleanness, or covetousness, let it not be once named among you, as becometh saints; neither filthiness, nor foolish talking, nor jesting, which are not convenient: but rather giving of thanks. For this ye know, that no whoremonger, nor unclean person, nor covetous man, who is an idolater, hath any inheritance in the kingdom of Christ and of God. Let no man deceive you with vain words: for because of these things cometh the wrath of God upon the children of disobedience"*—Ephesians 5:2-6. Consider for yourself how much of that constitutes vital parts of the way of life we so frequently find ourselves compelled to defend. That says a great deal about how we define good, and so about how we define God. It therefore reveals the religion of which our governmental form is a reflection.

Although our relationship has changed, the God of the Old Testament remains forever. We can infer that by the fact that the *First Commandment* makes it integral to the identity of the God and Father of our Master. *"I am the Lord thy God, which [has][17] brought thee out of the land of Egypt, out of the house of bondage. Thou shalt have no other gods before Me."* (See Exodus 20: 2.) Jude reminds us that we speak of the same God: *"I will therefore put you in remembrance, though ye once knew this, how that the Lord, having saved the people out of the Land of Egypt, afterward destroyed them that believed not"*—Jude 5. It's not enough to consider Him the supreme Lord; we must take Him as the *only* God, for Egypt was a land of idolatry. If we break that commandment, then our most passionate observance of the others will avail us nothing, for righteousness lies in whom we obey, not what

---

[17]   The KJV translates that as "have" which implies the Triune God doctrine which I do not accept. That is a very controversial subject which we have not the time to explore here. For the record, the Amplified Bible uses "has".

we obey. If we break that commandment we find ourselves figuratively back in the land of Egypt again, toiling in slavery for an earth-god without even realizing it! More immediately pertinent to our present discussion, the Jews' Egyptian captivity provides an excellent example of the similarity between the two Covenants directly related to delivering ourselves from evil.

Ironically, we can see that best exemplified in Pharaoh himself in the famous *Plagues of Egypt* episode. The first Plague (see Exodus, Chapter 9) frightened him into wanting to let God's Children go. *"And Pharaoh sent for Moses and Aaron and said unto them, I have sinned this time: the Lord is righteous, and I and my people are wicked!"*—Exodus 9:28. He acknowledged God's goodness, and confessed his own sin. What more could you ask for? Notice the parallel between that and one coming to Christ of his own volition seeking salvation. Moreover, note that he was motivated not by love but by fear, just as we find in those coming to Christ to avoid perdition. Yet consider what happens. In the very next verse he expresses a desire to allow the Jews to leave, but Pharaoh's heart hardens, and the very first verse of Chapter Ten tells us that, *"'I have hardened his heart.'"* Consider that carefully in correlation to John 1:13 and the description of the righteous: *"which were born not of blood, nor of the will of the flesh, nor of the will of man, but of God."* God would not allow Pharaoh to release His people, and therein lies the message for us all. We can in no way, deliver ourselves from evil be it external or internal, political or spiritual, even if we experience a desire to do so. Notice too what this does to the issue of good vs. evil. God used evil on a grand scale to His own good purpose: *"And I will harden Pharaoh's heart, and multiply My signs and My wonders in the Land of Egypt. But Pharaoh will not hearken unto you, that I may lay My hand upon Egypt, and bring forth Mine armies, and My people the children of Israel out of the Land of Egypt by great judgments. And the Egyptians shall know that I am the Lord, when I stretch forth Mine hand upon Egypt, and bring out the children of Israel from among them'"*—Exodus 7:3-5.[18] Paul makes the issue still clearer: *"For the Scripture saith unto Pharaoh, 'Even for this*

---

[18] Notice the parallel not only in effect but in intent to the Great Tribulations yet to come.

same purpose have I raised thee up, that I might shew My power in thee, and that My name might be declared throughout all the earth'''—Romans 9:17. Without a founding on divine Truth, we can never hope to understand that and as a result will inevitably misjudge it.

Since we define good as that which overcomes evil, we likewise define whatever means accomplishes that end as a commensurate good—ultimately yielding the attitude commonly known as "the ends justify the means," sometimes more formally known as *circumstantial ethics.* As we can plainly see in the world around us, that definition constantly spirals further and further away from any kind of objective or absolute moral standard even of our own device. There's a very valid reason for that. In the absence of absolutes, only relativity remains; in the absence of absolute good, only relative good remains, and it has no meaning without relative evil to which to contrast itself. That eventually yields our most common contemporary principle: *expediency.* We define good for ourselves, and then take as true whatever yields the preconceived results.[19] We find just such relative goodness at this nation's foundation. After centuries of perceived evils perpetrated by kings, emperors and other autocrats, the self-evident good of self-government seemed obvious—*by contrast.* In the absence of a divine authority goodness, like Truth, becomes a matter of opinion.

Idolatry runs far deeper in this one nation under God than most of us dare to imagine, for we are to serve God exclusively, as a matter of conscious conviction. When we don't, we serve His usurper by default. Think about that and then consider: even as we once fought evil doers in defense of the Faith because we believed that their evil threatened the cause of eternal survival, so we now fight them in defense of our social survival largely defined as the free market and the attendant devotion to the things of the earth. Notice how the two definitions of economy

---

[19] We find this phenomenon often repeated in the so-called "scientific method" of experimentation. It has been often noted that researchers in different parts of the world conducting the same experiments come to different conclusions based on what they initially sought.

merge. Given the value addition inherent in both the religious and political doctrines demanding our defense, that puts LOM in both senses at the core of each set of conflicts. What authority does that put at that core? Also consider this: nations don't go to war with each other; in virtually no case do the inhabitants of one land know and so loathe those of another as to seek to do them harm on a massive scale until so convinced by their governments. Moreover we are convinced to *want* to go to war by our government leaders just as we were by our religious leaders centuries ago—and just as Eve was cajoled into desiring the Forbidden Fruit centuries before that. This helps to illuminate an apparently contradictory duality. On the one hand, all powers are ordained of God, yet at the same time, it has been given to Satan to endow whom he will with the power, glory and prestige of secular leadership which, coincidentally enough, usually includes a great many pleasures and privileges associated with wealth.

Notice the parallel to the purpose behind the Jews' wilderness wanderings. The evils that befall us collectively and individually serve the purpose of seeing whether we will obey God or not. In a Christian context, it serves to test our love of the Truth as given by Christ rather than the *strong delusions* of self-evident truth. Perhaps most importantly, it means to see if we will forego judging those whom the Lord has ordained—something we can't do if we take good vs. evil as our philosophical baseline. Thus, it serves to see whether we will genuinely accept a love of the Truth and reject the illusions inherent in the world system given to good vs. evil. That in turn poses the question of whose dollars and cents embroil us in those conflicts. That grows far more pertinent when we remember that such conflicts are in diametric opposition to Christ's teachings which, by definition, makes them Antichrist. That in itself suggests the entire issue of good vs. evil as Antichrist. From there we can ask how we define the national interests and security we so commonly find espoused as the expedients of warfare, and we again return to the defense of our way of life featuring the things of the earth. *"The Spirit itself[20] beareth witness with our spirit, that we are*

---

[20] The KJV uses "itself" while the Holy Spirit is usually personified.

the children of God: and if children, then heirs; heirs of God, and joint-heirs with Christ; if so be that we suffer with Him, that we may be also glorified together. For I reckon that the sufferings of this present time are not worthy to be compared with the glory which shall be reveled in us"—Romans 8:16-18. We value the things of earth, including our security, comforts, pleasures and even survival, or we value the things of heaven; we cannot do both.

Clearly the Elite favor the former, and theirs is the voice of war. That war does not remain confined to external foes; highly vocal elements of the Elite have distrusted the common man since our inception. *"All communities divide themselves into the few and the many. The first are rich and well born; the other, the mass of the people. The voice of the people has been said to be the voice of God; and however generally this maxim has been quoted and believed, it is not true in fact. The people are turbulent and changing; they seldom judge or determine right. Give therefore to the first class a distinct, permanent share in the government. They will check the unsteadiness of the second; and as they cannot receive any advantage by change, they will therefore maintain good government."*—Alexander Hamilton. Governments are not neutral, nor do they spring out of thin air. Rather, they reflect the intellectual and moral climate of those framing it. That means that they usually represent the dominant economic concerns of the people involved, and constitutions and laws will surely reflect those interests, albeit perhaps unintentionally. The US proved no exception: the whole idea of independence revolved around the riches this nation promised, and the framers generally represented those most likely to benefit from them. In all fairness, some did profit and some did not, but virtually all of them were from the "upper class". Moreover, many wanted to make property ownership a prerequisite for voting privileges.

That also reflected the general climate of the times. A very considerable disparity between rich and poor had existed throughout the Colonies since the beginning. Since America remained a British colony, the Elite could use that fact to vilify the English while obfuscating their own abuses of power that would manifest after independence. Class struggles right out of Karl

Marx were the focal point of a great many upheavals and riots in the 150 years prior to the Revolution, always featuring a large population seeing itself as exploited by a much smaller wealthy minority who inevitably had both the law and the military on their side. The structure must reflect its foundation. LOM, chiefly defined as the Profit Motive, which played an integral role in our revolution from Great Britain, also prominently figured into our dealings with the Native Americans, with the Civil War, with the Spanish American War, and, as we'll touch on a bit later, played a large and surprising role in WWII. Virtually all of our conflicts and secret operations since then have been geared toward protecting or enhancing major American fiscal interests—what many have begun to call "Corporate America". In all cases we define our adversaries in terms of *"what can you do to me?"*, with financially harming the Elite chief among those concerns, and with concern over those who do the protecting falling further and further from the top of those concerns. During both the Revolutionary and Civil Wars we saw soldiers joining the ranks as a matter of economic expediency. We can see the same in the escalating use of professional security forces—mercenaries—such as those in Iraq and Afghanistan at an estimated cost of $120 billion per year. Death and destruction have become major money-makers and an increasingly lucrative market for soldiers of fortune more and more drawn from Third World countries. Personnel and material are essentially co-equated. Simply consider the huge number of deaths, injuries and mutilations, partly caused by unacknowledged but well documented use of forbidden radioactive weapons used largely because it proved a very inexpensive way of getting rid of radioactive waste. "What can you do for me" applies equally to the people carrying the guns, and if death proves more profitable than life, so be it; medals conferred posthumously are not expensive. Who do we serve? Simply consider how much money has been spent—and how much squandered on unfinished, unneeded, and unwanted projects—in Iraq before the American "withdrawal" of late 2010. In all cases we find physical and fiscal survival at the root along with the deliberately manufactured fear of man supplanting fear of God. *"For what shall it profit a man, if he shall gain the whole world, and lose his own soul"*—Mark 8:36.

Physical life, walking after the flesh, is a mirror-image to a walk with God and walking in the Spirit. While Christ cites *loving God with all our beings* as the number one commandment, He cites *"loving our neighbors as ourselves"* a very close second (see Matthew 23:39, for example.) Clearly unconditional love for our international neighbors has reached an historic low, supplanted by a growing fear and suspicion. More and more, the exhortation to *"come out from them and be separate"* is seen as consistent with walking in the Spirit. To that end, Christ's exhortation that we *love our enemies* is an excellent place to start, for in no other way can we so dramatically separate ourselves from the world and act as the light thereof. Think about it. Instead *of loving our enemies,* we march off to war on them for that same worldly reason: they pose a threat to our lusts of the flesh! Consider: on May 1, 2010, Faisal Shahzad tried to blow up an SUV full of bombs in Times Square for the specific purpose of killing as many people as possible for the simple reason that they were the enemy in a mirror-image to Christ's command. At his trial, according to the Los Angeles Times (10/06/10), he said: *"If I am given 1,000 lives, I will sacrifice them all for the sake of Allah fighting this cause, defending our lands, making the word of Allah supreme over any religion or system."* In addition to the obvious merging of religion and politics, that classifies Mr. Shahzad as both a martyr and a patriot. But if we look closely, can we not pose the question of in what significant manner we differ? Is that so different from Nathan Hale's famous, *"I only regret that I have but one life to give for my country"?* We seek nothing less than the imposition of the word of the Freedom God, making it supreme over any religion or system—and gaining hegemony in the Mideast while we're at it.

But there's more to it even than that. Our deepest convictions constitute our most basic sense of self, and a sufficient threat to those convictions constitutes a death threat every bit as real as its physical counterpart. True meekness coupled with the strength of the Spirit allows us to turn the other cheek when struck, even if the strike should prove fatal; pride demands that we strike back, or even act to prevent it by striking first. Which characterizes the patriot and what values does it reflect? As a result we have legitimized oppression, cruelty, enslavement, even murder, all of which stand in sharp opposition to the mercy and forgiveness central to true Christianity, but all of which have been manifest at one time or another by the official Church in manners that make modern-day Islam seem pretty tame. Much the same holds true politically as we can find amply evidenced in our treatment of the Native Americans, the Vietnamese, and in the very existence of contemporary "black bases" devoted to "enhanced interrogation techniques." Again we find our governmental form as a reflection of our national religion, and find that religion a mirror-image of true Christianity—which, again by definition, makes it Antichrist. Again too we find that goodness and righteousness do not mean the same thing, and at times are diametric opposites!

The real issues of the Spirit War have begun to reveal themselves in the aftermath of 9/11. With the advent of religious terrorism, we must now consider strictly enforced monotheism not only as detrimental to freedom, self-expression and other life-based values, but as an actual threat to *life itself*. If we take freedom defined as the absence of an absolute authority such as strictly enforced monotheism as our highest good, and define freedom as essential to survival, then we must end up calling God's absolute authority not only evil but an evil we must overcome in order to survive! We must likewise take the absolute love for that authority that Christ cites as the number one commandment as a similar evil which we must overcome for similar reasons. We trade eternal life for physical life quite consistent with pursuing earthly matters over heavenly. The survival imperative is the mark of the beast. Think about it. Isn't that essentially what the people do who take the literal mark as described in Revelations? *"And he caused all, both small and great, rich and poor, free and bond, to receive a mark in their right hand, or in their forehead: and that no man might buy or sell, save he that had the mark, or the name of the beast, or the number of his name"*—Revelations 13:16-17. Isn't it ironic that evolution, stressing survival above all other goods, literally casts us in the image of the beast. More disturbing still, some mainstream Christian religions have adopted evolution as "factual truth", relegating the Creation Story to "metaphor" status, calling it an attempt to explain scientific fact to those without a scientific grounding.

We've noted that there is a very big difference between one nation under God and one nation under Christ. We can of course find a plethora of false christs, all of whom have free reign in this climate of religious freedom, yet, *the* Christ is indispensible in making the identification of the true God certain. That means that our efforts to worship God without the Son amount to idolatry—which we likewise take as a self-evident good. Thus we find the principle problem with patriotism. *We cannot simultaneously believe the divine Truth at the foundation of Christ's church, and the self-evident truth at the foundation of this country, for the two conflict on every point.* That poses some very inconvenient questions in these politically correct times of ours. That's why we sub-titled this work, "Serious questions for the serious Christian": the harder the question the greater the necessity of posing it. If we don't believe the Truth, and act accordingly, then by definition we revere and serve a false god regardless of what we tell others or even ourselves. That is the essence of the Great Apostasy which is already well under way.

We'll find more difficult questions in the next chapter. We increasingly find lies and murder essential to our national security. Who has the Bible identified as the *father of lies?* To whom does it refer as a *"murderer from the beginning"?* Dare we take that satanic combination of characteristics as coincidental? No wonder we never ask toward what end we progress! Then again, we seldom ask where we've been, either. That's too bad, because in order to understand where we're going, we must understand where we originated. Popular opinion aside, this one nation under God has clearly *deistic*, not Christian roots, and that makes a world of difference.

Chapter Three

f we accept the premise that our governmental form is our religion enacted, then that governmental form must manifest the most basic spiritual beliefs of those framing the government. If that's the case, then we must ask on what spiritual beliefs we established this country, and who actually did so. Rather than a government of and by the people, this nation was elitist in its very inception.

Most Christian patriots point to the Puritans and other religious refugees braving an uncertain sea, seeking to establish a "Godly nation" on these new shores. While we remember the *Nina*, the *Pinta* and the *Santa Maria*, far fewer of us recall the *Susan Constant*, the *Godspeed* and the *Discovery*—the first European ships (with the very probable exception of the Vikings) to reach American shores at what would become Jamestown. They had a considerably different mission in mind and, as it turns out, one far more in keeping with what this nation would become. By the early 18th Century the Colonies had degenerated into a dumping ground for English undesirables, and the Puritan aura rubbed off rather readily. As a result, by the time of the Revolution, we didn't even *intend* to found a Christian nation and, while estimates vary, most experts agree that about 25% of the colonists considered themselves Christian.[21] Although religion and politics merged quite liberally, they did not always do so comfortably. For example, Thomas Paine, one of the most influential writers promoting the American Revolution, wrote: *"Of all the systems of religion that ever were invented, there is no more derogatory to the Almighty, more unedifying to man, more repugnant to reason, and more contradictory to itself than this thing called Christianity."* Notice the tacit assumption:

---

[21] Historian, Robert T. Handy maintains that, "No more than 10 percent— probably less— of Americans in 1800 were members of congregations

religions were "invented" which, by definition, makes them human constructs. Ironically, that's often true: in a great many cases religion and God's true worship have little or nothing in common. That's certainly not the first time the Christian religion has given Christianity a bad name. James Madison wrote in his "Memorial and Remonstrance against Religious Assessments":

"During almost fifteen centuries has the legal establishment of Christianity been on trial. What have been its fruits? More or less in all places, pride and indolence in the Clergy, ignorance and servility in the laity; in both, superstition, bigotry and persecution."
"What influence, in fact, have ecclesiastical establishments had on society? In some instances they have been seen to erect a spiritual tyranny on the ruins of the civil authority; on many instances they have been seen upholding the thrones of political tyranny; in no instance have they been the guardians of the liberties of the people. Rulers who wish to subvert the public liberty may have found an established clergy convenient auxiliaries. A just government, instituted to secure and perpetuate it, needs them not."

In his, "A Defence of the Constitutions of Government of the United States of America" [1787-1788], John Adams wrote: *"The United States of America have exhibited, perhaps, the first example of governments erected on the simple principles of nature; and if men are now sufficiently enlightened to disabuse themselves of artifice, imposture, hypocrisy, and superstition, they will consider this event as an era in their history. Although the detail of the formation of the American governments is at present little known or regarded either in Europe or in America, it may hereafter become an object of curiosity. It will never be pretended that any persons employed in that service had interviews with the gods, or were in any degree under the influence of Heaven, more than those at work upon ships or houses, or laboring in merchandise or agriculture; it will forever be acknowledged that these governments were contrived merely by the use of reason and the senses. " . . . Thirteen governments [of the original states] thus founded on the natural authority of the people alone, without a pretence of miracle or mystery, and which are destined to spread over the northern part of that whole quarter of the globe, are a great point gained in favor of the rights of mankind."*

Paine did not limit his vitriol to the institutional Christianity itself, and revealed his preferred view of Deism as virulently opposed to God's word. *"It is the duty of every true Deist to vindicate the moral justice of God against the evils of the Bible."* That's more revealing than might initially seem self-evident. Again we touch upon the issue of authority. Christians take the Bible as the revealed word of God Almighty and, therefore, as our ultimate authority. *"All Scripture is given by inspiration of God, and is profitable for doctrine, for reproof, for correction, for instruction in righteousness: That the man of God may be perfect, thoroughly furnished unto all good works"*—II Timothy 3:16-17. This is what Paine calls the *"evils of the Bible"* which the *"true deist"* must contest. Perhaps most prominent of those "evils", we must chose our allegiance to one master or the other, manifest in the dichotomy between the things of the earth and the things of heaven. *" . . .know ye not that the friendship of the world is enmity with God Whosoever therefore will be a friend of the world is th enemy of God"*—James 4:4. The world and "nature" are pretty nearly interchangeable, yet Adams maintains that we founded this nation on *"the simple principles of nature"* which, by definition, makes this country God's enemy. As we'll see presently, friendship with the world is what united the Thirteen Colonies into a cohesive nation.

Even as the Founders denied any inspiration from heaven, we made our denial of Christ official in the infamous *Treaty of Tripoli* of 1797, ratified by the US Senate, making it an official part of our national identity: *"As the Government of the United States of America is not in any sense founded on the Christian religion . . ."* Although that document had a very limited life span, it nevertheless demonstrates the viewpoint of the American government at the time. As if to make the matter sure, much to the dismay of Fundamentalists and Conservatives, President Obama stated that, *"One of the great strengths of the United States is . . .we do not consider ourselves a Christian nation or a Jewish nation or a Muslim nation. We consider ourselves a nation of citizens who are bound by ideals and a set of values."* In a different context, he made a similar statement: *"Whatever we once were, we are no longer just a Christian nation; we are also a Jewish nation, a Muslim nation, a Buddhist nation, and Hindu nation, and a nation of non-believers . . ."* Thus, again we must ask ourselves: can the Christian conscionably support a government that *officially* denies Christ? *"But whosoever shall deny Me before men, him will I also deny before My Father which is in heaven'"*—Matthew 10:33.[22] Think about it: to deny Christ is to deny the Truth He embodies, and we've systematically done that since our inception by embracing self-evident truth. Moreover, as Obama's statements clearly indicate, religious freedom takes that denial as a *virtue!* But we can find far more subtle examples of the same denial. For example, Senator John McCain, Obama's Republican opponent in the 2008 elections, maintained that voters should ask themselves, " *. . . will this person carry on in the Judeo-Christian principled tradition that has made this nation the greatest experiment in the history of mankind?"* Later he added that, *"I just have to say in all candor, that since this nation was founded primarily on Christian principles . . ."* It would be interesting to know what principles he had in mind, for the basic principles underpinning this "greatest experiment" are diametrically opposed to those espoused and exemplified by the Son of God as related in the Scriptures. Of course, those same Scriptures do warn about false messiahs, teachers and prophets, and in our unchanged state we have a natural affinity for the Anti-Truth they preach.

Again and again we find references to *the Christian religion*, which, with a few exceptions, is not at all the same thing as Christianity. *"Pure religion and undefiled before God and the Father is this, to visit the fatherless and widows in their affliction, and to keep himself unspotted from the world"*—James 1:27. While the first phrase deals with charity within the Christian community, for our current purposes, the latter phrase is the more salient. As implied by the observations cited above, and as manifest in the current *jihad* in response to the actions of the Crusaders past and present, in many cases the Christian religion has done far more harm to true Christianity than any of it opponents could ever have hoped to do. Ironically, one of the biggest examples

---

[22] The Amplified Bible adds "disowns Me"; to disown is to *refuse to acknowledge a connection with someone.*

of that damage is the very existence of this country. Beyond support for a governmental form diametrically opposed to how Christ defines righteousness, rather than remaining *unspotted from the world* (what Jude calls *"hating the garment spotted by the flesh"*—1:23), we have turned such spotting, the lusts of the flesh, into the world's most desirable and copied way of life—and still again, as a matter of desire. Yet, these are the principles to which Messrs. McCain and Obama refer.

We like to believe that "we all worship the same God", not noticing the inherent deception in that statement. God's *existence* is not the issue. *"Thou believest that there is one God; thou doest well: the devils also believe, and tremble"*—James 2:19. The real issue revolves around our relationship to Him, and it is there that we can definitively state that this is not, nor ever was, nor ever intended to be a Christian country. *Not once* in our founding documents do we find any reference at all to Christ, yet no one comes to, or even knows the true God without Him. *"All things are delivered to Me of My Father: and no man knoweth the Son, but the Father; neither knoweth any man the Father, save the Son, and he to whomsoever the Son will reveal Him'"*—Matthew 11:27 No one can serve God without Him, which means that we never intended this country to serve the true God. Rather than serving the cause of righteousness, we deliberately chose to serve the cause of goodness and, as we've seen, they do not mean the same thing. Consistently, when we do find references to Christ in some of the other writings of the era, they're almost entirely in a moral context to be used as either an ethical guide or for the basis of law. *"We have no government armed with power capable of contending with human passions unbridled by morality and religion. Avarice, ambition, revenge or gallantry would break the strongest cords of our Constitution as a whale goes through a net. Our Constitution is designed only for a moral and religious people. It is wholly inadequate for any other"*—John Adams. That equates religion with morality, just as we'd expect from a mindset of good vs. evil, and casts it as a means to a political end just as we'd expect from religion taken as a human construct. More importantly, given the definition above, do we make any effort at all to *keep ourselves unspotted from the world?*

If not, then what "religion" does he have in mind?*"Statesmen may plan and speculate for liberty,"* he went on to say, *"but it is religion and morality alone that can establish the principles upon which freedom can securely stand."* Notice how that echoes the allusion to divine freedom in the Patrick Henry quote above. Is democracy the self-evident truth that Christ said would make us free? *"And He that sent Me is with Me: the Father hath not left Me along; for I do always those things that please Him." As He spoke these words, many believed on Him. Then Jesus said to those Jews which believed on Him, 'If ye continue in My word, then ye are My Disciples indeed; and ye shall know the Truth, and the Truth shall make you free'"*—John 8:29-32.

How can we claim to *"do always those things that please God"* when our entire philosophical foundation revolves around pleasing ourselves? Whose "religion" is he describing? We worship God by obeying that most important commandment, that *we love God with all our beings*. If we do that, then it follows naturally that we would want to serve Him with all our beings, and that largely defines righteousness. By contrast, we can define idolatry as holding anything as an object of greater devotion or of greater adoration than God. Look at Philippians 3:18-19. *"For many walk, of whom I have told you often, and now tell you even weeping, that they are the enemies of the cross of Christ: whose end is destruction, whose God is their belly, and whose glory is in their shame who mind earthly things."* That's pretty emphatic and quite specific: set your mind on earthly things and you not only make yourself the enemy of both Father and Son, but also make your end destruction. Still again, on what did we found this country? How do we define the ideals that unite us that Mr. Obama had in mind? If we accept the common deistic belief that God set the universe in motion but does not participate in its affairs thereafter, then we define deism as a belief that *demands* that we immerse ourselves in worldly affairs, making my (our) will be done a legitimate political paradigm and life goal. In essence, it takes the divine right of kings and applies it to the common man.

Thomas Jefferson was a self-proclaimed *materialist*, which gives him something in common with Karl Marx, the founder of

Communism. A philosophy dating back to the ancient Greeks, *materialism* maintains the physical as the only reality while dismissing the supernatural altogether. In spite of lip service to the contrary, this one nation under God as a whole does just that, and has done so since our inception. Think about it: if Christ is the Truth, then there can be no other truth, self-evident or otherwise. More specifically, we either accept Christ as the absolute Truth, without compromise or concession, or we don't accept Him at all! *"For He whom God hath sent speaketh the words of God: for God giveth not the Spirit by measure unto Him. The Father loveth the Son, and hath given all things into His hand. He that believeth on the Son hath everlasting life: and he that believeth not on the Son shall not see life; but the wrath of God abideth on him"*—John 3:34-36. That belief entails a great deal more than simply accepting His existence, although religion, albeit unintentionally, often reduces it to just that. By definition true faith must found on divine Truth, and Christ is that Truth. Moreover, faith is not faith unless we act in accordance with it. Except in extremely extraordinary circumstances, our actions reflect what we really hold as true regardless of what we tell ourselves or others. *"Yea, a man may say, Thou hast faith, and I have works; shew me thy faith without thy works, and I will shew thee my faith by my works. Thou believest that there is one God; thou doest well: the devils also believe, and tremble. But wilt thou know, O vain man, that faith without works is dead?"*—James 2:18-20. If the devils believe in God—indeed, they are absolutely certain of His existence—then such a faith in and of itself cannot be what distinguishes the Christian. Note too that such devilish faith founds on knowledge similar to what we see in much of mainstream Christianity. More pertinent to our immediate discussion, we have founded this nation on self-evident truth which can yield only self-evident faith, normally known as *seeing is believing*. Coincidentally enough, that's also the basis for the truths common to both deism and empiricism, the foundation of science which most of us take as our ultimate truth. Obviously, too, it's the judgmental basis of good vs. evil. Nature's God, the natural man, natural perception, natural principles: what spiritual foundation does this suggest?

Self-evident truth, self-expression, self-determination all have *self* in common. By definition, *self* refers to an entity disconnected from and independent of the body of Christ. Thus, in a very fundamental way, the idea of self, and the Christian's ideal state are mirror-images. Given that, how can we take self-determination as anything but sinful? How can we advocate much less desire, much less seek self-sovereignty? How can we consider self-expression a virtue? If we constitute part of the embodiment of divine Truth, how can we take self-evident truth as anything short of Antichrist? How can we deliberately walk by sight rather than by faith? Yet, these are the ideals and principles that President Obama cited as uniting this non-Christian nation and with very good reason: these are the ideals and principles shared by virtually every American, "Christian" or not. Doesn't that still again conjure up the deadly image of the *broad and spacious way?* We must worship God in *Spirit and in Truth*, with Christ the Truth in question, the Holy Spirit the Spirit in question. If we do not worship Him in Christ, enabled by the Holy Spirit, we do not worship Him at all. Yet, worshiping God (or gods) in the flesh as we see fit is also one of those Obama principles that purportedly unite this nation and, more disturbing still, is also one of the "Judeo Christian principles" Mr. McCain apparently had in mind.

If it's true that we must serve one spiritual master or the other, then it's also true that we must obey one or the other, for service subsumes obedience. That too is more important than most of us acknowledge, for as we've noted, good vs. evil stresses *what* we obey, while Truth vs. Anti-Truth stresses *whom* we obey. *"Little children, let no man deceive you: he that doeth righteousness is righteous, even as He is righteous. He that committeth sin is of the devil; for the devil sinneth from the beginning. For this purpose the Son of God was manifested, that He might destroy the works of the devil. Whosoever is born of God doth not commit sin; for his seed remaineth in him: and he cannot sin because he is born of God. In this the children of God are manifest, and the children of the devil: whosoever doeth not righteousness is not of God . . ."*—I John 3:7-10. We all sin as an unavoidable part of being human. This refers to the extremely

113

important difference between sin that we can't avoid, and *willful sin*—i.e., sin as a matter of conscious, habitual choice and active desire which again brings us back to Eve in the Garden. Bear in mind that Satan's temptations, the "works" John refers to, won't always look evil, and will often appear good, even as the tree of knowledge looked good to her, and even as self-determination seems good to most of us. But bear in mind that all sin really amounts to the same sin: consciously, deliberately, desirously defying God's will—the essence of what we define as freedom, and what we preach as the political holy of holies to the entire world! Original Sin wasn't a one time event; it has manifested as the foundation of this one nation under God. Since we can succinctly summarize righteousness as Thy will be done, that means that those who deliberately defy God's will are not of God, *and are of the devil instead!* Of what sin was Satan guilty from the beginning? His lack of Truth manifested in the desire to first deny and then usurp God's absolute authority! How does that define self-determination and a government systematically devoted to defying that will underpinned by a religion devoted to usurping God's authority? How must we answer our title question?

We cannot choose to follow the Lamb, but must be called by the Father to do so. We can however choose to follow His usurper of our own wills. Which reflects freedom from God's authority? Which reflects my will rather than Thy will be done? Which reflects delivering ourselves from evil? Which has the greater appeal to the *natural man?* In other words, which reflects all of the major characteristics of self-determination? If Satan and his cohorts guise themselves as *an angel of light* and as *ministers of righteousness* respectively (see II Corinthians 11:12-14), then we should expect them to offer us many means to salvation—which sounds like a very accurate definition of both religious freedom and the broad and spacious way leading to destruction. Political correctness notwithstanding, we can no longer afford to ignore the stark Truth: we either worship the living God by way of His Son as described in the Scriptures, or we worship Satan! People can whine and moan all they like about how intolerant and unfair that seems, they can react with hate and think they do

God service by harassing those who espouse it, but that does not change the facts.

How we react to that fact, however, very largely defines us as Christians. Unlike virtually every other religion and philosophy on earth, that does not mean that we march off to war against the world's infidels as misguided attempts to force the unwashed into the fold demand. As intimated by the quotes beginning this chapter, throughout the centuries Christianity has been targeted for criticism almost exclusively due to the excesses of its alleged representatives, ranging from militaristic Popes to deranged avengers bombing abortion clinics, all of whom share judgmentalism in common. Ironically, here we find perhaps the darkest side of the saving souls misconception, for its misguided efforts have created much hatred and intolerance. We must emphasize *misguided* efforts. Evangelism per se is a vital part of God's work and, on a personal note, I salute the true evangelicals for a gift which I do not possess. Nevertheless, as with everything else, evangelism too can be and has been perverted to the Evil One's purposes. Look again at II Peter 2:1-2: *"But there were false prophets also among the people, even as there shall be false teachers among you, who privily shall bring in damnable heresies even denying the Lord that bought them, and bring upon themselves swift destruction. And many shall follow their pernicious ways; by reason of whom, the way of Truth shall be evil spoken of".* The countless battles and contentions over the issue of saving souls has indeed caused the Truth to be evil spoken of in a great many quarters, most dramatically in the Mideastern *jihadists.*

It's ironically fitting that Peter should mention those who *"deny the Lord that bought them,"* since he did just that. Yet, at the same time, he makes a very good example of how subtle yet vital the difference between goodness and righteousness can prove. While we can judge good and evil by appearances alone, especially when we define the terms, we cannot so judge righteousness and unrighteousness. That too is a legacy of Original Sin. Righteousness reflects in behavior, but behavior is not its essence. The Pharisees, after all, put on the outward *appearance* of righteousness, as do Satan's *ministers of righteousness.* Think about it. Why does Christ tell us *to resist not an evil person?* Why did He offer no rebukes of any kind to the Romans who tortured and killed Him? Why the emphasis on *loving our enemies*, on *recompensing no one evil for evil,* and all the other utterly illogical exhortations we find scattered throughout the New Testament? Because, as epitomized most dramatically by Saul/ Paul and Judas Iscariot, we have no way of knowing how a given individual, regardless of outward appearances, figures into God's overall plan. The same held true for Pharaoh (see above). We must always bear in mind that God sometimes uses evil to His own good purposes, and that can include individuals. That plan, external appearances notwithstanding, is *always* good, in spite of any overt evils. *". . .but we glory in tribulations also: knowing that tribulations worketh patience; and patience, experience; and experience, hope: and hope maketh not ashamed; because the love of God is shed abroad in our hearts by the Holy Ghost which is given to us"*—Romans 5:3-5. By definition, a tribulation is an evil, yet it works toward a divine good and so, rather than resisting it, we should welcome it as another manifestation of God's love for us. The *natural man* cannot hope to understand that for he cannot hope to take divine issues seriously enough to do so. But the Holy Spirit grants us the wisdom to see that delivering ourselves from evil really amounts to delivering ourselves from God's plan, which is a very basic way of resisting His will.

Again we can see the difference between goodness and righteousness, especially as we define the former. If we take the good as that which overcomes evil, we must deliver ourselves from evil in order to consider ourselves the good. That means that we must defy God in order to consider ourselves the good just as we find in our social progress manifest in overcoming "outdated" laws of a Biblical origin. Who do we serve? Consistent with self-determination defined as self-deification, we end up putting ourselves in God's place just as any other form of idolatry does. If we equate goodness with righteousness, then we must overcome evil in order to be righteous which ultimately makes us self-righteous—just like the Pharisees. If only the righteous are saved, then we must overcome evil in order to earn salvation. We thus end up saving ourselves just as a great many mainstream denominations preach in countless subtle ways, most commonly manifest in "fighting sin" and "resisting temptation". This country was founded on just that idea. The Puritans and their kin sought to establish a "Godly nation," and in our own eyes we have created a "great nation", but in actuality the United States of America stands as Satan's greatest triumph! Think about it. This land devoted to the Freedom God is an elaborate house of mirrors which in its every aspect goes against the teachings of Christ and His Apostles!

If we don't keep the First Commandment, as well as Christ's most important commandment, our most valiant efforts to keep the others will avail us nothing. Yet, nationally we have entirely ignored those commandments. Instead, we have officially taken Nature's God as this nation's deity and as our cynosure while openly embracing a wide variety of idols. In short, we quite literally cast this nation in the image of the beast! No wonder national security—survival—plays such an overwhelmingly preponderate part in our thinking, and why that security includes not only our lives but all that we associate with them. No wonder LOM rules our every decision! No wonder we can call ourselves one nation under God, but don't dare call ourselves a nation under Christ. Look at Matthew 8:19-20: *"And a certain scribe came, and said unto Him, Master, I will follow thee withersoever thou goest."* Christ responds by saying, *"'Foxes have holes, and the birds of the air have nests, but the Son of man hath not where to lay His head.'"* He was telling the scribe wither He went in more than a physical sense by making it clear that He was utterly divorced from the natural world. The following verse reconfirms that: *"And another of His disciples said unto Him, Lord suffer me first to go and bury my father.*[23] *But Jesus said unto him, Follow Me; and let the dead bury their dead.'"* We must include the physical family in with the things of the world we value more than God. *"'He that loveth father or mother more than Me is not worthy of Me; and he that loveth son or daughter more than Me is not worthy of Me'"*—Matthew 10:37. Everything we associate with physical life falls into the same category, and a devotion to any or all of it constitutes enmity with God. *"For they that are*

---

[23] According to the Amplified Bible, he asked Christ to let him stay with his father until he died.

after the flesh do mind the things of the flesh; but they that are after the Spirit the things of the Spirit. For to be carnally minded is death; but to be spiritually minded is life and peace"—Romans 8:5-6. We find this essential message reconfirmed a number of times throughout the New Testament. Those *who follow Christ are dead to their mortal lives* (see Colossians 3:3), and so the survival imperative no longer applies to either their lives nor to what they associate with them including both their possessions and their loved ones.

Consider a rather famous incident recounted in Mark 4:37-41. *"And there arose a great storm of wind, and the waves beat into the ship so that it was now full. And He was in the hinder part of the ship, asleep on a pillow: and they awake Him and say unto Him, Master, carest thou not that we perish? And He arose, and rebuked the wind, and said unto the sea, 'Peace, be still.' And the wind ceased, and there was a great calm. And He said unto them, 'Why are you so fearful? How is it that ye have no faith?' And they feared exceedingly, and said one to another, what manner of man is this that even the wind and the sea obey Him?"* Notice that they both feared the storm and feared the One able to calm it. (We find the same reaction in Matthew 14:26). In Revelations, chapter fifteen, we find the seven angels holding the final seven plagues singing "the song of Moses": *"Who shall not fear Thee, O Lord, and glorify Thy name? For Thou only art holy; for all nations shall come and worship before Thee; for Thy judgments are made manifest."* We cannot truly love God without fearing Him, for rather than fear of survival, this fear is more of a kind of jaw-dropping awe which serves to reflect the Truth of His majesty.

The Disciples, by contrast, did not manifest that kind of fear as suggested by their question of what kind of man He was. Instead, they feared for their lives while Christ took a nap. When He asks them how it is that they have no faith, we must ponder one of the most basic questions this work means to address: *faith in what?* Faith, the synthesized totality of what we believe, lies at the heart of our introcosms, and so at the very foundation of our identities. In essence, then, our answer to that question defines whose children we are, God's or Satan's. To change the essence of our faith is to change the essence of our natures, and only God can do that by way of the baptism of the Holy Spirit. Such is the nature of true faith as opposed to simple belief. Yet to receive that faith in sufficient measure, the Disciples' fear still founded on the survival imperative which meant that they considered their lives a greater good than that which they perceived as a threat to them. We can also see this reflected in the Revelations' account of the Great Plagues of the Tribulation. *"And men were scorched with great heat, and blasphemed the name of God, which hath power over these plagues: and they repented not to give Him glory"*—Revelations 16:9.Notice how that establishes evil as originating with God and to a good and loving purpose! The storm arose according to God's will; it also abated at that same will. Thus, they were both threatened and survived due to God's will! *If we live or if we die, we are the Lord's.* Consider the imagery: they sought to deliver themselves from this evil—to save themselves—by literally coming to Christ in the flesh. Sound familiar? That too invokes Christ's question while raising another. What prompted their actions, love or fear? Love of God and fear for our own survival are polar opposites and utterly incompatible! *"'Whosoever shall seek to save his life shall lose it; and whosoever shall lose his life shall preserve it'"*—Luke 17:33. Sadly, that's what many coming to church seek, but they do so with preserving their eternal lives in mind, i.e., motivated by fear rather than by love which, if you'll pardon the expression, puts them in the same boat as the Disciples. Such a belief reflected a lack of faith in the very Truth He embodied, in the very reason for His earthly sojourn and, presumably, the very reason for them being on the boat with Him!

We Christians are called to live in the world but not as part of it. *"Dearly beloved, I beseech you as strangers and pilgrims, abstain from fleshly lusts, which war against your souls . . ."*—I Peter 2:11. That brings up a subtle but important point. Although clearly having much in common, "country" and "nation" are not entirely synonymous. Connotatively, the former refers to the land itself while the latter usually refers more strongly to the people occupying the land. *"But ye are a chosen generation, a royal priesthood, an holy nation, a peculiar people; that ye should shew forth the praises of Him who hath called you out of darkness into His marvelous light; which in time past were not a people, but are now the people of God: which had not obtained mercy, but now have obtained mercy"*—I Peter 2:9-10. Notice how the phrase "royal priesthood" intimately associates religion and politics. Perhaps most important of all, however, that we define that people *as those who have obtained God's mercy and praise Him for that fact.* That is the essence of the free gift of Grace available by our faith in Christ. We can in no way divorce that gift from that Person, for without Him there is no gift! We cannot genuinely accept God's word as espoused by His Son without the appropriate foundation; we cannot accept His spiritual Truths while holding earthly concerns as our baseline values or self-evident truth as our ultimate authority. *"But the natural man receiveth not the things of the Spirit of God: for they are foolishness unto him: neither can he know them, because they are spiritually discerned"*—I Corinthians 2:14. Moreover, neither can we look at issues in any other than a good vs. evil format, thereby denying the very Truth that Christ embodies. If we take the physical as our basic definition of reality, as deism and Nature's God must, then we cannot fathom eternity and, more importantly, find ourselves quite incapable of taking it as anything more than a largely useless abstraction. Yet taking that time frame into account is utterly essential to taking the things of heaven in contrast to the temporal concerns of physical existence as our guiding light. *"While we look not at the things that are seen, but at the things that are not seen: for the things that are seen are temporal; but the things that are not seen are eternal"*—II Corinthians 4:18. Consider the inherent irony. We like to think that reason rules us but, if we cannot even *conceive* of eternity, how rational is it to consider ourselves adequate judges of it? Yet just that attitude has played a cardinal role in Christianity's history. No wonder the illusion of progress seems so real.

Christianity initially appealed almost exclusively to the poor and uneducated to whom the Truth was divinely revealed. It's difficult if not impossible to overstress the importance of that qualifier. Although their "betters" treated this new religion with skepticism (hell, these idolaters worshiped an *invisible* god!), they also found it intolerable that the poor and illiterate could know something they didn't. As Christianity's influence began to rise, (as early as the Second Century,) so arose intellectual criticism of it which some saw as threat to the faith. Note that carefully, for it plays a huge role in what was to follow. That threat to the faith actually meant a threat to the content of the faith, which comes down to what we know. The trouble is, we cannot separate what we know from the means by which we acquire our knowledge, and therein we find the problem. Ironically, the initial defense of "the Faith" founded on reason. With the best of intentions, *apologists,* most of whom were skilled philosophers, rose to the defense of their beliefs and, although obviously not intentionally, thereby acted in an Antichrist-like manner. It certainly seemed right. *"But sanctify the Lord God in your hearts: and be ready always to give an answer to every man that asketh you a reason of the hope that is in you with meekness and fear: having a good conscience; that whereas they speak evil of you, as of evildoers, they may be ashamed that falsely accuse your good conversation in Christ"*—I Peter 3;15-16. There is, however, that all-important important qualifier. *"'Settle it therefore in your hearts, not to meditate before what ye shall answer: For I will give you a mouth and wisdom, which all your adversaries shall not be able to gainsay nor resist'"*—Luke 21:14-15. Christ's is what we call a "mystery religion" with *mystery* defined as *"any truth that is unknowable except by divine revelation"* (Dictionary.com.) *"How that by revelation He made known unto me the mystery; (as I wrote afore in few words, whereby, when ye read, ye may understand my knowledge in the mystery of Christ) which in other ages was not made known unto the sons of men, as it is now revealed unto His holy apostles and prophets by the Spirit . . ."*—Ephesians 3:3-5. Notice how that parallels Christ saying, *"'Every one that is of the Truth heareth My voice'"* (see above). Suddenly the division between the human spirit and the Holy Spirit as what unifies us grows considerably wider. In short, we *cannot* understand the mystery of God's plan for our redemption without the Holy Spirit, any more than we can accept that magnificent gift without that same Spirit. Neither can we explain it to anyone else lacking that Spirit. *"Which things also we speak, not in the words that man's wisdom teacheth, but which the Holy Spirit teacheth; comparing spiritual things with spiritual"*—I Corinthians 2:13. Given such radically differing epistemological and cosmological baselines, the apologists could hope to reach only the vaguest common ground with their antagonists. That common ground turned out to be morality—the very foundation Adams found essential to a constitutional government (see above) and what many people most readily associate with Christianity. While it's difficult to say which came first, that fateful compromise reflects the Church's move from emphasizing Truth to emphasizing goodness (morality). Far less noticed, but far more importantly, that also reflects the Church's move from emphasizing righteousness to emphasizing goodness while laying the foundation for the eventual co-equation of the two which played a part in Christianity's subsequent fragmentation.

Again, it must have seemed right. By pretty much any definition the intention, desire and attempts to save souls must be taken as good, especially given perdition as the contrasting evil. Moreover, if we define the good as that which overcomes the evil, then saving souls from perdition must be taken as both the definition and the proper role of the good. If we equate goodness with righteousness, then doing such must not also be the proper role of the righteous, but must be the means by which we attain righteousness. Any time we deliberately alter the Word of God, regardless of the purity of our intentions, to that same extent we deny the Truth Christ embodies and, therefore, deny Him. With so much at stake, the temptation to do so can sometimes prove almost overwhelming, but the intention to pursue goodness, and the intention to pursue righteousness are two entirely different things. We can will ourselves into goodness, especially defined as behavior modification, by myriad means, including plain, old-fashioned will power. The fact that we cannot will ourselves to righteousness poses an obvious question: which would seem the more desirable and worthwhile pursuit to the *natural man* given to self-determination? Which is more conducive to life and its associated concerns? Unwittingly, the seeds of self-rule had been planted, the temple of the God Life sanctified. Not surprisingly, the cross—the virtually universal symbol of Christianity—has historically been used as a life sign and even the symbol of life gods.

It must have *seemed* good, but survival always seems good to the unenlightened to the extent that we may call the desire for survival a primary characteristic of the unenlightened. By removing religious principles from revelation to a matter of learning, such philosophical agreement gave rise to the hope of saving heathen souls by way of conventional teaching and, of course, by way of the human spirit. Consistently enough, as we'll explore in more detail a bit later, it also served the purpose of allowing the physical church to survive and flourish as a political entity dedicated to worshipping God in the flesh. Religion and politics merge still again. Although it certainly didn't seem like it at the time, and took several centuries to come to fruition, since virtually the entire world was under the heel of some authoritarian or another, it likewise eventually added legitimacy to self-rule. Think about it: that compromise essentially made self-determination the focal point of the entire mainstream Christian religion that worships the Father in the flesh. As that implies, it simultaneously made revolution against God's rule a primary Christian characteristic. No wonder it seems so righteous for us to replace divine Truth with self-evident truth in order to justify our governmental form! If you think about it, self-evident truth and its spiritual counterpart, deism, amount to believing in the flesh. More revealing, we cast ourselves as the ultimate authority in both cases in a clear example of self-deification. Since we must consciously serve God or we serve His usurper instead, we therefore make *Satan* our ultimate authority in both cases!

By linking our salvation to what we learn, we turn what we learn into the source of our righteousness while casting those devising those doctrines as the root of righteousness. In a broader sense, we then turn our intelligence into the source of our righteousness and salvation just as evolution cites our intellectual capacity as saving us from extinction. No wonder the clergy-laity distinction seems so legitimate and even vital, with its power base founded squarely on the mark of the beast! If we can claim ourselves as the source of righteousness, as the *good people go to heaven* doctrine clearly implies, then we can readily consider ourselves capable of choosing our own leaders from "God" on down. No wonder my will be done seems so righteous both ecclesiastically and politically. More pragmatically, knowledge-based faith can thus be imposed on the *natural man,* which essentially means that we can force the unwashed into salvation. That accounts for much (if not all) of the Christian religion's bloody history, as well as for a good deal of the legitimate criticism resulting from it. Much the same holds true for the mounting international criticism aimed at the United States for taking a similar attitude toward democracy and the American way of life.

We have placed so much emphasis on faith that we often refer to religions accordingly: *people of different faiths,* for example. In each instance, we differentiate those people on the basis of their faith's content. Ironically, the specifics don't really matter. Faith based on knowledge is a contradiction in terms as evidenced by the devils who acknowledge God's existence cited above. Faith, by definition, means a belief in something *that can neither be seen nor logically demonstrated.* (See Hebrews 11:1.) Knowledge-based faith, however, is central to worshipping God in the flesh, even though the flesh has been shown inadequate to the task (see above). But most tragic of all, what better way to keep believers from seeking the Truth than to convince them that they've already found it? *"'...for wide is the gate, and broad is the way, that leadeth to destruction, and many there be which go in thereat...'"* Billions of "Christians" have been so convinced, and their numbers increase every day, for what we find depends upon what we seek. Given deception as Satan's primary tool, wouldn't we expect such a gate to be marked, "Salvation"? What else would we logically expect from those posing as *"ministers of righteousness"?* Consider the subtly involved: we seek salvation, thereby leaving the door open to anyone promising it, when we should seek God's mercy that allows for that salvation and limits our search to Him. We should ask ourselves upon whom He shows that mercy. If we do that much, we find the humility and submission to His authority and will exhorted throughout the

New Testament at the core of the answer: *the meek shall inherit the earth.*

While not obviously related, belief based on knowledge is frightingly similar to empiricism which literally amounts to *walking by sight* and, ultimately leads to our belief in our own reason—another characteristic absolutely essential to self-determination. From there it's a simple step to likewise believe in our own wisdom, and with extremely rare exceptions, we universally use that as our guiding principle. *"Let no man deceive himself. If any man among you seemeth to be wise in this world, let him become a fool, that he may be wise"*—I Corinthians 3:18. Does that suggest the *strong delusions* Paul mentions? After all, he cites them in direct opposition to receiving a love of the Truth. Think about it: by putting our faith in excogitated doctrine, we put our faith in excogitation itself in a manner very similar to how we put our faith in scientific revelations, statistics, studies and so on. Doesn't that suggest being wise in this world? Yet how else could we define the self-evident truth we find as the spiritual foundation of this country? How else could we define the Nature's God we hold as our official deity? Our governmental form is our religion enacted. The American combination of religious and political freedom is no coincidence; we can also make a strong case that, taken together, the traditional Christianity amply represented in this nation's nascence constitutes a major part of that *strong delusion*. Think about it. By definition, a strong delusion will prove difficult to detect. Indeed, without divine perception it will prove *impossible* to detect. The deceived is unaware of the deception in large part because we believe what we want to believe. If we have no love of divine Truth, then we have a love of Anti-Truth in its stead. Just as we must serve one master or the other, so we will devote ourselves to one or the other. Hence, our title question.

Efforts to deliver ourselves from evil inevitably deliver us to it instead. Religious freedom's efforts to save souls by founding on reason and the products of the human mind provide an especially good case in point. Based on reason, those adopting the scientific discipline have good reason to believe as they do, especially by contrast to what many take as the "religious view".

For example, while religious freedom reflects a badly fractured view of existence, the science resulting from intellectual freedom does the exact opposite. We could look upon science's different branches as different denominations in the Church of Reason, yet in spite of their sometimes radically different subjects and methods, all of those branches tightly interrelate in a huge and extremely complex latticework of knowledge with the overall structure only as strong as the weakest piece, and with all the pieces always open to challenge. By contrast, religious freedom offers an extremely splintered view of existence, with a large number of deital powers ranging from a harsh authoritarian eager to condemn even the slightest transgression to an indifferent Prime Mover to an Ultimate Good Guy god who eventually saves everyone. No wonder the self-enlightened take science as their foundation for truth. No wonder religious concessions to its revelations seem so right. Good intentions notwithstanding, the apologists' metaphysical and epistemological concessions to their philosophical adversaries has borne the inevitable fruit.

Still, although Satan can warp and distort our perception of God's preexistent Truth, he cannot fundamentally alter it. Since scientific cosmology and deism are so similar, especially in contemporary America, let us look a bit more deeply at scientific theory in light of the proposition *"by their fruits we may judge"* (Matthew7:20.) More specifically, let us again consider the question of whether we actually seek self-destruction without realizing it. Consider: if physical life without Christ is actually death, and if most of us worship the God Life and all that it represents, then it seems that we do indeed seek self-destructiveness. Since we can essential equate worship of God with service to Him, that means that by serving Death as our end we actually worship Death, as clearly evidenced in our ever increasing global arsenals and the preponderance of virtual deaths in our entertainments. Think about it. War and related industries not only prove enormously profitable for a select few, they and their peripheries also account for a major part of our global economy. Indeed, should global peace suddenly break out, billions of dollars in corporate profits would evaporate along with millions of jobs. As the economy crashed, the whole fabric of our social structure would unravel, and the *author of chaos* would reveal himself as our actual deity.

But in a more abstract sense, we can reveal that deity any way simply by observing that, in general, science deals with the physical to the total exclusion of the supernatural in a manner very similar to our efforts to separate church and state. However, while we can ignore the Truth, we cannot escape it any more than we can escape the consequences of not accepting it. Given that, consider a grim curiosity. Scientists have yet to extrapolate the final fate of the universe to their satisfaction, but have reduced it to two basic scenarios. They now seek "dark matter" which remains beyond our ability to detect directly—ironic in itself given science's normal emphasis on observation—but which they have inferred due to observable gravitational influences. Without this dark matter, scientists say that the universe will simply continue to expand. The galaxies will grow ever more isolated until the very fuel of existence itself is completely expended resulting in universal death—what they call "the Big Chill." If, on the other hand, they can find the necessary dark matter, then the universe will eventually collapse in on itself in "the Big Crunch". Some speculate that this might yield another Big Bang—the cosmological counterpart to reincarnation—but in either case, physical evidence points to universal destruction as the ultimate perfection—"death more abundant" taken to its logical extreme. It would appear as if Nature itself takes self-destruction as its ultimate ideal. What does that suggest about those who seek guidance from Nature's God? What does that suggest about those who take that god as their creator? Fruit must follow the pattern of its seed.

What does that suggest about our definition of progress? One can, after all, progress toward the gallows. Does that definition also reflect an unacknowledged desire for Death? Think about it, again in light of our governmental system as our religion enacted. We take *easier is better* as a primary characteristic of that progress, and so as an unqualified good. But, consider again Luke 13:24: *"Strive to enter in at the strait gate; for many, I say unto you, will seek to enter in, and shall not be able."'* While *strive* means to put forth great effort, religious freedom strives to make salvation easy. Perhaps even more telling, most if not all of the concessions with paganism have been aimed at the same end by making Christian Truths more palatable to pagan tastes. Rather than the elect chosen by God—which finds an obvious mirror-image parallel to the Elite running the world as well as their spiritual counterparts devising doctrine—it strives to open salvation to anyone willing to mouth the appropriate phrases, drink the appropriate beverage, obey the appropriate rules, and proclaim the appropriate doctrine. All of the above are matters of our own choice, our own will, and are therefore inherently unrighteous while reflecting the essence of democracy: self-determination. Doesn't that also sound like a pretty good definition of the Great Apostasy? Who advocates self-determination? The answer to that question answers our title question.

Nowhere in the New Testament do we find the issue of self-determination more eloquently illustrated than in the persons of Simon Peter, the one on whom Christ said *He would build His church* (Matthew 16:18), and Judas Iscariot, the one who betrayed Him. What has this "rock", so re-named by Christ Himself, to tell us about that church? Bear in mind that Christ says that *wise men build their houses on the rock, while the foolish do so on shifting sand* (see Matthew 7:26). Presumably, then, Peter symbolized that kind of wisdom, but what is the nature of that wisdom? Consider: if any man in history could have saved himself, it would have been him. Still more pertinently, if any man in history could have followed Christ of his own volition, it surely must have been him. When Christ went to Gethsemane, some of His disciples, including Peter went with Him. He told them to sit and wait for Him while He prayed, yet they could not do it. *"What,'"* Christ said to Peter, *"could ye not watch with Me one hour? Watch and pray, that ye enter not into temptation: the spirit is indeed willing, but the flesh is weak'"*—Matthew 26:40-41. Indeed, it was weak, for Peter and the disciples fell asleep a second time.

But the human spirit had yet another tale to tell. Just after Christ was taken in Gethsemane, in spite of his sincere vows to remain true, *Peter denied the Lord three times before the cock crowed,* just as Christ had foretold (see Matthew26:33.) Christ tells us that *if we deny Him, He will deny us* (see Matthew10:33,) so, at least by surface appearances, we must take Peter's denial as a serious breech of God's Law. Yet think about it. By denying Christ, Peter did *not* deny Him in a very specific sense: he followed God's word as given to him by his Master in spite of his most ardent and passionate desires to the contrary. As we found earlier in the heart of Pharaoh, *we cannot do good of our own resources regardless of the sincerity of our desire to do so.* (For a full discussion of this phenomenon, see Romans, chapter seven.) This man was Christ's favorite and yet, in spite of years of learning, in spite of a passionate desire, and in spite of the best the human spirit could conjure, he could not prevail. *"But as many as received Him to them gave He power to become the sons of God, even to them that believe on His name: which were born not of blood, nor of the will of the flesh, nor of the will of man, but of God"*—John 1:12-13. In spite of his learning, which far exceeded that of contemporary experts yet which lies at the foundation for virtually all of the mainstream Christian religion, deserted him and left him powerless, even as it will to those clinging to it as their hope. Yet, ironically, he thereby taught us all an important lesson. Left to his own power, he demonstrated that we *can't* deliver ourselves from evil by our own wills, and certainly not by the power of the human spirit, but must rely *entirely* on the Lord. More specifically, we rely totally on the Lord's *mercy.*

In Matthew 16:13, Christ asks His disciples, *"'Whom do men say that I, the Son of Man, am?'"* They replied that most took Him to be one of the prophets. He then asks them, *"'But whom say ye that I am?' And Simon Peter answered and said, Thou art the Christ, the Son of the living God."* Christ seemed very pleased by that response, and replied, *"'Blessed art thou, Simon Barjona: for flesh and blood hath not revealed it unto thee, but My Father which is in heaven. And I say also unto thee, thou are Peter, and upon this rock I will build My church; and the gates of hell shall not prevail against it'"*—Matthew 16:17-18. Consider that very carefully. *Christ has just defined His church as built upon divine revelation.* That is the "rock" on which *the wise build their houses,* and the means by which they avoid the *"shifting sands"* of doctrinal concessions to changing times and social norms. That means that any church not built on that foundation is false at best, Antichristian at worst. Moreover, He has likewise defined any other system as being at least associated with the gates of hell, which He specifically says will not prevail! To *prevail* means to "to prove to be effective" (Encarta).

What specifically will not prove to be effective? *"Then charged He His disciples that they should tell no man that He was Jesus the Christ."* The Amplified Bible phrases it still more strongly: *"Then He sternly and strictly charged and warned the disciples to tell no one that He was Jesus the Christ."* There's a very sound reason for that: that constitutes the diametric opposite of the divine revelation upon which He just established His church. Simply put, *flesh and blood profits nothing* and cannot reveal Christ. We can't have the Father without the Son, but neither can we have the Son without the Father: *"'No man can come to Me except the Father which hath sent Me draw him: and I will raise him up at the last day. It is written in the prophets* [Isaiah 54:13] *And they shall all be taught of God. Every man therefore that hath heard, and hath learned of the Father, cometh unto Me'"*—John 6:44-45. One very significant exception did not heed that command, nor take that Truth to heart, and that failure has rippled through all the centuries since.

Consider an episode that happened not long before the betrayal in the home of a man referred to as *"Simon the leper."* Here *"a woman"* (identified in John 11:2 as Mary, the sister of Lazarus) poured very expensive oil onto Christ's body for, as He explained to the astonished Disciples, the purpose of His burial. He counted it as such a notable deed that He said, *"'Verily I say unto you, wheresoever this gospel shall be preached in the whole world, there shall also this, that this woman hath done, be told for a memorial of her'"*—Matthew 26:13. Judas and some of the others had argued that the oil could have been sold, and the money given to the poor, just as goodness as we commonly define it would mandate. Indeed, in another famous incident which we'll deal with presently, *Christ's encounter with the rich man seeking eternal life,* He instructed him to do just that. *"'If thou wilt be perfect, go and sell that thou hast, and give to the poor...'"*—Matthew 19:21. Hence, we find a very subtle example of the difference between goodness and righteousness. We can summarize that difference with a single question: what motivates our actions, a desire to do good, or a desire to serve God? They are not always the same: we serve our fellow man by serving God; it doesn't work the other way around, and this makes an excellent case in point. Appearances notwithstanding, Mary's actions served Truth rather than goodness. While selling the oil and giving the money to the poor would have served the generally accepted definition of goodness, Mary's action quite literally acted in accordance with the Truth. She properly answered our Basic Question, *what is my purpose in life*, by proclaiming the glory of God Almighty in perhaps its most dramatic manifestation. After all, even though He died a most ignoble death, Christ was nevertheless a *king*, and this woman anointed Him accordingly. Doing so with the expensive oil proclaimed that Truth for those who could see it while requiring divine sight—the God-given ability to see the Truth—in order to do so. Notice how that brings a number of threads together: *Christ's church built on divine revelation*, the idea that *we walk by faith and not by sight*, the difference between physical and spiritual perception, the *carnal mind's inability to please God*, and so forth. Aside from Christ and His immediate associates, that action went utterly unheralded at the time, but that too works in accordance with the Scriptures. I Peter 2:12 exhorts us to do our goods deeds so that *"they* [the Gentiles] *may, by your good works which they observe, glorify God in the day of visitation."* It may take that long for them to realize what they had witnessed. That implies that those good deeds don't always seem good to normal perception at the moment they happen, as certainly must have proven true of Christ's crucifixion. Indeed, that was the essence of Judas' repentance: he regretted his role in taking the physical life of an innocent man while totally disregarding the Truth that only spiritual discernment could reveal.

Judas is called the *"son of perdition"* by Christ Himself in John 17:12, and again by Paul in II Thessalonians 2:3-4, who does so in a very specific context: *"Let no man deceive you by any means: for that day* [the Day of the Lord] *shall not come, except there* come a falling away first, and that man of sin be revealed, the son of perdition; who opposeth and exalteth himself above all that is called God, or that is worshipped: so that he as God sitteth in the temple of God, shewing himself that he is God." In the previous verses, he also says that this had already begun even in his time. Where do we find the connection between Judas' betrayal and the Great Apostasy? It is said that Judas "betrayed" Christ. That word can also mean to *unintentionally reveal something*, and that applies to both Judas Iscariot, and to his unintentional followers. Who are those followers? Consider John 6:63-66 where Christ says, "*'It is the Spirit who gives life; the flesh profits nothing. The words that I speak to you are spirit, and they are life. But there are some of you who do not believe.' For Jesus knew from the beginning who they were who did not believe, and who would betray Him. And He said, 'Therefore I have said to you that no one can come to Me unless it has been granted to him by My Father.' From that time many of His disciples went back and walked with Him no more.*" Perhaps it's not more than a coincidence, but that last phrase, *"From that time many of His disciples went back and walked with him no more",* occurs in John 6:66—the number of the Beast. Yet, if you think about it, walking no more with Him and the Great Apostasy have much in common. Consider too that, as with the *mark of the beast*, the *number of the beast* relates to survival just as holding salvation as Christianity's proper focal point does. Just because those disciples no longer walked with Him doesn't mean that they no longer sought survival. But, motivated by fear, they would find themselves very prone to letting *"any man deceive them"*, and deception is Satan's stock in trade. More pertinent to our current discussion, notice that He groups together those *"who did not believe"* with *"who would betray Him,"* while making the latter both plural and in the future tense. That casts those who do not believe in the same mold of the son of perdition. That of course poses the question of what they did not believe which, given the context, we may take as the fact *that no one can come unto Christ unless the Father so draws him,* and that *the flesh profits nothing.* Coincidentally enough, such disbelief is integral to the doctrines of much of the mainstream Christian religion. If we consider the image of Judas bringing the Jewish thugs to

Christ, we can see it as a diametric mirror-image: although they were so drawn in order to fulfill God's ultimate plan, they were drawn in the flesh and not so drawn to the very salvation they would play a role in actuating.

Finally, consider a very cryptic exchange in John 21:20-22. *"Then Peter, turning about, seeth the disciple whom Jesus loved following; which also leaned on His breast at supper, and said, 'Lord, which is he that betrayeth Thee?' Peter seeing him saith to Jesus, 'Lord,' and 'which is he that betrayeth Thee?' Peter seeing him saith to Jesus, 'Lord' and 'what shall this man do?' Jesus saith unto him, 'If I will that he tarry till I come, what is that to thee? Follow thou Me'".* By this point you would think *"Follow thou Me"* would be unnecessary to the Apostle on whom He'd chosen to build His church. Thus, we may conclude that He said that much more for our benefit than for Peter's. Moreover, He said it as a differentiation. Notice the context: Peter asked Christ about the nature of Judas' *future* betrayal. Christ answered him by telling him to ignore Judas and follow Him instead! The differentiation is clearly between Judas who led men to Christ in the flesh and the Son of God who told us that we must be so drawn to Him by the Father. In which mold has the vast majority of the Christian religion cast itself? Why has it done so if not due to the survival imperative translated into spiritual terms? Does that not cast such as false messiahs and prophets who have gone out from Christ's true disciples? Does that not cast them as *ministers of righteousness?* By seeking salvation per se rather than God's mercy, we seek the Gift rather than the Giver. Thus, we serve ourselves and not our God just as self-determination mandates.

Consider a refrain of a passage already cited, this one in Luke 9:59-62. *"And He said unto another, 'Follow Me'. But he said, 'Lord, suffer me first to go and bury my father.' Jesus said unto him, 'Let the dead bury their dead: but go thou and preach the kingdom of God.' And another also said, 'Lord, I will follow thee; but let me first bid them farewell, which are at home at my house'. And Jesus said unto him, 'No man, having put his hand to the plow, and looking back, is fit for the kingdom of God.'"* We find an echo of that in His encounter with *the young man seeking eternal life* (see below). Christ loved him as well, but he was unable to give up his worldly values and so was unable to follow Christ. The same held true for Judas. As the fact that he carried the group's purse suggests, he was given to the world and in the end could not relinquish the appropriate virtues and values. What else might we expect from a *"devil"?* (See John 6:70). A great many putative Christians have the same problem. But also notice John 21:23: *"Then went this saying abroad among the brethren, that that disciple should not die: yet Jesus did not say unto him, He shall not die; but, If I will that he tarry till I come, what is that to thee?"* That saying implied that Judas led to eternal life, but that is not what Christ actually said, and certainly not what He'd meant. But that casts Judas as the one leading people to Christ in the flesh under the common misapprehension that he thereby leads them to eternal life. Thus we reveal one of the most basic of divine Truths: the *strait and narrow gate* is quite impossible to find without divine empowerment just as the Apostles could not detect a devil in their very midst without the same empowerment. The flesh indeed profits nothing; we live by the Sprit and that alone, even as we follow Christ by the same means. *"For as many as are led by the Spirit of God, they are the sons of God"*—Romans 8:14.

Yet the seeds of Anti-Truth embodied in Judas following Christ in the flesh were cast forth, finding fertile ground among those given to self-determination and the power of the human spirit. In a sense, we could cast Judas Iscariot as the founder of the mainstream Christian religion as well as the true Father of our Country. Those who betray Him are those who do not believe that that *the flesh profits nothing* and, more importantly, that *"'No one can come to Me unless it has been granted to him by My Father.'"* The follow self-evident truth, truth they want to believe, rather than the divine Truth embodied in the Way to salvation! That single element is common to the entirety of mainstream Christianity united by the human spirit, and is the centerpiece of the Great Apostasy! That holds entirely consistent with the fact that Christ would build His Church on the divine revelation epitomized in Simon Peter, which was specifically contrasted to the fleshly perceptions of others who took Christ as a prophet, and who now consider Him a great man or spiritual leader. Without that kind of revelation, we can neither see not accept the true Son of God just as Judas could see Him only as a political activist and troublemaker. Consider the nature of Judas' betrayal in light of perception. He revealed Christ's identity to those possessing only natural sight in the same manner that we do to those who have not been called by the Father. That's what makes physical perception, especially judging good and evil based on seeing is believing, so deadly. It's also what enables the *wolves in sheep's clothing* to do their thing. Even worse, it's what allows those wolves to get their followers to participate in their apostasy while packaging it as righteousness. By definition, the sheep's clothing strongly implies a Christ-like outward appearance which masks their true rapacity. Those whom the Father has not called can attempt to follow Him only in the flesh, and fear of perdition can drive them to do just that. Thus we can find a link between the mark of the beast and those wolves, for such fear can ultimately lead only to obedience as the fulfillment of the Law which, righteous appearances notwithstanding, leads us right back to the *Synagogue of Satan.*

Many have speculated that Judas may have been motivated by *philios,* and sought to betray Christ because he'd come to see Him as a troublemaker who threatened the peace and stability of his nation. The priests with whom he colluded faced something of a dilemma. They could readily see and hate Christ as one who threatened their privileged positions in the community and, given Roman rule, perhaps even their identity as a nation. On the other hand, if He really were the Son of God, then He *had* to die in accordance with prophecy. *"Then gathered the chief priests and the Pharisees, and told them what things Jesus had done* [performed many miracles]. *If we let Him thus alone, all men will believe on Him: and the Romans shall come and take away both our place and our nation. And one of them, named Caiaphas, being the high priest that same year, said unto them, 'Ye know nothing at all, or consider that it is expedient for us, that one man should die for the people, and that the whole nation perish not.' And this he spake not of himself: but being high priest that year, he prophesied that Jesus should die for that nation; and not for that nation only, but that also He should gather together in one the children of God that were scattered abroad"*—John 11:46-52. Again we find religion and politics intimately interwoven, just as the *Kingdom of God* suggests.

Given that he may have had the wellbeing of his countrymen in mind, couldn't we classify Judas as a *patriot?* Given that he took the delivery of his people from this troublemaker (i.e., this evil) unto himself, wouldn't we now consider him a hero in much the same way we would have considered Peter a hero for defending his beloved Master with the sword in Gethsemane? Doesn't that parallel the American desire to deliver the world from the evils of tyranny? Notice that in the above passage, some of the priests maintained that, if left alone, all men would believe on Christ due to His miracles. To that the High Priest retorted, *"'Ye know nothing at all'"*. He separated the spiritual from the physical, and saw Christ as who and what He was. His vision of righteousness, which amounted to prophecy, was the diametric opposite of the others' vision of goodness just as secular truths are the diametric opposite of spiritual truths. Suddenly, our Basic Question, *who do we serve*, takes on a good deal more importance. It likewise seems a good deal less self-evident, especially if we think in terms of good vs. evil. *"If ye love Me, keep My commandments. And I will pray the Father, and He shall send you another Comforter, that He may abide with you forever; even the Spirit of Truth; whom the world cannot receive, because it seeth Him not, neither knoweth Him: but ye know Him; for he dwelleth with you, and shall be in you'"*—John 14:15-17. Can a nation officially denying its allegiance to Christ hope for that Spirit's guidance? Since the world *"knoweth Him not,"* nor even sees Him, we cannot live as part of the world and still hope to receive Him as an indwelling part of us. Moreover, once having received Him, we can no longer walk in the flesh, abiding by the world's norms and conventions, for such are hostile to the Truth.

You may have noted the irony of the fact that Judas is the *"son of Simon"* (John 6:71) which was, of course, Peter's name before his re-christening. That's symbolically more important that many of us might realize. Consider Revelations 2:17: *"He that hath an ear, let him hear what the Spirit sayteh unto the churches; to him that overcometh will I give to eat of the hidden manna, and will give him a white stone, and in the stone a new name written, which no man knoweth saving he that receiveth it'".* As that suggests, the contrast between Peter and Judas, in spite of a surprising number of similarities, epitomizes perhaps the most important Truth of them all: *God will have mercy on those on whom He will have mercy!* Consider: in Luke 22:31, Christ says to Peter, *"'Simon, Simon, behold, Satan hath desired to have you, that he may sift you as wheat: But I have prayed for thee, that thy faith fail not: and when thou are converted, strengthen thy brethren.'"* Notice that, although He had previously rechristened him "Peter", He here refers to him as "Simon" since he has yet to be converted—i.e., he has yet to receive the baptism of the Holy Spirit. By contrast, He says of Judas, *"'But behold, the hand of him that betrayeth Me is with Me on the table. And truly the Son of Man goeth, as it was determined: but woe unto the man by whom He is betrayed'"*—Luke 22:21-22. Remember that Jude speaks of *"ungodly men"* who have *"crept in unawares"* and who deny Christ but who *"were before of old ordained to this condemnation"* (Jude 1:14.) Notice how that corresponds with *"as it was determined"* in the verse above. *"'I will have mercy on whom I will have mercy, and I will have compassion on whom I will have compassion'".* That applied to Judas as it did to Peter, and as it did to His own Son and as it does to everyone else. In a sense, that single verse summarizes reality and the Truth of Christ! Think about it. Christ perfectly kept the Law in both flesh and Spirit, and died anyway, only to be raised from the dead by the power and mercy of our Heavenly Father. That summarizes the Grace Economy. Acknowledging that is absolutely integral to accepting the Truth that Christ embodies, but there's more to it that that. His true righteousness lies in His submission to His Father's will. *"'Therefore doth My Father love Me, because I lay down My life, that I might take it again. No man taketh it from Me, but I lay it down of Myself. I have power to lay it down, and I have power to take it again. This commandment have I received of My Father'"*—John 10:17-18. Notice how that parallels the idea that *he who would save his life shall lose it* (see above) which clearly relates to the survival imperative and to the most basic aspect of walking after the flesh. We must similarly lay down our old lives in this world, with all its lusts and concerns, to take up our new lives in Christ both now and at the Final Day. That is integral to our walk with God and walking in the Spirit.

If we combine that lack of mercy on this "devil" with the fact that he alone of all of His disciples brought people to Christ in the flesh, what lesson can we learn? Consider what happened to Judas after the fact. *"Then Judas, which had betrayed Him, when he saw that He was condemned, repented himself, and brought again the thirty pieces of sliver to the chief priests and elders, saying, 'I have sinned in that I have betrayed innocent blood.' And they said, 'What is that to us? See thou to that.' And he cast down the pieces of sliver in the temple and departed, and went out and hanged himself"*—Matthew 27:3-5. Notice that it still again reminds us that Judas had betrayed his Master, which puts a great deal of emphasis on that betrayal while directly associating that betrayal to his guilt over having spilled *"innocent blood".* He had acted in accordance to the Truth that Caiaphas had seen, but could only see his own actions in terms of good vs. evil, just as had proven true throughout the Old Covenant. In a very basic sense, he denied the Truth. Ironically, he also epitomized a bitter Truth found in II Peter 2:20: *"For if after they have escaped the pollutions of the world through the knowledge of the Lord and Savior Jesus Christ they are again entangled therein, and overcome, the latter end is worse with them than the beginning."* Therein we find a powerful lesson for us all: there is no mercy in the Old Covenant where *the penalty for sin is death.* Similarly, there is no mercy for those who reject Christ's Truth about the nature of Grace, and that most certainly includes those who would rather accept the Anti-Truth of self-determination, politically or ecclesiastically. Self-determination does not allow for the guidance of the Holy Spirit and so, by definition, consists of walking after the flesh just as worshipping God in the flesh suggests.

In a sense, we live much as did the early Christians under Roman persecution: living our faith in the face of mounting opposition which, although far more subtle than what the martyrs had to endure, is no less deadly. Most of it doesn't seem hostile; we do, after all, include Christianity in with religious freedom. That explains why we can readily dismiss the threat, but in a way that makes it all the more dangerous. Bear in mind that Christ warned against false prophets and messiahs who might be able to *deceive even the elect* (Mark 13:22).While that again highlights the struggle as between Truth and Anti-Truth rather than good vs. evil, it also hints at an extraordinarily convincing subtly. Without a full commitment to the Truth, without loving it with all our hearts, minds and so forth, we may well fall prey to those imposters, just as many have already done. The Adversary uses a vast array of evils not toward the conquest of good, but as the means of eroding the Truth. To that end, in addition to using shock troops readily definable as evil by pretty nearly any standard, his Propaganda Machine also lets loose innumerable *"little foxes"* (Song of Solomon 2:15) bent on trampling our vineyards day by day, while hoping that most of them will go unnoticed or unidentified. As part of being human, we live lives beset by all manner of temptations and lusts of the flesh, the gross and obvious sins acting to obfuscate the more subtle ones. If we think in terms of good vs. evil, with sin naturally cast as the latter, we can find ourselves blinded to what may well prove more devastating iniquities directly related to self-determination and so to idolatry.

That illustrates a Truth we need to take to heart: *the whole good vs. evil mindset is in itself a deception aimed at luring us from the strait and narrow way!* Our relationship to the things of the earth provides an excellent example. There's nothing inherently "wrong" with material possessions per se any more than there's anything wrong with money per se. As with money, the problem lies not in the possessions themselves, but in our relationship to them, for we can define idolatry as holding anything of greater importance or as a subject of greater reverence and service than God. *"Charge them that are rich in this world, that they be not highminded nor trust in uncertain riches, but in the living God, who giveth us richly all things to enjoy; that they do good, that they be rich in good works, ready to distribute, willing to communicate; laying up in store for themselves a good foundation against the time to come, that they may lay hold on eternal life"*—I Timothy 6:17-19. Notice how the *"foundation"* echoes Christ observation about the *"rock"* on which the wise build their homes. Bearing in mind that "wealth" is a highly subjective term—even the poorest American is wealthy compared to those in some parts of the world—regardless of our relative income, we dedicate ourselves to the things above as a defense against the distractions and cares of the world that can so readily lead us astray, and which wealth can so readily amplify. To reiterate, we engage in idolatry if we hold *anything* as an object of greater love and devotion than God. Again refer to the rich man seeking eternal life cited above, and note that he found it impossible to abandon his wealth both fiscal and spiritual. We must not allow earthly concerns, profound or mundane, to supersede our devotion to God for doing so amounts to idolatry. Again, good vs. evil cannot hope to comprehend that. If, however, we look at idolatry in terms of Truth vs. Anti-Truth we can begin to understand that it constitutes a violation of the most basic Truth of them all: only God is God. *"And Moses said unto God, Behold, when I come unto the children of Israel, and shall say unto them, The God of your fathers hath sent me unto you; and they shall say to me, What is His Name? what shall I say to them? And God said unto Moses, I AM THAT I AM: and He said, Thus shalt thou say unto the children of Israel, I AM hath sent me unto you"*—Exodus 3:13-14. The Amplified Bible embellishes that to include: *"I AM WHO I AM and WHAT I AM and I WILL BE WHAT I WILL BE".* Doesn't that define self-determination? Doesn't self-determination literally amount to self-devotion at the expense of a devotion to God? Doesn't that constitute self-deification? No wonder we believe that we can both rule and save ourselves! Given that, we can clearly see any conscious effort to modify God's definition to suit our own whims as a matter of self-deification/idolatry which again casts Anti-Truth as our true Adversary and as the legitimate definition of evil.

If we look closely, we can see that Peter and Judas both committed mirror-images of the same sin with Christ's Truth the central issue. The one denied an association with Christ—clearly an Anti-Truth—while the other acknowledged it—ironically, also an Anti-Truth. Peter's association with Christ was spiritual, as reflected in the exchange about *whether he loved Christ* in John 21:16-17. Judas had but a physical relationship to Christ, as suggested by the manner in which he betrayed Him: with a chaste kiss of friendship reminiscent of the hypocrisy of the Pharisees. Consider that carefully: by definition, he was a "Christian" in that he followed Christ, yet he acted in accordance with Old Covenant conventions thereby making himself part of the *Synagogue of Satan*, just as Christ calling him a "devil" would suggest. Christ is the Truth incarnate and therefore our relationship to Him revolves around the divine Truth He embodies. That divine Truth is the New Covenant which supersedes the Old. That means that our relationship to the Father also revolves around and is totally dependent upon that Truth. Not embracing that fact means that we lack the same Truth as Satan lacks: God's ultimate authority. Remember that Paul warns of the *strong delusions* sent by the Father against those who did not accept *a love of the Truth*, and that's where we find the primary difference. That which we love is that which we seek, but it goes further than that. That which we love is that with which we desire to spend our time and to which we desire to devote our lives. In essence, who (what) we love is who (what) we serve. As a result, giving up the things of the world—including the peace and security of our nation if necessary—is not a burden but a matter of preference, for we can begin to see earthly affairs as what *spots the garment*, as what fouls our relationship to Father and Son alike, and we find ourselves with an ever increasing desire to relinquish such things. Both love and sin are matters of the heart that eventually reflect in the flesh. Accordingly, while we begin to define such things as the tangible, we eventually mature enough to realize that even deadlier intangibles can readily fall into the same category.

Peter deeply regretted his denial as soon as he realized what he had done, even though it had caused Christ no direct harm. By contrast, only when he saw that Christ was condemned to death did Judas repent himself, and then for the wrong reason! *"I have sinned in that I have betrayed the innocent blood!"*—Matthew 27:4. Although true in a sense, even "innocent" implies good vs. evil, and so good vs. evil reveals Judas' unwitting followers as those sharing the Satanic lack of Truth, and replacing it with good vs. evil directly related to the survival imperative. In terms of Truth vs. Anti-Truth, he had acted in accordance with God's divine plan for our salvation—*and counted it as an evil!* That mirrors Peter's earlier concern about Christ's wellbeing when Christ referred to him as Satan (see above). Do you also see the similarity between that and the Apostles in the boat (see above)? All of the above share in common loving "goodness" more than Truth. Whenever and to whatever extent we value *anything,* including our lives, our wellbeing, or even our visions of goodness more than we value our relationship to God's divine Truth, to that same extent *we are idolaters.*

That's the lesson we can learn from the Roman martyrs. Clearly those emperors interfered with, abridged, sometimes entirely negated their religious freedom as well as their basic human rights. And yet, these martyrs, some of Christ's best known and highly regarded representatives, did nothing to retaliate, to resist, or even to protest. Then again, they didn't need to, for they worshipped the Father *in Truth and in Spirit,* not in the flesh, and the mightiest Empire in the world could do nothing to stop them. Think about that and then consider how dependent contemporary worship is on political freedom and "tolerance". If human rights and religious freedom were the holy issues we like to believe them to be, you would think the martyrs would have died in that cause. Instead, they did exactly the opposite. They *did not resist an evil man* regardless of his evil, and regardless of the threat he posed, for they realized that we cannot simultaneously fear man and love God. As a result, they spread this new religion based on Truth throughout the Empire in spite of its most ardent efforts to curb it. Rome's persecutions, even including the most heinous torture and barbaric deaths, did not constitute a sufficient reason to disobey the exhortation to *"bless those who despitefully use you"* (Matthew 5:44) any more than Pharaoh's persecutions constituted adequate reason for the Jews to attempt to deliver themselves from his evil (see below). As a result, *"...they overcame him* [the Devil] *by the blood of the Lamb, and by the word of their testimony; and they loved not their lives unto the death"*—Revelations 12:11. Pay particular attention to that last phrase, for it refers to the *Second Death. "He that leadeth into captivity shall go into captivity: he that killeth with the sword must be killed with the sword. Here is the patience and the faith of the saints"*—Revelations 13:10. Christ is described as having a *"sword with two edges"* (Revelations 2:12). More frightening, in Revelations 2:16 He says, *"'Repent; of else I will come unto thee quickly, and I will fight against them with the sword of My mouth'"*. The Roman Christians not only died for their convictions, they had the courage to *live by them*. They not only tolerated death, but also the *threat of death*, not only of self but of loved ones as well, all for an abstract ideal that other religions couldn't even comprehend. Why is that distinction so important? The martyrs' acquiescence to Roman demands would have appeared good in that it saved lives. It was *unrighteous,* however, because it denied God not only as the supreme deity, but as the *sole* deity. That is the one deadly issue that religious freedom, no matter how we guise it, cannot circumvent.

It's no coincidence that we're called the *children* of God. As spiritual entities, even the most devout are little more than young adolescents, with the vast majority of us well behind that. As we've mentioned, and as we find throughout the New Testament, our primary task is to grow, and to mature as part of the body of Christ. Yet most of the world, including the vast majority of those professing Christianity, have now embraced both democracy and religious freedom, both of which feature *my will be done* as their most basic component, and have taken it as a matter of progress. Think the implications. An infant's entire existence totally revolves around MY WILL BE DONE—*NOW!!!*[24] Is it coincidental that we see a simultaneous rise in global violence, all centered on that same issue? Don't most if not all of our most serious contentions come down to the question of who has the right (and might) to impose their will on whom? Isn't that the essential definition of "hegemony" which crops up evermore frequently in the news? Doesn't that really amount to a schoolyard squabble over by whose rules we'll play, a heavily armed version of "King of the Mountain?" Of course we cast these conflicts in terms of good vs. evil, but those terms remain forever relative. As a result, we likewise always define those concepts in

---

[24] That is, by the way, a pretty good indication that we are born into Original Sin.

terms of our own desires and perceived needs of the moment, very seldom taking long term consequences into account. Hence our foreign policy of expediency and the introduction of a new political term: *blowback.*[25] Not surprisingly, that's not what Paul advises: *"See then that ye walk circumspectly, not as fools, but as wise, redeeming the time, because the days are evil. Wherefore be ye not unwise, but understanding what the will of the Lord is"*—Ephesians 5:15-17. That's another characteristic common to young children: the inability and lack of desire to defer gratification. Can we call it coincidental that we've made instant gratification a major hallmark of our overall progress? *"When I was a child, I spake as a child, I understood as a child, I thought as a child: but when I became a man, I put away childish things"*—I Corinthians 13:11. If only the righteous are saved, and if righteousness comes about as a matter of spiritual maturity, what do we actually strive to attain by seeking eternal youth? Perhaps we seek self-destructiveness after all.

As a major hallmark of both our definition of progress and of our racial dematuration, we find more and more emphasis on play and recreation in our idealized way of life. If you look up the word *recreation* in the thesaurus, you'll find *regeneration* and *rebirth* as the first two offerings (*Microsoft Encarta.*) Dictionary. com offers "something created anew" as its second definition of the word. That poses the question of in whose image we are *re-creating* ourselves, and what kind of re-birth we seek. That gains a good deal more pertinence when we realize that, jointly, our recreations are often called "diversions"—a term with definite military/war applications. Microsoft Encarta defines that application as, *"a mock attack aimed at drawing enemy attention and troops away from the place of the intended main attack."* Consistently enough, that application founds on *deception*, and we know who most commonly uses that weapon in the intangible but all-too-real Spirit War. That in turn poses the question of from what those recreations intend to divert us, and what constitutes the main attack. Given that the Spirit War's issues are Truth vs.

---

25   In case you're not familiar with it, blowback refers to a decision, usually secret, that has unforeseen and undesirable long term consequences.

Anti-Truth, we should logically expect an attack on divine Truth largely characterized by turning us from it. Sure enough, the vast majority of those diversions—especially television, motion pictures, video games, music and literature—stress the eternal conflict not only in terms of good vs. evil, but in terms that are both readily ascertainable to the physical senses, and which always feature life and associated values as the primary goods. Seemingly trivial, this acts as one of the Propaganda Machine's primary cogs that continues pumping across this basic message every minute of every day to as many people as it can reach. Given the addictive quality of those diversions, it can reach a great many, which again hearkens unto the *broad and spacious way.* But consider a larger and more serious aspect of this issue. In addition to judging the good guys and the bad guys in the material itself, these diversions also constitute a major part of our criteria for judging other governments and social structures along the same lines. Simply put, if another nation is not as able to recreate as we are, we judge them as not as "advanced" as we are, and certainly not as free.

We do love that word, "advanced." By definition, the term means "more highly developed" but, when you think about it, have we really more highly developed anything except our ability to delude ourselves? Perhaps deluding ourselves and diverting ourselves come down to the same thing. Think about it. If we must serve one master or the other, and if we can dichotomize that service as physical vs. spiritual, then which do we serve by "advancing" in physical terms? *"'Labor not for the meat which perisheth, but for the meat which endureth unto everlasting life which the Son of Man shall give unto you: for Him hath God the Father sealed'"*—John 6:27.That holds especially true when we note that we advance in physical terms at the expense of spiritual advancement—again, just as we'd expect from anti-growth.[26] Doesn't that sound like the description of the scoffers James refers to in James 1:2: *"Ever learning, and never able to come to the knowledge of the Truth"*? Doesn't that also sound like those trying to come to Christ by way of man-derived doctrine, where

---

[26] The general acceptance of evolution and modern cosmology makes an especially good case in point.

we worship God on our own terms and to the extent that we choose? Consider a single question: in spite of the huge and growing number of putative Christians in the world, can we honestly claim to have advanced toward godliness as a race?

It should be obvious to what Truth James refers, and we can readily contrast that to the self-evident truths science and human wisdom continue to learn as integral parts of our advancement. Have we considered that we advance toward oblivion? Consider II Peter 3:10-12: *"But the day of the Lord will come as a thief in the night; in which the heavens shall pass away with a great noise, and the elements shall melt with fervent heat, the earth also and the works that are therein shall be burned up. Seeing then that all these things shall be dissolved, what manner of person ought ye to be in all holy conversation and godliness, looking for and hasting unto the coming of the day of God, wherein the heavens being on fire shall be dissolved, and the elements shall melt with fervent heat?"* That puts our second Basic Question, what is my purpose in life, in a more immediate and dramatic context: *what should I do with my time?* In II Peter 1:5-8, he addresses the question of what kind of people we should be: *"And beside this, giving all diligence, add to your faith virtue; and to virtue; knowledge; and to knowledge temperance; and to temperance patience; and to patience godliness; and to godliness brotherly kindness; and to brotherly kindness charity. For if these things be in you and abound, they make you that ye shall neither be barren nor unfruitful in the knowledge of our Lord Jesus Christ."* To reiterate, in the most basic sense the Christian's purpose is the same as any living thing: to grow, and for a very valid reason. A living thing cannot remain static: it must either grow or wither. To grow implies maturation, yet we can make a very strong case that humanity is actually retrogressing into a kind of universal infancy. Maybe that's from what all those endless entertainments intend to divert us. We sometimes hear people say, "You take life too seriously." *Au contraire:* most of us don't take life nearly seriously *enough*. Simply notice that the word "sober", meaning "marked by seriousness, gravity, solemnity" and so on, crops up no fewer than a dozen times in the New Testament. In each instance we see it as a definition of how we should conduct ourselves and, perhaps still more importantly, how we should view life itself. Consider this question as a life guide: if Christ were to return right this moment, what would you want Him to find you doing?

Do we count *all as loss except for the knowledge of Christ*—or do we pigeonhole acquiring that knowledge into weekly time slots geared toward our convenience so we can more efficiently keep up with more important concerns such as career, family, football games and so on? Which characterizes the American way of life we so zealously defend with the sword at every opportunity? Such questions separate the Christian from the pagan, for the latter are incapable of taking them seriously. But more, they separate the true Christian from the social Christian which, for all practical purposes, is also a pagan often guised as a minister of righteousness—or, far more commonly, of self-righteousness. We can serve only one master, and if that Master is the living God, then we must do so with *all our hearts,* regardless of what we do. *"And whatever ye do in word of deed, do all in the name of the Lord Jesus, giving thanks to God and the Father by Him"*—Colossians 3:17. If we believe the Truth, why would we do anything else? Think about it. If the *whole world and the things in it are destined to burn up,* what does that suggest about those who devote their lives to those things? If such things have such a limited value, what profit can we seek from pursuing them? Perhaps we seek self-destructiveness after all.

If a of *love of the things of the earth is enmity toward God,* then in whose image are we re-creating ourselves as a matter of national policy? If we can equate "pagan' with "Gentile", then consider:*"This I say therefore, and testify in the Lord, that you henceforth walk not as other Gentiles walk, in the vanity of their mind, having the understanding darkened, being alienated from the life of God through the ignorance that is in them, because of the blindness of their heart . . ."*—Ephesians 4:17-18. No wonder we've adopted so many pagan customs, holidays and symbols. The *natural man* must lean on natural perception—just the blindness of heart the Apostle had in mind. Given the numerous references we find to that man, especially his inability to please God, we can at least suspect nature itself as part of the *strong delusions.* Moreover, we can suspect that delusion to have something to do with the difference between goodness and righteousness. Consider: spread among the species, animals break every one of God's commandments possible for them to break, including theft, murder, covetousness, adultery and failure to honor parents, all toward the ultimate good of survival—*the mark of the beast.* Spread among the races, we do the same thing to the same end. Physical survival is appropriate to the beasts, for they have no share in the Kingdom of Heaven. The same holds true for those taking the Mark of the Beast, and who worship its image. Consider the convolution resulting from that. While we also break the same commandments to the same end, the more idealistic among us have long maintained that we eventually must overcome our "animal natures" to ensure our survival. Ironically, we do overcome our animal natures, but not in the way the idealists would like to believe. While those beasts do indeed commit those sins, they are quite *unable* to break the First Commandment: *they cannot, and do not seek my will be done and, so, do not have any God before the Father.*[27] We do so all the time, often in ways that do not seem self-evident.

That was the point of the story of Balaam. You may recall that Balak, king of Moab, saw the Children of Israel, recently released from Egypt, at his doorstep after a resounding victory over the Amorites. In a classic case of fearing man rather than fearing God, he called upon Balaam, *"For I wot that he whom thou blesses is blessed, and he whom thou cursest is cursed"*—Numbers 22:6. He offered the prophet a considerable profit in oxen, cattle and human glory and renown in return for his blessings and his curse upon Israel. After a famous incident of *Balaam's donkey speaking God's word to him* (see Numbers 22:23ff), he found himself constrained to speak only what the Lord instructed him to say—which was not what Balak wanted to hear. Again and again he beseeched Balaam to curse the Jews, offering him money and honor—the best he had. Yet Balaam finally had to say, *"How shall I curse whom God hath not cursed? Or how shall I defy whom the Lord hath not defied?"*—Numbers 23:8. Yet,

---

[27]   While science calls it "instinct", most serious theologians believe that animals are directly governed by God.

good vs. evil demands that we do just that and on a daily basis: a nation of law bent of justice demands that we must both judge and condemn. No wonder freedom from God's authority seems so right. More pertinently, no wonder we can take freedom from God's authority as a major *good!* We cannot judge people, conditions or circumstances without simultaneously judging the authority behind them. That of course calls into question the whole issue of freedom per se.

Perhaps that's one thing the diversions we so relish intend to keep us from seeing. Given that most of Washington's activities take place behind doors tightly closed to the general electorate, we can legitimately ask in what sense we are free. At the same time however, we do remain free to chose what TV programs we'll watch, what music we'll listen to, which games we'll play, which church we'll attend, which political party we'll support and so on, all with an ever increasing selection. That give us the illusion of freedom of choice when in fact we have virtually no freedom of choice in matters directly affecting our national or personal destinies. Isn't that a trifle odd for a nation devoted to self-determination? But consider a deeper, more subtle element. A number of studies have long demonstrated the addictive qualities of television, video games, motion pictures, and even music. Much more current studies have begun to reveal a very similar relationship to computers, blackberries, cell phones and other electronic gadgets, with people often demonstrating genuine distress very similar to drug withdrawal when deprived of them. Although not very popular, this has even led some groups to counsel a reduction in the usage of these items, led perhaps most emphatically by exhortations to "kill your TV." That seems highly unlikely to happen, and again we encounter desire, with desire for deception leading the way. Who is the master of deception? Have we not equated self-evident truth with Anti-Truth? If fruits must follow the pattern of their seeds, can we call it coincidental that the nation built on that self-evident truth also leads the world in the production of increasingly convincing diversions guised as entertainment while at the same time leaning evermore heavily on deception, duplicity and prevarication politically? Think about it: the word *hypocrite* shares an etymological link to the Greek word for *actor*, with pretending to be something one is not the common denominator. Isn't hypocrisy the *"leaven"* Christ warned us to avoid in Luke 12:1? In addition to our huge entertainment industry featuring just such people, doesn't that also pretty well epitomize our government and society? After all, we officially promote a "drug free America," and yet pharmaceuticals rank among the nation's most profitable and competitive industries, and critics call America the most legally drugged nation in the world. More pertinent to our immediate discussion, our way of life in this land of the free essentially comes down to a large and growing number of electronic addictions and dependencies, all of which we count as integral to our status as a free country. That makes *dependence* an inherent part of the *independence* which we use as our definition of freedom. Doesn't that sound a bit like a drug addict or an alcoholic denying the problem while trying to justify the addiction? *"Ye are they which justify yourselves before men; but God knoweth your hearts: for that which is highly esteemed among men is abomination in the sight of God'"*—Luke 16:15. If the structure must reflect its foundation, what must we infer about our foundation of freedom?

If our freedom leads to a nearly universal and growing series of addictions and dependencies, should we not question the nature of that freedom? After all, by definition a dependency or an addiction makes the object of that dependency or addiction a powerful authority. Doesn't that sound like someone keeping us *"alienated from the life in God?"* (Ephesians 4:18). If our "freedom" is actually yielding progressive slavery—i.e., a progressive dependency on a huge raft of addictions and amenities (not to mention more laws than any society in history)—whom might we suspect behind that freedom? Can we take it as coincidental that a majority of early American settlers were indentured servants? Can we take it as coincidental that many other subsequent immigrants found themselves in literal slavery, while still more found themselves in virtual slavery at the hands of the rich and powerful Elite? Think about our freedom, and wonder how much has actually changed? How many things do we find ourselves forced to do in order to maintain our "healthy" economy? Does that not suggest servitude to Mammon? After all, most of us literally "work for money". Don't most of us seek a way to do so more lucratively? Indeed, for many that becomes their primary life goal. If our way of life is our faith enacted, what does that imply about the object of that faith? If our governmental system is our religion enacted, what does that suggest about the national religion underlying this country? If we want the things that *choke the word*, and desire the things of the earth that constitute *the friendship with the world* that James cites as *enmity towards God*, what must we conclude? How then must we answer our title question?

Given Satan as the *"father of lies"*, doesn't it seem logical to assume that he would attack divine Truth with those diversions? Consider: every work of fiction, print, video, or celluloid, includes an *implied cosmology:* an origin that either includes or excludes the Creation, and therefore the whole issue of salvation and righteousness. Even more commonly, they all perpetuate the good vs. evil myth. As perhaps the greatest example of both, consider those multi-million dollar fairy tales we take as such vital parts of our way of life. Don't they all share the same moral? Crime may not pay, but sinning surely does. Sinners win the prizes, get the girl, receive the fame, and, for all practical purposes, live happily ever after. Those portraying them win the accolades and praise of their peers, and gain the status of virtual demigods, often living lives of conspicuous consumption and revelry. Who has taught us that as desirable? Just as we've pigeonholed God's worship into specific time slots and conditions, His service into specific function and roles, so we've limited our answer to our Basic Question, and made our service to Him a matter of requisite rituals and rites, performed at specific times and under specific circumstances. In short, for most people Christianity is a "Sunday thing."What occupies us the rest of the time?

Given the word's military application, we should seriously consider that both the war and the entertainment industries taken as a whole rank very near the top of the country's most lucrative endeavors. That makes both extremely important to our entire economic and social structure. That also means that the former is largely geared to protect the latter, while the latter very frequently glorifies the former. Ironically, though strangely consistent with the mirror-imagery we've found, physical warfare itself acts as a diversion from the far deadlier Spirit War of which the entertainment industry is the major player. Consider the similarities. Is it coincidental that any form of fiction must incorporate conflict which is inevitably defined as good vs. evil? Is it coincidental that such fictional conflict is evermore frequently portrayed as mortal? Based on the subject matter of the vast majority of our entertainments, as well as the profitability of both those entertainments and their military counterparts, we can legitimately wonder whether we truly even *want* peace.[28] Adolph Hitler took a very similar view in *Mein Kampf:* "*In actual fact the pacifistic-humane idea is perfectly all right perhaps when the highest type of man has previously conquered and subjugated the world to an extent that makes him the sole ruler of this earth . . .*" Remember that term "hegemony"? It shows up in the news, especially the analytical pieces, with increasing frequency these days, often associated with the "American Empire." Think about it: taken to its logical extreme, global hegemony would amount to just the kind of scenario Hitler describes. Ironically, that would make America exactly the kind of authority against which we so self-righteously rail, and suddenly the definition of *actor* as a *hypocrite* doesn't seem quite so coincidental.

"*Seek and ye shall find*" has a huge number of applications, all dependent upon what we want to find. The devotees of Nature's God, which includes the vast majority of the world's population, seek the things of the earth for they can hold nothing else as valuable. That doesn't put us in the best of company. "*And seek not what you shall eat or what you shall drink, neither be of doubtful mind. For after all these things do the nations of the world seek: and your Father knows that you have need of these things.*'"—Luke 12:30-31. Again note that the problem lies not in the things themselves but in our relationship to them. Also note the parallel between the "nations of the world" and what

---

[28]   Many have noted that should peace on earth suddenly appear, the world's economy would be in serious trouble, especially in terms of very massive unemployment.

Satan offered Christ in the wilderness.[29] Bear in mind that LOM reflects our relationship to money—its' the *love of* money, not money itself that we find at that root. That likewise applies to other earthly values. *"Again, the kingdom of heaven is like unto a merchant man, seeking goodly pearls: who, when he had found one pearl of great price, went and sold all that he had, and bought it'"*—Matthew 13:45-46. He sold all of his material possessions—earthly values—in order to possess the heavenly pearl of great price. Readily overlooked, that also implies Christ's Truth as entailing just that cost. The merchant man knew that could not have both, but more importantly, he did not *desire* both, nor did he seek both. Ironic, isn't it, that we live in a corporate state where virtually every major decision, and every conflict is heavily influenced if not entirely determined by the Elite who have no use for such a pearl. How can a Christian take pride in such a nation? How can a Christian actively support such a nation?

Although that pearl consists of wisdom, it doesn't necessarily entail knowledge as we generally conceive it. While knowledge of God's word clearly plays a part in our spiritual growth, it doesn't ultimately matter whether we know the Truth. What matters is that the Truth knows us. *"Verily, verily, I say unto you, he that entereth not by the door into the sheepfold, but climbeth up some other way, the same is a thief and a robber. But He that entereth in by the door is the shepherd of the sheep. To Him the porter openeth; and the sheep hear His voice; and He calleth His own sheep by name, and leadeth them out'"*—John 10:1-3. That's something of a Christian *cliché*, but an important concept nevertheless. Just as we cannot have the true God without the Truth embodied in His Son, neither can we separate our love of God from our love of and devotion to that Truth. Since we normally desire that which we love, that love subsumes a desire for divine Truth which in turn defines what we seek, earthly goods or pearls of great price. Just as we cannot serve both God

---

[29] It's also worth noting that while some translations read "nations of the world" others read "Gentiles" and still others read "heathens." Taking the three together we may infer *Gentile* to mean a heathen nation.

and Mammon, and just as we cannot live by both the Truth and self-evident truth, so neither can we ascertain divine Truth by means of physical perception and the human spirit. That places deism, the spiritual and largely the philosophical foundation of this country, at diametric odds with the word of God. By definition that makes that foundation *Antichrist*. If we find Antichrist at our foundation, how then must we answer our title question? If we, as Christians, are *not to conform to the world*, refusing to conform to our national norms is a very good place to start. We live in this world, and in deference to God, we obey its rulers up to the point where doing so contravenes obedience to God. Those who rule us, whether we approve of them or not, deserve our obedience, our respect and our prayers, not due to any inherent qualities but, again, in deference to the One who has ordained them. But, we cannot actively participate in such a government, for doing so automatically lends our sanction to the basic concepts underlying it: my will be done, and LOM.

While we have demonstrated America's spiritual roots as deistic rather than Christian, we can nevertheless find an influence of the Christian religion in our origin. If we take the Reformation as a legitimate revolution against the self-evident evil of an overly oppressive theocratic political entity, then it logically follows that we can resist *any* political entity we deem overly oppressive and do so with equal legitimacy. Obviously this was not Martin Luther's intent,[30] but legitimizing freedom from Papal authority, regardless of the validity of his action, set the template for political freedom as a divinely sanctioned good at the same time.[31] While religious freedom amounts to freedom from an authoritarian church, it also ultimately means freedom from God's absolute authority, for He establishes those leaders just as He establishes their political counterparts. That does not necessarily guarantee their spiritual purity as the *infallibility of the Pope doctrine* likes to believe. After all, God also ordained

---

[30] Of course there were a number of other very prominent Reformers as well, but Luther has become the poster boy in the popular consciousness.

[31] It's interesting to note that Luther was denounced as an enemy of the Holy Roman Empire at the Diet of Worms in 1521.

Saddam Hussein, Adolph Hitler, and King Ahab. Thus, we find the same kind of quiet rebellion that we find with secular leaders: we obey to the point where doing so contravenes service to God and His Truth, while all the while showing the appropriate respect to those who in essence represent God's will. Good vs. evil cannot understand that, and that led to some unforeseen, unintended, but inevitable consequences. If our spiritual leaders do not lead due to God's will, as the Popes had long maintained, then how can we assume that our political leaders do so? If our political leaders do not rule due to divine authority, on what authority do they do so? Once we eliminated God as the authority behind our political and religious leaders, we began to question where such authority properly originated. This lead to the concept of the consent of the governed, a very basic form of self-determination, which we then applied to spiritual leadership as well. The seeds for today's political and religious freedoms had been planted, the spiritual economy of Antichrist instituted, and the Great Apostasy begun—all with the very best of intentions. It took several centuries to come to fruition; Europe remained dominated by monarchies for centuries after Luther. Nevertheless, we can find the roots of today's freedom movement right here. Do not misunderstand our intention: we do not mean to vilify Luther, the Catholic Church or any other entity, including the United States government. Quite the contrary, all of the events in our global history served an indispensable part in God's overall plan. Our purpose is not to indict, and certainly not to condemn, but to *warn*. We make these points to reveal a far more fundamental and deadly fallacy directly related to self-determination.

By inadvertently establishing religious and political freedoms as a divine ideal, Luther unwittingly established the idea of an identity separate from a part of Christ's body as a divine ideal, even though such was not his intention and very probably in conflict with his personal beliefs. By definition, that also included an entity separated from the Truth which Christ embodies, thereby laying the foundation for self-evident truth to take its place. Already we can see the similarity between self-evident truth—i.e., truth divorced from its divine source—and self-excogitated doctrine—also divorced from its divine source—that would dominate religious freedom and come to essentially define the Christian religion. It's likewise not hard to see how self-evident truth fits into this scheme. Catholic doctrinaires had already begun the process with political survival in mind (see below) and again politics and religion merge.

This again poses some serious questions for the Christian. If even *Christ's doctrine was not His own* (see John 7:17), then how can we accept, or even seek, our own? Again too we find elevating personal salvation to Christianity's focal point the culprit. The self-evident good of eternal survival outweighed the Truth of divine revelation. As a result, the problem revolved around trying to teach inherently spiritual truths to those given to the flesh just as worshipping God in the flesh demands. No wonder self-determination grew into such a popular political ideal: we cannot separate our political system from the religious beliefs underlying it. Given that religious freedom can't function without the freedom to believe as we please, we cannot have religious freedom without self-evident truth. If self-evident truth then gains a pseudo-divine sanction from religion, how can we wonder that we accepted it as a political good with the same justification? No wonder America likes to believe itself mandated with a "divine destiny" even while discounting Christianity as part of that destiny. That means that we cannot have religious freedom or political freedom without Anti-Truth—i.e., without Antichrist—just as the freedom from His authority inherent in those concepts suggests. The Great Apostasy did not begin with Luther, but it did gain momentum, and a whole new level of deceptiveness through his efforts. It has now come to full fruition in this one nation under God, and so powerful has the deception grown that virtually no one seems to notice—or to care.

Both groups, the Reformers and the Papacy, played an indispensible part in God's plan and, in spite of themselves, revealed a divine Truth for those with the eyes to see it. While, based on good vs. evil, much has been written to vilify the Catholic Church, for the most part its leadership consisted of men dedicated to their vision of the Almighty and they did the best they could. Similarly, Luther did not intend this end: regardless of our opinion of him as an individual, or even as a clergyman, we cannot doubt his sincerity. On the other hand, neither can we deny his dogmatism: he was as convinced of the validity of his own doctrine (his own official infallibility) as the Mother Church and Holy Papa had been of theirs, and therein we find the deadly good vs. evil commonality, not within the men themselves so much as within their respective religious structures. In each case, eternal life comes down to knowledge capable of being imparted to anyone by way of the human spirit. No matter how you look at it, that ultimately comes down to us saving ourselves, and virtually every mainstream denomination shares that same fallacy in common. As a result, due to the same human wisdom, we've officially gone to the other extreme. Religious freedom, unintentionally sparked by this contention, teaches that it doesn't really matter what or even *whose* truth we embrace, because we all worship the same god. Do you notice a familiar motif beginning to develop? We have two extremes, with the proper course a narrow way between them: *"Because strait is the gate, and narrow is the way, which leadeth unto life, and few there be that find it"*—Matthew 7:14. Of course few are finding it, for few are seeking it! Religious freedom allows us to chose our own experts so deemed due to their ability to spoon-feed us whatever we want to believe in response to religious exclusivity trying to foist upon us what we do not want to believe. Is that what Christ meant by worshipping God in *Truth and in Spirit?* Does that reflect what Christ actually taught? Does that reflect God's will? Given the overwhelming popularity of the religious approach, doesn't that more closely resemble the *broad and spacious way* than the *narrow gate?* Many billions are finding it, and few even suspect the delusion, for the deceived does not recognize the deception. That's largely why we've written this.

Who do we serve? Consider: in Matthew, chapter 15, Christ and His disciples sit down to eat, and the Pharisees jump all over them for dining with unwashed hands. In verses 18-20, Christ responds to them: *"But those things which proceed out of the mouth come forth from the heart; and they defile the man. For out of the heart proceed evil thoughts, murders, adulteries, fornications, thefts, false witness, blasphemies: these are the things which defile a man; but to eat with unwashen hands defileth not a man.'"* Appropriately enough, how often do we see exhortations to "wash your hands" as a major means of preventing disease? Indeed, we have a huge cosmetics industry directly related to making us "feel clean" and to removing even the slightest trace of offensive smells. We have perhaps a still larger industry dedicated to beautifying ourselves, again in an effort to please each other. *"'Woe unto you, scribes and Pharisees, hypocrites! For ye make clean the outside of the cup and the platter, but within they are full of extortion and excess. Thou blind Pharisee, cleanse first that which is in the cup and the platter, that the outside of them may be clean also'"*—Matthew 23:25-26. Shall we call it coincidental that our whole electoral process as well as most of our merchandising depends almost entirely on image—i.e., on superficial appearances? Can we call it coincidental that we judge by those same appearances?

But there's more. Our national deficit now stands at something over $12 *trillion* and is presently predicted to reach 100% of our GDP by 2020. We could reasonably consider that an "excess." But more revealing still, why has it gone so high? Over and over again, our government creates an endless parade of false flag operations geared toward engendering fear which allows the Elite to wring excessive amounts of money from the public into the coffers of those charged with saving us. There's nothing new about this. In 1957, General Douglas MacArthur observed: *"Our government has kept us in a perpetual state of fear—kept us in a continuous stampede of patriotic fervor—with the cry of grave national emergency. Always there has been some terrible evil at home or some monstrous foreign power that was going to gobble us up if we did not rally behind it by furnishing the exorbitant sums demanded. Yet, in retrospect, these disasters seem never to have happened, seem never to have been quite real."* Doesn't that sound a good deal like extortion?[32] The "patriotic fervor" the good General mentioned, has largely fallen out of fashion. Then again, we no longer need it. Fear can be manufactured quite readily, and deliberately used to achieve specific ends

---

[32] Dictionary.com defines *extortion* as: "The crime of obtaining money or some other thing of value by the abuse of one's office or authority"

without patriotism as an intermediary. In short, rather than love of country, today's power brokers appeal directly to the survival imperative. Protecting us from manufactured fear—isn't that what we used to call a "protection racket"? What else might we expect from a government born of lawlessness? But, using the threat of damnation and setting itself up as the sole protection from it really amounts to the same thing, and the Mother Church acquired a good percentage of its financial and real estate holdings as a result of it.

The merging of the two economies is no accident any more than it's coincidental in this one nation under Mammon. Again, let us pose our Basic Question, *who do we serve.* The innumerable concessions the Christian religion has made to paganism and superstition have made the way to salvation broad indeed, turning it into a veritable ecclesiastical marketplace where one can shop until they drop for the doctrine that best suits their needs and desires. More importantly, rather than increasing the value of divine Truth, as real spiritual growth does, we end up making it all the more difficult to find while simultaneously making it seem less worth the effort. Even worse, the proliferation of Christianity's fragments leaves many a neophyte sincerely seeking the Truth wondering which of these multitudinous paths is the right one. Yet, we consider this confusion a major virtue! Who do we serve? Who is the author of confusion? *"For God is not the author of confusion, but of peace as in all the churches of the saints"*—I Corinthians 14:33.

He makes that statement after detailing a proper worship service (see the chapter's preceding verses) which stands in sharp opposition to the clergy/laity distinction as well as the whole idea of dogmatic doctrine per se. *"And it shall come to pass in the Last Days, saith God, I will pour out of My Spirit upon all flesh: and your sons and your daughters shall prophesy, and your young men shall see visions, and your old men shall dream dreams: and on My servants and on My handmaidens I will pour out in those days of My Spirit; and they shall prophesy"*—Acts 2:17-18 quoting from Joel 2:28-29. Such a Pauline congregation amounts to those speaking who feel moved by the Holy Spirit, as opposed to passively listening to an expert giving a lecture.

With the exception of a few sects, that adhocracy has been lost, and that should be a matter of considerable concern, as a very possible part of the Great Apostasy. *"If any man think himself to be a prophet, or spiritual, let him acknowledge that the things that I write unto you are the commandments of the Lord"*—I Corinthians 14:37.

The concern goes beyond the content of the doctrine espoused by the respective experts and addresses a far broader and more serious problem. Superficially, such a congregation would seem a group of people all expressing their opinions, and in a unity of the human spirit that would be the case. Here, however, we speak of a unity of the Holy Spirit, with both the speakers and the listeners motivated by that Spirit. As the lack of a church *service* implies, for such people Christianity is far more than a formalized doctrine or set of rituals, and much more than a Sunday thing. Rather, it constitutes a way of life where we realize that our every waking moment is dedicated to praising, thanking, and glorifying either the Lord or the Adversary. Our every thought and word is a kind of prayer aimed at one master or the other; our every action is an act of devotion. Our every desire reflects whom we love and whom we seek to serve. Every moment of every day we answer the question of whether we *"hunger and thirst for righteousness"* or whether we lust after the things of the earth. Come the Day of the Lord, we will have to answer our Basic Question: what have we taken as our purpose in life? That in turn comes down to one of two answers: we have either served God, or we have served His usurper.

That of course brings up the question of what constitutes that service? Recall the *parable of the ten virgins* recounted in Matthew, chapter 25. Ten maidens with their lamps awaited the Bridegroom, but since He tarried, they all slumbered. At midnight, however the cry went out that the Bridegroom approached. All ten arose and trimmed their lamps, but only five of them thought to bring oil with them. *"And the foolish said unto the wise, "Give us of your oil; for our lamps are gone out." But the wise answered, saying, "Not so; lest there be not enough for us and you: but go ye rather to them that sell, and buy for yourselves." And while they went to buy, the Bridegroom came; and they that were ready went in with Him to the marriage: and the door was shut. Afterward came also the other virgins, saying, "Lord, Lord, open to us." But He answered and said, "Verily I say unto you, I know you not." Watch therefore, for ye know neither the day nor the hour wherein the Son of Man cometh"*—Matthew 25:8-13. Notice a very important point easily overlooked: remaining virgin—not engaging in idolatry—in itself is not enough. That mirrors a passive "belief in God" even as the sole supreme deity. The oil represents, again if you'll pardon the pun, a burning love of and desire for God's Truth, not only as a mental construct or a set of "beliefs" but *as the purpose of our lives.* That's not to say that we can't help and exhort each other—indeed, that's part of the purpose of this work—but, ultimately we will all face the Judge and answer those questions one at a time. Then we will see the folly of "righteousness by association" (sharing the oil) we find so common in mainstream Christianity: "I'm a member of the XYZ Church, therefore I am righteous." Moreover, we'll see the folly of depending on a religious service—on someone else worshipping God for us—as opposed to making that worship so central to our lives as to *become* our lives. Indeed, our worship of and service to God essentially amount to the same thing. Taken together they constitute our way of life, for our way of life is our faith enacted. True faith does not consist of goodness, at least not as we normally define it, but of divine Truth.

That difference has a far more common application than most of us realize. Turning from overt sin does not necessarily mean that we've turned toward God, though good vs. evil would lead us to believe so. Thus we find the Reformation's fatal flaw and its connection to this one nation under God. Without intending it, by turning from the Mother Church's overt evils, Luther began a chain reaction in which we eventually replaced the divine right of kings with the divine right of the individual. If we take human rights as a divinely sanctioned good, we must take their violation as a commensurate evil, as an affront not only to us but to God. Politics and religion blend again. Human rights violations inevitably center on the political entities doing the violating, which casts those entities not only as evil, but as God's enemies. Do you see the inherent fallacy? How can they be God's enemies if

God ordained them? Notice how that very subtly incorporates the divide and conquer motif, yielding a house divided against itself just as we see in Christianity's fragmentation. This lends a tacit sanction to the idea that God ordains the "good" powers, which readily translates into those powers of whom we approve which cast us as God's judge! Would you consider *that* blasphemy? If we accept good vs. evil as our guiding principle, and accept individual rights as a divine good—and we do occasionally refer to them as "God given rights"—then we must likewise take those abridging those rights as an evil against which we may legitimately rebel with a self-evident divine sanction. Moreover, if we define good as that which overcomes evil, then we define them as those against whom we *must* rebel and defeat at any cost if we are to call ourselves the good. Our own Declaration of Independence states that, while unwarranted in doing so for *"light or transient causes"* the people, from whom power rightfully derives, have the right and the responsibility to overthrow sufficiently oppressive governments. *"Governments are instituted among Men, deriving their just powers from the consent of the governed. That whenever any Form of Government becomes destructive of these ends, it is the Right of the People to alter or to abolish it, and to institute new Government . . ."*

It's not hard to see the connection between that and the pursuit of happiness as our national purpose. But if we Christians seriously put to ourselves that Basic Question, what is our purpose in life, we find a considerably different answer. *"But God be thanked, that ye were the servants of sin, but ye have obeyed from the heart that form of doctrine which was delivered to you. Being then made free from sin, ye became the servants of righteousness"*—Romans 6:17-18. The *Amplified Bible* expands that last phrase to mean, *"of conformity to the divine will in thought, purpose and action."* All sin amounts to the same sin: deliberately defying God's will. At the same time, we can define righteousness in four simple words: *Thy will be done.* Indeed we do need to defend our title to that freedom, not with force of arms but with earnest efforts to *bring every thought into the captivity of Christ*, thereby making Thy will be done an essential part of our lives utterly germane to walking in the Spirit. The natural man, empowered by the human spirit and given to conventional liberty, can't hope to understand that, and this nation was founded by such men for such men. Think about it: no other rights make any sense without the rights to self-expression and, even more basically, the right to believe as we will, and live accordingly. In that regard politics and religion, especially religion as redefined by the Reformation, inextricably intermingle, for that is no doubt its profoundest legacy. The self-evident truth that power legitimately originates with the governed fueled our rebellion and has guided our nation ever since, creating that curious duality of a secular state with a divine destiny. Largely due to our influence, it has guided virtually the entire world ever since. That means that self-evident truth, not divine Truth, has guided the world ever since. Doesn't that sound like a pretty good definition of the Great Apostasy? Doesn't that reflect the idea that the *whole world is under the sway of the Evil One?*

But simply believing something doesn't make it true, regardless of how evident it might seem, and that constitutes a very basic difference between belief and true faith. Given that Christ is both the Truth and the Life, we can see this difference demonstrated in a very subtle yet profound manner. Virtually all of the mainstream Christian religion bases it faith on knowledge, while in fact they are basing their *beliefs* on knowledge. Think about the difference. We can have reasons for believing as we do. *"I believe him because he's never lied to me." "I believe it because it sounds reasonable." "I believe it because it's happened before"* and don't forget our favorite, *"Seeing is believing."* True faith, faith granted by the Holy Spirit, is quite different: *"Now faith is the substance of things hoped for, the evidence of things not seen"*—Heb. 11:1.[33] But if we look a bit more deeply we can see belief associated with death, faith with life. How so? Even though we may have beliefs, we'll never "know for sure" until death—i.e., until it's too late. Faith is exactly the opposite. When we have an unquestioning and unquestionable certainty that the Bible speaks the Truth and that we have died to our old selves

---

[33] The Amplified Bible adds ["faith perceiving as real fact what is not revealed to the senses"]

to resume life anew in Christ, then we have been baptized by the Holy Spirit and granted the gift of *true faith*. No power on earth can give us that faith; no power on earth can take it away, although the Deceiver constantly seeks a way of beguiling us into giving it away. By contrast, belief can be demonstrated while true faith cannot (and does not need such a demonstration). *"Then certain of the scribes and of the Pharisees answered, saying, Master, we would see a sign from Thee. But He answered and said unto them, An evil and adulterous generation seeketh after a sign, and there shall no sign be given to it, but the sign of the prophet Jonas: For as Jonas was three days and three nights in the whale's belly; so shall the Son of Man be three days and three nights in the heart of the earth'"*—Matthew 12:38-40.

Again, although adultery refers to marital infidelity, it also refers to spiritual unfaithfulness, and it is to that sin that Christ chiefly alludes. We have used that same sort of unfaithfulness, that same demand for a sign, to drift ever further from God's word ever since. Consider: so long as we base our judgments on good vs. evil and physical perception, we can provide plenty of empirical evidence that religious and political freedoms are divinely inspired, and use those justifications as the foundation for our belief system. Just look around! In those places where they've been given a chance, political and religious freedoms have to a very large extent done away with the blatant regal and ecclesiastical excesses of yore. Let's face it, Europe under Papal influence was anything but a pleasant place, and we find ourselves hard pressed to find love as an integral element. The same could be said about a number of monarchies, as well as about the hard-line Islamic theocracies of today. Notice how that amounts to just the kind of sign the Jews demanded. Then again, given our "seeing is believing" mindset, we should expect to demand a physical sign. No wonder all of our entertainments define good and evil in such readily recognizable forms: they teach us to judge accordingly. Of course Christ explicitly told us *not to judge by appearances* (John 7:24), but that has long ceased to matter to most.

Nevertheless, Christ had a very good reason for that command. By luring some of us into blatantly dramatic evils at one end of the good/evil spectrum, Satan can obfuscate the more subtle, but often more serious evils at the other extreme. For example, if we compare a child molester to the child's loving parents, whom must we deem as good, and who as evil? Yet, if those parents are deists or atheists or somehow surround the child in perpetual Anti-Truth, can we not make the case for spiritual child abuse that ultimately proves far more destructive? In a similar sense, self sovereignty can seem good *by contrast* by eliminating the overt evils of religious intolerance and political despotism, while masking the far more serious underlying sin of resisting God's ordinations and the resultant idolatry. Turning away from overt evil doesn't necessarily mean that we've turned toward God, but good vs. evil largely blinds us to that. Thoughts and ideas do not and cannot remain confined to their initial context. By equating goodness with righteousness, we eliminate affronts to our fellow man by replacing them with affronts to God and call it virtue! This has a far more serious spiritual application than might seem self-evident. As mentioned earlier, we must bear in mind that our bodies are the temple of God where we Christians worship the Father. Before the Antichrist can *install himself physically in the Jerusalem Temple* (II Thessalonians 2:4), he must first do so spiritually by insinuating his way into the hearts of his followers. Indeed, that's one of the major objectives of the Spirit War. Suddenly the whole notion of diversions takes on a considerably darker complexion. " . . .*lovers of pleasures more than lovers of God . . .*"—II Timothy 3:4. We could also add, lovers of deliberately manufactured untruths more than lovers of divine Truth. No wonder he quite emphatically tells us *"from such turn away"* (II Timothy 3:5.)

Those diversionary untruths are nearly all based on seeing is believing. Indeed, motion pictures and television found on the *"willing suspension of disbelief"* with "willing" the operative term. We not only believe what we want to believe, we demonstrate that in our natural state we want to believe untruth! Yet, deism is based on *seeing is believing*, and the vast, vast majority of us accept that as our primary if not sole criterion for truth. Ultimately, science also rests on the same principle, and even more of us take it as our final truth. Isn't that what we'd expect from an "*angel of light*" who specializes in deception? Yet, think about it. Why does Paul make a point of telling us that we "*walk by faith, and not by sight*" in II Corinthians 5:7? In countless ways, we are encouraged to judge both good and evil by overt characteristics in another image of *the broad and spacious way*. Who do we serve? If we equate such discernible goodness with righteousness, how can we avoid falling for Satan's masquerade? How can we avoid falling for his very realistic *ministers of righteousness?* Just as the Apostles could not see a devil in their very midst even when he went out from them to betray Christ because they lacked the proper discernment (see John13:26-29), so we cannot see the apostate spiritual leaders all around us without similar perception. Does that make you feel a bit vulnerable? All of a sudden, *deliver us from evil* makes a good deal more sense, for evil hides in manifold deceptions which we cannot discern, all geared toward undermining the Truth and removing us from it. "*Wherefore also it is contained in the Scripture, Behold, I lay in Sion a chief corner stone, elect, precious: and he that believeth on Him shall not be confounded* [Isaiah 28:16.] *Unto you therefore which believe, He is precious: but unto them which be disobedient, the stone which the builders disallowed, the same is made the head of the corner.* [Psalms 118:22]. *And a stone of stumbling, and a rock of offense, even to them which stumble at the word, being disobedient: whereunto also were they appointed*"—I Peter 2:6-8. For God to deliver us from evil is for God to define the evil as well as the righteousness to which we are delivered. If we define truth for ourselves, as we do with self-evident truth, then we must define righteousness for ourselves. Clearly that makes us disobedient—idolaters, to be exact. How clear an example of self-deification do we need?

Especially with the advent of the Tea Party in 2010, we more and more frequently hear conservative Christians expressing wishes that America could return to its founding values. *Wake up, people!* We now experience the inevitable fruit of the seeds we planted upon this nation's inception. Face the facts! We put Anti-Truth, aka self-evident truth, in Christ's place, Satan, aka, Nature's God, in the Father's place, my will be done, aka democracy, in place of Thy will be done, service to Mammon, aka the Profit Motive, in place of service to God, and religious freedom, aka idolatry, in place of piety! How must we answer our title question? We believe that question will grow increasingly more pertinent as the pace of American secularization simply continues to increase. Ironically, a good deal of that secularization is guised as spiritual, again just as we would expect from an Adversary who specializes in deception.

That has a long precedent directly related to the two definitions of economy. We have long taken our prosperity as a sure sign of God's approval. However, beginning in Korea, and greatly exacerbated in Vietnam, that aura began to rub off. More importantly, since then the junction between the Corporate State and the official government has begun to reveal itself, and we begin to confront the unbridled avarice that founded and rules this one nation under Mammon. Again we confront the concept of authority, and ironically the secular state of America helps to reveal a spiritual Truth in spite of itself: we gradually begin to realize that we the people are largely if not entirely impotent. *"I am the Vine, ye are the branches: he that bideth in Me, and I in him, the same bringeth forth much fruit: for without Me ye can do nothing'"*—John 15:5. Illusions of physical efficacy, of which displays of military might are an especially dramatic example, are naught but more *strong delusions.* Yet, it is upon those physical displays of power that we evermore completely base our national identity. At the same time, more and more the government retreats into secrecy, always with the same excuse: *national security.* Yet, in spite of those efforts, more and more those dirty little secrets begin to see the light of day. As a result, more and more the electorate is left wondering just what our "elected" officials actually do in our name, and whose security they actually have in mind. As epitomized by the political climate as of this writing (late 2010), we again see that classic divide and conquer motif, with the United States ideologically torn asunder by a raft of domestic woes reminiscent of the Vietnam Era. But more subtly, with that realization, the myth of self-determination defined as a representative democracy likewise begins to fade. More and more we find people looking for an efficacious leader who can get us out of what increasingly seems an inextricable mess not only nationally but globally, yet suitable candidates seem very scarce. Thus, we encounter a theme we'll deal with in more detail presently: the subtle erosion of our belief in our ability to govern ourselves. Here we can see a parallel to the pre-Reformation Church which grew ever more domineering, making itself a strawman destined to fall to the plaudits of many who took goodness as their cause. Perhaps still more pertinently, we can also see a parallel to the Jews at the time of Christ's appearance. Fed up with Roman dominance, they expected a militant Messiah come to right wrongs, dispense justice, and to deliver them to their erstwhile glorious relationship to the Father. Note the sinister echo to the desire to return to the values founding America, and combine that with similar cries for efficacious leadership. *Beware!* The coming Antichrist may well offer just that, and a great many will flock to his banner in opposition to a glaringly obvious raft of evils. We've already seen a few examples of extremely false spiritual leaders, roaring lions such as Jim Jones, David Koresh, Sun Yet Moon, but we could hardly describe them as wearing sheep's clothing. Even so, they also constitute a warning: if a good many otherwise reasonably intelligent people can be taken in by prophets as blatantly false as they are, how many more will fall for the more convincing ones yet to come? More importantly, how many *have already done so?*

We live in the most dangerous and painful times in human history, and the *Birth Pangs* (see I Thessalonians 5:3) haven't even begun yet. It's a bit beyond the scope of this work, but given the universal acceptance of good vs. evil, we believe that the digression is worthwhile. For the world has never experienced—nor will it ever experience—a greater evil than what is commonly called *"The Tribulation".* Consider Mathew 24:21-22: *"'For then shall be great tribulation, such as was not since the beginning of this world to this time, no, nor shall ever be. And except those days should be shortened, there should no flesh be saved: but for the elect's sake those days shall be shortened.'"* The eternal conflict is between Truth and Anti-Truth, not good and evil, and this provides ample evidence. Consider: if we believe that evil originates with Satan, what must we believe about this ultimate evil? How many of those given to that mindset will be able to see this tribulation as a manifestation of God's *divine love?* Daniel 12:10 foresees this event and comments: *"Many shall be purified, and made white, and tried; but the wicked shall do wickedly: and none of the wicked shall understand; but the wise shall understand."* Again, that directly relates wisdom to divine Truth, foolishness and wickedness to Anti-Truth. Throughout the Old Testament, especially Proverbs, we are exhorted to seek heavenly wisdom. In Chapter 3, James defines that wisdom. *"Who is a wise man and endued with knowledge among you? Let him shew out of a good conversation his works and meekness of wisdom. But if ye have bitter envying and strife in your hearts, glory not, and lie not against the Truth. This wisdom descendteh not from above, but is earthly, sensual, devilish. For where envying and strife is, there is confusion and every evil work."*—James 3: 13-16.

By disavowing any *"inspiration from heaven"* or *"interviews with the gods"*, we clearly disavowed any wisdom that *"descendteh from above"*. As a result, we've made *"envying and strife"* essential to our political process and so to our very definition as a nation. Politely called "bi-partisanship", rather than having the good of the nation as a whole at heart, the party out of power commonly hopes and works toward the failure of the party in power so that they can trade places. Perhaps nowhere in recent history can we see this more blatantly manifest than in the Conservatives' relationship to Barak Obama. Fittingly enough, most of that rancor[34] focuses on the economy. Taking consumerism as a kind of envying, and taking competition as a kind of strife, we've also made them essential to our social definition both domestically and internationally. We can see this socially manifest in the proliferation of games where the objective is no longer to play and enjoy oneself but to win, often "at any cost". More seriously, this country is no longer a democracy or a democratic republic, and most probably never was. America has devolved into a

---

[34] We did not choose that word lightly: seldom if ever if we see such bitter animosity of one party vs. the other with, many suggest, race a major contributor, but with religion—is Obama a "secret Muslim"?—not far behind.

confederation of competing power groups, all with their own, often sharply conflicting agendas, all finding "power politics" essential to meeting those agendas. In short, they too must win at any cost. Whose ultimate agenda does that follow? Given money as power, can it surprise us that the super wealthy Elite run the country? Consider the fruit this has produced, often cited as those "American values" that some hold so dear. We have developed an enormous military-industrial complex and a huge standing army geared toward protecting what we have, even though we acknowledge that we hog a hugely disproportionate percentage of the world's resources. Even more telling, we not only constantly lust for still more, but find acquiring still more absolutely essential to our economic survival. That eventually makes conquest essential to that end, and suddenly the parallels to Constantine's empire don't seem so far fetched. More seriously, LOM and the mark of the beast come together figuratively just as they eventually will literally under the reign of the Antichrist.

If we accept foolishness as our premise, we can reach only foolish conclusions. As a result of adopting good vs. evil as our guiding moral premise, even at the end many won't recognize Messiah when He does return, clad in glory beyond description as the *Conquering King*. On the contrary, many will go to battle *against* Him, only to finally discover the true identity of the Freedom God. Just as the Jews didn't recognize Him for who He was when He came in *His Humble Servant* manifestation, so those who say they are Jews and are not—the *Synagogue of Satan*—given to the same good vs. evil mindset, will likewise fail to accurately see Him until the very end. Then we will understand the nature of our revolution; then we will understand the nature of our desire for freedom, and see it as an extension of Satan's heavenly rebellion. Then we will understand why we cannot serve both the master of the world, and of Heaven. Perhaps most of all, we will see what service to each entails—and that, nationally, we have in fact sought self-destruction as our unstated ideal.

Good vs. evil casts Satan as evil's originator, God as the originator of good. Yet, in Revelations 16, as part of the Tribulation, we find God pouring out His wrath quite liberally in a variety of very unpleasant events, and in each case we have angels saying something to the effect of, *"You are righteous, O Lord, the One who is and who was and who is to be, because You have judged these things."* (16:5.) By contrast, in v. 9 we find, *"And men were scorched with great heat, and they blasphemed the name of God who has power over these plagues; and they did not repent and give Him glory."* Notice the operative verb: *repent.* Even this cruelty is motivated by love, just as a loving parent will sometimes cause a child to experience a painful spanking to make a point. The angels don't sing praises for God's actions themselves—there's no sadistic glee involved any more than you find masochistic glee involved with the martyrs praise of the same misfortune.[35] In both cases, they sing praises for His *judgments,* and for the righteousness inherent in them! We must always bear in mind that righteousness doesn't even exist except in God's eyes. Any efforts to deem ourselves righteous amounts, by definition, to self-righteousness.

We've noted that LOM has an unconventional application as well as a fiscal one. We can see that perhaps most clearly in the quantitative value addition we often find associated with good vs. evil. Perhaps nowhere in history do we find a more eloquent example of that than in World War II. It remains America's favorite war, and with good reason: nowhere else do we see the lines of good and evil so readily discernible to the physical senses and human reason. As slavery gave the American Civil War a moral aura (see below,) so the Shoah did the same for the Second World War, even though it played no part in its origins. But unlike any other global conflict, WWII features the veritable quintessence of evil, the most notorious bad guy since Judas Iscariot: Adolph Hitler. No matter that his foe, and our erstwhile ally, Joseph Stalin, killed more than three times as many of his countrymen, (and for a time allied himself with Hitler,) in the popular consciousness Hitler embodies evil to the extent that many have accepted him as a sure Antichrist.[36] But more than

---

[35] Even secular historical accounts recount some of the martyrs marching off to their grisly demises with songs of praise and thanksgiving on their lips.

[36] In point of fact, this one nation under God has actively supported a number of dictators who performed purges and mass murder

the Shoah and associated pogroms, we can cite several instances of church and state merging in Hitler's character. We can, for example, cite a number of examples of his blasphemy against both Father and Son, especially when favorably comparing himself to them. Not content with that, he and his propaganda people launched a deliberate deification campaign epitomized by a saying common to school children during his reign. *"Jesus and Hitler were both persecuted. But while Jesus was crucified, Hitler became Chancellor."* But most significant to our current discussion, with the possible exception of Rasputin, no world leader or historical figure has ever gained greater notoriety due to their personality than *Das Fuhrer.* Although usually defined as the epitome of evil, many who met him personally reported an other-worldly air about him, a strange, almost mesmerizing charisma characterized by a tremendous *force of will.*

How curious.

What if we look past good vs. evil? What if we look past the blatant militarism, look past the obvious abridgments of human rights, the terrorism and gross cruelties, and seek the essentials? What if we look at this conflict not in terms of good vs. evil, but in terms of Truth vs. Anti-Truth? Once we begin looking at WWII in those terms, one stark commonality immediately leaps out at us: we find the essence of democracy, my will be done, coming closer to reaching idealization in Nazi fascism than in this land of the free, embodied not in a Christ-like figure, but in a commonly acknowledged Antichrist. Could that be the whole purpose of WWII? We must bear in mind that, for all his cruelty and despotism, Hitler was nevertheless appointed by God to that specific position for that specific purpose just as He appointed Pharaoh to hold His people in their Egyptian captivity and subject them to similar cruelties. *"For by Him were all things created, that are in heaven and that are in earth, visible and invisible, whether they be thrones or dominions or principalities or powers*

---

very similar in style if smaller in scope than *das Führer.* Moreover, in terms of percentages, our treatment of the Native Americans came closer to genuine genocide than did Hitler's "Final Solution." We point this out to emphasize the deceptive quality inherent in good vs. evil even with such a blatantly self-evident evil as this.

. . ."—Colossians 1:16. In a sense, that makes Nazi Germany "one nation under God." The same holds true for Iraq, North Korea, China and any other "rogue state" you might wish to mention.

Of course freedom lovers would maintain that democracy actually reflects *our* will be done, the will of the people, as opposed to the egomaniacal dictates of a psychopath. They would further argue that our system has safeguards built in to protect against just that, George Bush notwithstanding. Yet, those safeguards did not prevent a number of very prominent American business leaders and industrialists, George Bush's family included, from dealing with and facilitating Hitler's rise to power. It didn't prevent them from availing themselves of the huge profits to be made by exploiting labor under the fascist regime free of labor laws, where workers were paid slave wages for long, long hours and were forbidden to quit. Those safeguards did not prevent some of those industrialists from continuing that association well into the war, ending it only after it became clear that Hitler would lose, or until the US government got wise to them and forcibly closed them down. Neither did those safeguards prevent a coterie of radical corporate heads from attempting a *coup d'état* to remove FDR from the White House and to institute a fascist government in this country!

But even those specifics pale in comparison to the real commonality. In the essence of the opposing governmental systems, we find no difference at all! Again look past the superficialities of the Shoah and other overt evils, and then consider that Hitler attempted to deliver his people from what he perceived as evil even as the Founding Fathers did. That of course means to substitute his truth for divine Truth, again, just as the Founding Fathers did. His truths no doubt seemed self-evident, and his course no doubt seemed wise to him even as they did to the millions of Germans who voted for him, who thronged to see him, and who hung on his every word and who saw him as the savior of their nation. He too found conquest essential to his nation's economic survival, culminating in global hegemony. Lastly, he too saw his people as having a special, even divine destiny, and in spite of his radically inconsistent demeanor and actions, did not hesitate to invoke "Providence" or even "God". *"I can thank God at this moment that He has so wonderfully blessed us in out hard struggle for what it right...*"—Speech in Berlin, Oct. 6, 1939. Wars fought with guns and bombs act as smokescreens obfuscating the far more subtle Spirit War, and WWII proved no exception. Think about it. We can readily see the deceptive element inherent in good vs. evil simply by remembering that Satan and his followers masquerade as Christ's representatives (see above) and therefore seek to be taken as the good. More specifically, they seek to be taken as the relative good, and to that end they ingeniously manufacture relative evil to which to contrast themselves. Good vs. evil, especially when coupled with physical perception, immediately focuses our attention on the Nazis, begging us to judge them. If we take life and what we associate with it as our foundation, we must take death as the corresponding evil. Given that, how can we hope to avoid being deceived? We take life and death, and so good vs. evil, as the Truth.

Yet God uses death to His own good purposes as epitomized by the death of His own Son. But more, look at Acts, chapter five and the tale of *Ananias and his wife.* The early apostolic followers had agreed to sell all their possessions and to hold the money in common. Ananias and his lady decided to try to keep a little for themselves but Peter, empowered by the Holy Spirit, saw through the deception. *"'You have not lied to men but to God.' Then Ananias, hearing these words, fell down and breathed his last."*—Acts 5:5-4. Notice that lying to God, which we could define as faithlessness, was a crime worthy of instant death. Bear in mind that Revelations 21:8 lists *"all liars"* among those to find their share in the lake of fire. That in itself has serious implications for those finding prevarication necessary to our national security. Notice too that the amount of money had nothing to do with it, just as LOM has no direct relationship to greed per se. The scale is different, but just as God appointed Peter to that apostolic position for that particular purpose, so He likewise appointed Hitler to the Chancellorship for his particular purpose. Given that, we can see both as examples of the same Truth: that God often uses evil, including death, to His own ends just as we can frequently find throughout the both Testaments.

As an example, in John, chapter nine, Christ and His Apostles came across *a man blind from birth.* One of the disciples asked, *"'Rabbi, who sinned, this man or his parents that he was born blind?'"* to which Christ replied *"'Neither the man nor his parents sinned, but that the works of God should be revealed in Him.'"*—John 9:3. Notice how that in itself blends a blessing with a curse. God used an evil to a good purpose: the man was born blind specifically so God could heal him and impart a message to all of us by way of His Son. Consider: Christ healed a very great many people, so we should wonder why the emphasis on this particular man. For openers, notice how Christ's response puts the premium on the heavenly as opposed to the physical—and shows it as perfectly reasonable. Think about it. What are a few years' suffering compared to playing an important part in Christ's teachings? *"For I reckon that the sufferings of this present time are not worthy to be compared with the glory which shall be revealed in us"*—Romans 8:18. Those given to the God Life can never understand that, nor can those taking the pursuit of happiness as their lives' grail. Similarly, physical perception, fittingly enough, the nature of his affliction, could never reveal this poor fellow as more than cursed. That held especially true in the Jewish culture of the time, which often saw such a handicap as a sign of disobedience or inherent unrighteousness.

The good news/bad news continues in John 9:32. While the Pharisees examine him, trying to figure out who cured him, the man tells them: *"Now we know that God does not hear sinners; but if anyone is a worshiper of God and does His will, He hears him. Since the world began it has been unheard of that anyone opened the eyes of one who was born blind. If this Man were not from God, He would do nothing."* To that the Pharisees responded, *"'You were completely born in sins, and are you teaching us?' And they cast him out."* They could see only with *physical perception,* appropriate to a dedication to keeping the Law in the flesh and in ironic contrast to the man's affliction. That in itself links seeing is believing and a dependence of physical perception to the *Synagogue of Satan. "Jesus saith unto him, 'Thomas, because thou hast seen Me, thou hast believed: blessed are they that have not seen, and yet have believed'"*—John 20:29. *"God does not hear sinners,"* yet those who appeared sinless to physical perception could not see, understand, or accept the Truth. Who does that cast as the sinners? Lack of sin does not characterize a good person but a righteous person, with Thy will be done the core of that righteousness and lack of sin. Christ strongly implied that the blind man had been preordained of God to serve this specific role and to find salvation. He heard that they had cast the man out of the synagogue and, when He found him, He asked, *"'Dost thou believe on the Son of God?'"* (John 9:35). The following exchange proves very illuminating. *"He answered and said, who is He, Lord, that I might believe on Him? And Jesus saith unto him, Thou hast both seen Him, and it is He that talketh with thee. And he said, Lord, I believe. And he worshipped Him."* In spite of his physical sight, the man still could not see the Son of God even as He stood before him. Neither could he worship Him until he had been granted that privilege. Self-determination demands the diametric opposite: we grant ourselves the privilege to worship God, to become His children, and to reveal His Truth.

No wonder we chose self-determination as our political form: our governmental system is our religion enacted. Unable (and naturally disinclined to) perceive much less comprehend divine Law, we instead more and more commonly find ourselves obeying the law of the jungle: the law we express each time we invoke national security as a justification for our actions. For example, although we hear a great deal of rhetoric about bringing Osama bin Laden and his cohorts to "justice," the speakers usually make it quite clear that the wanted poster reads *"Dead or Alive"*—and that they'd quite frankly prefer the former. From the opening days of the Iraqi War, we personally targeted Saddam Hussein with the specific intention of killing him, just as we did on a number of occasions with Fidel Castro in the 50s and 60s. Neither are those isolated incidents. How often has our government resorted to "black ops" against government leaders it found intolerable? How many clandestine wars do we fight today? Perhaps more telling still, how often does the fiscal wellbeing of large corporate interests figure into (if not entirely define) that intolerability? When does killing in the name of national security become premeditated murder? We can likewise find a domestic precedent. Consider how that parallels the same kind of justice done to Lee Harvey Oswald by Jack Ruby as the act upon which the current Presidency founds. It doesn't matter whether Lee Harvey Oswald acted alone, or as part of a massive international conspiracy, or even if he played no part at all in the assassination of John F. Kennedy. The fact remains that our national leadership founds on murder, both of the President and of Oswald, (and, arguably of Jack Ruby as well) surrounded by secrecy and deception. If fruit must follow the pattern of its seeds, what does that imply about the seeds from which this country sprang and upon which it now rests?

But perhaps Osama bin Laden has another, more subtle similarity to Oswald. Well substantiated rumors maintain that our intelligence apparatus could have captured him on at least one occasion, and perhaps more. If that's so, then we must wonder whether we really *want* to capture him. After all, he makes an excellent poster boy for an ongoing War on Terror that makes select sections of the Elite very, very wealthy, and wealth, like power, never voluntarily relinquishes itself. That in turn brings up another and much more serious question directly associated with the very definition of this nation of law: do we really want justice? If fruit must follow the pattern of its seeds, and if this country were born of sedition, how can we expect such seeds to produce as a harvest a nation dedicated to justice? Consider American history. How much justice did we show to the Native Americans whose lands we usurped whenever they became desirable? How many treaties did we break or ignore in the process? What justice did we show to countless Africans imported as slaves who, even after their presumed emancipation, continued to find discrimination at virtually every turn? How much justice did we show the Mexicans when we arrogated their territory north of the Rio Grande on flimsy pretexts just so we could fulfill our "Manifest Destiny"? How much justice did we show Spain when we went to war with her over equally specious grievances, including the self-inflicted wounds on the USS Maine? What definition of justice did we serve by forcing countless American born Japanese into essential concentration camps at the onset of WW II? How just was our involvement in Southeast Asia, with the "police action" originating in the trumped up Gulf of Tonkin incident? What was the difference between our invasion of Iraq to sack Saddam Hussein and the actions of a lynch mob out after vigilante justice?

Scariest of all, this brand of justice is a matter of official national policy. The New National Security Strategy, released in September 2002, stated that, the United States *"will take the actions necessary to ensure that our efforts to meet our global security commitments and protect Americans are not impaired by the potential for investigations, inquiry, or prosecution by the International Criminal Court (ICC), whose jurisdiction does not extend to Americans and which we do not accept."* We are not a nation of law so much as we are a nation of *our* laws—and ours alone! Do you see how that autocratic authority smacks of the self-deification inevitably resulting from self-determination? That means that our every international interaction is based on that law which means that we tacitly seek to become exactly the kind of global authority against which we presumably rebelled! If we do so in the name of God, then we seek divine global authority, very much in keeping with the "prince of the world" who is quite likely the author of our Manifest Destiny. Consider the duplicity involved. On the one hand, we preach peace, global stability, and most of all, self-determination, yet at the same time we demand that stability be by our standards, under our dictates, and that self-determination to our benefit. No wonder a good deal of the world sees the United States as "imperialist."

Yet, this is logically inevitable. If we take survival as our highest good, then we must take whatever facilitates that survival as commensurate goods—legal or otherwise. Notice that the "efforts" mentioned in that document include the death, detainment and mistreatment of pretty much anyone we deem an enemy, including those who act in accordance with their own law, and including the leaders of presumably sovereign states! Survival taken to its logical extreme comes down to my survival at the expense of yours—the diametric opposite of the unconditional love central to Christian theology. These are the principles to which Obama and McCain refer and again we must pose our title question.

Consider what just might rank as the most prominent of those principles. We defined ourselves as a nation of law, yet rebellion remains a fundamental part of our national experience. We likewise define the good as that which overcomes the evil, but in some instances those evils are the laws themselves. Every so often we see an outdated edict as an evil that some iconoclast finally finds the courage to challenge. That one characteristic essentially defines many of our cultural heroes whom we hold responsible for the majority of our social progress, most assuredly including the Founding Fathers. How curious: as a nation of law dedicated to justice, we admire and take as examples worthy of emulation those who break the law, and at the same time define breaking the law as the good! After all, that's what we celebrate every July 4[th,] the holiday most intimately associated with patriotism—and almost as intimately associated with a wide variety of "sales events". By definition, that makes that lawless rebellion the primary reason why patriots love their country. Celebrating lawlessness: doesn't that sound eerily similar to those who *"take pleasure in unrighteousness"?* That means that those who break the law define justice for us just as that which defines evil defines good for us. No wonder those laws make us ever freer to break God's commandments. As a result, we hold rebellion *itself* as a primary source of our goodness.[37] Who is the *"evil man"* who seeks only rebellion in Proverbs 17:11—the one who will be visited by a *"cruel messenger"?*

Again consider Revelations 12:7-9: *"And there was war in heaven: Michael and his angels fought against the dragon; and the dragon fought, and his angels, and prevailed not; neither was their place found any more in heaven. And the great dragon was cast out, the old serpent called the Devil and Satan, which deceives the whole world; he was cast out into the earth, and his angels were cast out with him.* We find the birthplace of freedom in the act of Original Sin but, if you'll pardon the expression, we find Original Sin's genesis in that heavenly rebellion. Consider a frightening curiosity: one of the earliest and most popular

---

[37] Although usually not in a political context, consider how often we use "revolutionary" as a high compliment to some sort of innovation.

symbols of American independence was the *Gadsen flag:* a coiled rattlesnake labeled with the warning, *"Don't tread on me"*. If we truly believe God's word, then we can take the consequences of defying it seriously. If we don't, then we literally *cannot* consider what we have done as a major infraction of God's sovereignty, and instead end up with rationalizations such as, *"He couldn't mean that . . .",* or *"Do you really believe that God means . . .?* We therefore can't take the accompanying warning seriously either, and there's nothing we can do about it! We can serve only one master and the Freedom God and the True God are diametric opposites, just as my will and Thy will be done are diametric opposites. If we chose the former we exclude the latter just as we do in choosing Mammon over God. Notice how that links the Freedom God to an obsession with the things of the earth. Again the two definitions of economy merge, just as they did in our rebellion against Great Britain.

By demanding justice, the Freedom God binds us to the Law just as the Old Covenant does; by featuring forgiveness and mercy, the True God frees us from the Law, expecting only that we dispense what we have received. In perhaps the profoundest mirror-image of them all, only by seeking the things of heaven and recognizing their value can we accept forgiving our enemies as a blessing *to us.* Clearly that applies only to the spiritual and the eternal, but that's also the basic difference between the Freedom God and the true God. *"Lay not up for yourselves treasures upon earth, where moth and rust doth corrupt, and where thieves break through and steal: But lay up for yourselves treasures in heaven, where neither moth nor rust doth corrupt, and where thieves do not break through, nor steal: For where your treasure is, there will your heart be also'"*—Matthew 6:19-21. Forgiveness for our sins amounts to one of the greatest of those treasures, and we gain that treasure in heaven by dispensing it on earth. The Freedom God, dedicated to the treasures of the earth, cannot hope to see that and, typical of the mirror-imagery we've seen throughout, demands justice (retribution) instead. Moreover, in our natural, unchanged state, the state Nature's God urges us to retain, we can't even care about such issues.

That brings up one of the most damaging yet most commonly overlooked of all sins: *indifference.* In spite of the superficial dissimilarities, the re-definition of God central to religious freedom almost always removes Him from the focal point of our lives, and ends up reducing Him to little more than an incidental or, in the case of this one nation under God, a virtually meaningless figurehead. In essence, we have made a new covenant of our own in which we say how, when and *to what extent* we'll worship Him. No wonder we've isolated that worship to specific "houses," where we properly do so only at prescribed times, under prescribed circumstances, and with prescribed clerical supervision. Why do you suppose Paul tells us to *"Pray without ceasing"* in I Thessalonians 5:17?[38] Clearly it would prove a trifle impractical to spend 24/7 on our knees with folded hands and closed eyes, but that's not what he meant. We live in a *deital kingdom* and, whether we care to acknowledge it or not, we render the appropriate service to one of two spiritual monarchs, the true King or His usurper on a minute-by-minute basis, and that's where we all fall short. *"There is none that understandeth; there is none that seeketh after God"*—Romans 3:11. Obviously some of us do seek after Him, but not nearly to the extent that we should, and that includes people like Paul and Peter! Where does that leave the rest of us? Consider the surrounding verses that speak of the Old Testament Jews and wonder how accurately that reflects the contemporary world, America in particular. *"As it is written, there is none righteous, no not one: There is none that understandeth, there is none that seeketh after God. They are all gone out of the way, they are together become unprofitable; there is none that doeth good, no not one. Their throat is an open sepulcher; with their tongues they have used deceit; the poison of asps is under their lips: whose mouth is full of cursing and bitterness. Their feet are swift to shed blood: destruction and misery are in their ways: and the way of peace have they not known: There is no fear of God before their eyes"*—Romans 3:10-18.[39] That seems a rather accurate

---

[38] Also see Ephesians 5:18-21

[39] He quotes from too many different Old Testament sources to comfortably list them. Any reference Bible will show them.

reflection of the modern world. We like to think of ourselves as wise and rational, yet when you come right down to it, what other than seeking after God is of even passing importance? Yet, the most pious among us can always find other things to interest us, other things to demand our time and attention, and take us away from what should be our sole life's pursuit. We seek what we truly desire. Thus, those desires play a dominant role in who we are and how we spend our lives. The more we love God, the more we seek His Truth in a self-perpetuating cycle and, perhaps as importantly, the more we seek the things of heaven in general in a similar cycle. Rather than a "religion" defined as an arbitrary set of beliefs that largely come down to dos and don'ts, often complemented by an equally arbitrary set of rites and rituals performed at the appropriate time and place under the appropriate supervision, our relationship to Father and Son becomes a very intimate and personal way of life. That not only pretty well summarizes Christ's earthly existence, but also His relationship to His Apostles.

Sadly, the opposite holds equally true which helps to explain the increasing secularization of human society as we've "progressed" through the ages. Consumerism, where we emphasize consumption per se even over the specifics, is the logical outgrowth of a longstanding preoccupation with the things of the earth. Consider this definition of progress: over the centuries we've gone from considering poverty enough of a virtue to take vows to that end to considering it the root cause of most of our social ills. Notice how that fits nicely with the consumerist belief that *stuff*, regardless of the specifics, is the key to happiness, contentment, and even world peace. That ultimately makes money, or more specifically LOM, the key to those ideals—no wonder we call it the Almighty Dollar! No wonder our first response to any kind of overt evil is to throw money at it! That serves a sinister purpose indeed: it moves idolatry from a matter of deception, where we can claim the role of innocent victim, into the realm of active desire often bordering on if not amounting to *lust*. Think about what that materialistic preoccupation has cost us. Not one of us is able to worship God and serve Him exclusively, but instead of seeing that as a reason for lamentation, our way of life makes that inability a matter of preference, which makes it a matter of conscious choice and ultimately even of pride. We *"take pleasure in unrighteousness"* and call doing so good!

That's what the Spirit War is all about. For, make no mistake, we live in a war zone that is really an extension of Satan's heavenly rebellion. That war centers on the essence of Original Sin: good vs. evil as we define the terms. Human history is littered with attempts to not only deliver ourselves from evil, but to deliver ourselves to goodness, and, in every conflict, each side considered itself the good, its adversaries the evil. Consider the objective and how effective it has proven. We have all but eliminated even the possibility of absolute Truth—Christ—and, at the same time, have all but eliminated the very concept of absolute good—God—as well. In the process, we have reduced both to matters of opinion and perspective which casts intolerance of such subjective concepts as a crime that creates strife and endangers life. It's utterly impossible to divorce politics from religion because the state of "atheism"—without God—is impossible; acknowledged or not, willingly or not, we render service to one deity or the other just as we are the children of one or the other. The question—the only question—is which God?

Chapter Four

t must surely rank as one of history's great ironies that this one nation under God found itself for so long at odds with the "Godless Commies," especially the Soviet Union. In the most fundamental sense, God's economy is Communist, and that applies to both definitions of the word. All that exists belongs to the "government," (see I Corinthians10:26 quoting Psalms 24:1,) and God is the autocratic leader of a self-perpetuating "party," who will most certainly not allow other parties to compete with His authority.40 That means that, at least in terms of desire, we and the Communists both sought a state of transcending that authority in favor of our own. The Communist philosophy, at least according to Marx, called for the eventual elimination of all central government defined as a distinct ruling class in favor of a stateless and classless society reflecting the pure will of the people. Isn't that the essential definition of idealized democracy? Doesn't that accurately reflect a government "of the people, by the people and for the people"? After all, Thomas Jefferson, maintained that *"the government is best which governs least"* with apparently something of that nature in mind. Doesn't the idea that *"all men are created equal"* imply such a classless state? The Communists declared themselves atheist, while the United States declared itself one nation under God, yet both declared freedom from God's authority in favor of my will be done. Which nation, then, was actually "godless"? Which added the Pharisaical element of hypocrisy?

Clearly having the entire population vote on every single issue would prove unmanageable, so America settled on the idea of a democratic republic where elected representatives vote in our stead, and are both guided and restricted by law

---

40   The Amplified Bible makes numerous references to being affiliated with Christ's "party".

rather than the whim of the majority.[41] But consider a curiosity. We chose Nature's God as our national deity, yet nowhere in the natural world do we find anything even remotely resembling a democracy, much less a democratic republic. On the contrary, among social species, we find a very distinct hierarchy, often with a single dominant individual, and seldom more than a small coterie exercising virtually autonomous rule over the group. Doesn't it seem odd that "Nature's God" would so lead us away from nature, especially given that Adams maintained that America was based on the principles of nature (see above)? But has it? Although we still call ourselves a democracy, in fact the federal government has steadily grown more autocratic over the past half century or so, and we can find more than ample evidence of rule by the super-wealthy Elite long before that. Of course the idealized Communist state of decentralized government never happened either for the simple reason that, once established, power will only very reluctantly relinquish itself and in nearly all cases seeks to enhance itself instead. We've seen it happen in the Soviet Union, and in Communist China among other places, but also experience it happening in this country. Doesn't that suggest an unacknowledged commonality? Consider: in spite of our purported desire and reverence for personal freedom, the Federal Government's control has steadily increased since our inception with the rate of that increase quickening as well.

The comparisons between Communism and "The Leader of the Free World" go still further. *"'He that speaketh of himself seeketh his own glory: but He that seeketh His glory that sent Him, the same is true, and no unrighteousness is in Him'"*—John 7:18. Combine that with John 8:44, where Christ describes Satan: *"When he speaketh a lie, he speaketh of his own: for he is a liar, and the father of it.'"* What more fundamental falsehood could we seek than our own glory? That brings up an interesting and almost entirely overlooked point. Why do we call it "God's word"? Why is the Christ, who defined Himself as The Truth, also called

---

41 The Founders did so because they greatly feared democracy as "mob rule" or rule by the lowest common denominator. Someone once described democracy as "two wolves and a lamb voting on what to have for dinner."

the Word (see John 1:14). Combine those and we come up with the answer: every word that originates from any source other than the living God of Israel amounts to a lie! *"The Lord knoweth the thoughts of man, that they are vanity"*—Psalms 94:11. Yet, we have made speaking of ourselves the first of our Constitutionally guaranteed rights *granted by our creator*, and lumped it together with freedom of religion. Rather than the "influence of the gods", the Founders relied on philosophers who, by definition, speak of themselves, thereby seeking their own glory. No wonder "Proud to be an American" followed so naturally.

Appropriately enough, those who interpret the Scriptures without divine guidance do the same thing. Here we find the heart of our title question. All forms of idolatry ultimately come down to self-deification; all forms of self-deification ultimately come down to devil worship. Since we must serve one master or the other, my will be done ultimately comes down to Satan's will be done, again just as we saw with Even in the Garden. Dare we call it coincidental that we have continued to define good and evil for ourselves as a direct legacy of Original Sin? Can we call it coincidental that those definitions have drifted ever further from those expressed by the Son of God? Dare we call it coincidental that our definition of good has virtually eliminated any vestiges of Christ's number one commandment: that we love God with all our beings, and at the same time has done the same to the secondary commandment that we love our neighbor as ourselves? Doesn't that in fact make us as "Godless" as the Commies ever were? *"I believe in one thing only,"* declared Joseph Stalin, *"the power of human will."* The Communists, by virtue of officially declaring themselves atheistic, officially rejected *Thy will be done* and, by default, adopted *my will be done* as their philosophy. By declaring ourselves a democracy, we do the same thing. If we acknowledge God as the universal sovereign then we come to realize that Thy will be done is not an option or a preference but a fact: God's will *will* be done, illusions of efficacy or self-determination notwithstanding. *"The lot is cast in the lap; but the whole disposing thereof is of the Lord"*—Proverbs 16:33. Once we fully realize that, then we also realize that God appointed

Hitler, Stalin, Bush, Obama, and the rest for the specific purposes they served.

The Soviets clearly made themselves the opponents to all things divine, including the "opiate of the people". We cast ourselves as the champions religious freedom, but again we both accomplished much the same purpose even as we saw with the Islamic terrorists above. Think about it. We've defined true religion as keeping ourselves *"unspotted from the world"* (James 1:277. How does religious freedom accomplish that? Do we expect the kingdom of God to be a constitutional monarchy where we can send our representatives to advise Him on issues such as good and evil, salvation and the nature of the universe? Do we expect His power to derive from those He governs? Do we expect Him to reign over us as a result of our consent and for only as long as He continues to earn that consent by acting in accordance with our wishes? Do we expect His kingdom to be polytheistic, with each of us free to define Him in our own terms and, so, free to relate to Him on our own terms? Do we expect Christ to advocate freedom from His Father's authority? If not, then why do we Christians advocate it now, and do so in His name as per the Patrick Henry quote cited earlier? Now is also part of eternity, you know. Do we expect to accept or reject the Son of God at our whim and still find favor with the One who sent Him? We take that denial as one of our most laudable characteristics, and President Obama made it a matter of our official national identity (see above). That defines the "ideals and values" he put in place of Christianity as what unites us. If the coming kingdom is to be characterized by love of and devotion to God, and to Him alone, how can we claim ourselves part of that kingdom if we don't demonstrate that love and devotion now? We dedicate ourselves to the things of heaven or to the things of the earth, and that includes worshipping God in *Truth and in Spirit!* By separating Church from state, we separate God, and, at least as importantly, His Son, from our daily affairs. Doesn't that make us Antichrist by definition? If our governmental form is our religion enacted, how must we answer our title question?

Like it or not, we live in an absolute existence. *"'He that is not with Me is against Me; and he that gathereth not with Me scatttereth abroad'"*—Matthew 12:30. Carefully consider what He says next: *"'Wherefore I say unto you, all manner of sin and blasphemy shall be forgiven unto men: but the blasphemy against the Holy Ghost shall not be forgiven unto men"*—Matthew 12:31. This episode began with Christ healing people on the Sabbath which the Pharisees saw as a blatant disregard for the Law. Christ exposed their hypocrisy. *"'What man shall there be among you that shall have one sheep, and if it fall into a pit on the Sabbath day, will not lay hold on it, and lift it out? How much then is a man better than a sheep? Wherefore it is lawful to do well on the Sabbath days'"*—Matthew 12:11-12. As a direct result, the Pharisees counseled together about how to destroy Him. *"But when Jesus knew it, He withdrew Himself from thence: and great multitudes followed Him, and He healed them all: and charged them that they should not make Him known: That it might be fulfilled which was spoken by Esaias the prophet, saying, 'Behold My servant, whom I have chosen; My beloved in whom My soul is well pleased: I will put My Spirit upon him and He shall shew judgment to the Gentiles. He shall not strive nor cry; neither shall any man hear His voice in the streets'"*—Matthew 12:18-19. Notice that this interaction with the Jews intended to show judgment to the non-Jews—the pagans. That defines the true Son of God as one about whom no one hears from another man, and that reflects God's judgment which, by definition, means that it reflects God's will. Consider Luke 13:24-27: *"'Strive to enter in at the strait gate: for many, I say unto you, will seek to enter in, and shall not be able. When once the master of the house is risen up, and hath shut to the door, and ye begin to stand without and to knock at the door, saying, Lord, Lord, open unto us; and He shall answer and say unto you, I know you not whence ye are: Then shall ye begin to say, we have eaten and drunk in Thy presence, and Thou hast taught in our streets. But He shall say, I tell you, I know not whence ye are: depart from Me, all ye workers of iniquity'"*. That casts those who eat and drink in His presence—which has obvious implications for the Eucharist—and, more immediately pertinent, those who hear His words from other men *as workers of iniquity who will be excluded from the kingdom of heaven!* The dictionary defines *blasphemy* as assuming to ones self the qualities or rights of

God. Thus, we may define blasphemy against the Holy Spirit as assuming to the human spirit the qualities belonging to Him alone—i.e., substituting the human spirit for the Holy Spirit. A religious unity based on the human spirit does just that; it is a unity based on the unholy spirit which, by definition, makes it Antichrist.

Yet, that is exactly the nature of the religious freedom we champion as a nation. Religion and politics merge still again. We didn't add the term "One nation under God" to the Pledge of Allegiance until 1954, partly as a reaction to the Soviets. We thereby took the protection of religion unto ourselves, forcing our citizens to swear fealty as an act of patriotism in both public schools, where it was usually mandatory, and at various public gatherings where, while not compulsory, failure to do so resulted in considerable peer disapproval. Consider how closely that parallels Hitler's demands for public fealty at similar gatherings.[42] Consider, too, how it parallels the demands made by the Romans on the early Christians. That's a closer parallel than we might dare to imagine, for again, *God* is not the issue. We did not make mention of His Son, and that amounts to doing the exact opposite of what we intended. Calling ourselves One nation under God without including His Son means that we claim direct access to God. That either applies only to the Old Covenant Jews or we speak of another deity. In the former, we again find ourselves in the *Synagogue of Satan*. In the latter, we again find ourselves in the *Synagogue of Satan*. In either case, without Christ we are just as "Godless" as the Commies. *"Who is a liar but he that denieth that Jesus is the Christ? He is antichrist that denieth the Father and the Son. Whosoever denieth the Son, the same hath not the Father: he that acknowledgeth the Son hath the Father also"*—I John 2:22-23. To acknowledge the Son is to acknowledge the Truth that He embodies—Truth that is not His but His Father's.

That Truth is all-encompassing. If you think about it, Christ's total divorcement from physical rites and rituals as necessary

---

[42] Initially, the Pledge was to be recited accompanied by the "Bellamy Salute" which had to be altered since it bore a very strong resemblance to the Nazi salute.

to God's worship is quite consistent with *worshipping God in Truth and in Spirit*, with His detachment from worldly things in general, and with His exhortations for us to eschew worldly pursuits. He thus likewise divorced His church from worldly pursuits, including activism and political affiliations. So who has led us to believe that we must worship Him by way of those rites and rituals while involving ourselves in such affairs? That grows especially pertinent when we realize that *"they that are in the flesh cannot please God"* (Romans 8:8.) Consider what John says pertaining to our virtually universal acceptance of doing so: *"If there come any unto you, and bring not this doctrine, receive him not into your house, neither bid him God speed: For he that biddeth him God speed is partaker of his evil deeds"*—II John 1:9-10. By supporting religious freedom we do exactly what John said not to do: we wish those not bearing Christ's doctrine Godspeed and therefore partake in their evil deeds—idolatry, to be exact! We even fight and kill our fellow man in order to maintain our "right" to do so as an essential part of our way of life, and an integral part of our definition of greatness! How must we answer our title question? Our separation of church and state forces us to choose between the ideals of the Christ, and the expediency of political and social survival, and the *natural man* chooses in favor of the latter *every single time*. He must, for he has no choice but to obey his introcosmic natural laws. No wonder we've taken Nature's God as our national deity.

As the world spirals down into a deepening pit of violence and animosity, one matter will gain greater and greater pertinence. If Christ promises *"peace, not as the world giveth,"* (John 14:27), what should we logically expect from His mirror-image? If the *whole world is under the sway of the evil one*, whom must we name as the author of our contentions? Perhaps even more importantly, what is the Deceiver's motivation for doing so? What would happen if one arose who could put a stop to them once and for all? How could we not consider him good? How could we not see him as wise? Given the many wonders and counterfeit miracles surrounding him, how could we not take him as divine? We don't intend this as prophecy in any kind of specific sense, but rather as examples to illustrate a point. If we seek external peace, finding it will spell our destruction, for external peace is just one more of the things of the earth Christ tells us to eschew. *"And if the house be worthy, let your peace come upon it: but if it be not worthy, let your peace return to you. And whosoever shall not receive you, nor hear your words, when ye depart out of that house or city, shake off the dust of your feet. Verily I say unto you, It shall be more tolerable for the land of Sodom and Gomorrah in the day of judgment, than for that city'"*—Matthew 10:13-15. We seek Christ's internal peace rather than that of the world just as we seek other heavenly values rather than the values of the earth.

Detractors have historically, and with a certain legitimacy, criticized Christianity as being "anti-life" in that it limits our pleasures and creative potential. Integral to Christian faith, we believe that the afterlife will feature far greater joy than we could ever even imagine in this life. *"If ye keep My commandments, ye shall abide in My love; even as I have kept My Father's commandments, and abide in His love. These things have I spoken unto you, that My joy might remain in you, and that your joy might be full'"*—John 15:10-11. We also believe in far greater potential than we could ever hope to realize here: *"Verily, verily I say unto you, He that believeth on Me, the works that I do shall he do also; and greater works than these shall he do; because I go unto My Father'"*—John 14:12. In Matthew 17:20 we find a refrain of the same idea in a very famous verse: *"If ye have faith as a grain of mustard seed, ye shall say unto this mountain, Remove hence to yonder place; and it shall remove; and nothing shall be impossible unto you."* That enough "potential" for you? Even so, the vast, vast majority of the world's population takes Life as their god, and adopts the appropriate value system prominently featuring instant gratification. Forget about divine wisdom for a moment; in strictly pragmatic terms, how logical is that? Consider James 4:14. *"For what is your life? It is even a vapor that appears for a little time and then vanishes away."* What kind of wisdom drives us to trade eternity for the equivalent to a week-end in Vegas? Does that sound like an advisor who has our best interests at heart? We Christians live in the world, but not as part of it: *"I have given them Your word; and the world has hated them because they are not of the world, just as I am not of the world. I do not pray that You should take them out of the world, but that You should keep them from the evil one. They are not of the world, just as I am not of the world."*—John 17:14-16. If Christ and His closest associates are not part of the world, then the rest of us must follow suit. *"If ye be risen with Christ, seek those things which are above, where Christ sitteth on the right hand of God. Set your affections on the things above, not on the things of the earth. For ye are dead, and your life is hid with Christ in God"*—Colossians 3:1-3. So long as we love the earth, we must follow the appropriate value system. From that system we will derive the appropriate definitions of good and evil and, so, of vice and virtue. We must therefore call enmity toward God our greatest good and expect to inherit the Kingdom of Heaven as a result of acting as His enemies! Doesn't that pretty well describe Satan's agenda? Doesn't that pretty well describe the national philosophy of the United States of America, born bereft of the influence of heaven?

If we define Original Sin as a desire for freedom from God's authority then we can find that rejection best epitomized at Christ's crucifixion. It was, after all, a matter of democracy in its purest (and most deceptive) form.[43] Remember that *Pilate couldn't find any fault at all with Christ, and said so* (see John 18:38.) He in essence pleaded with the Jews to allow him to let Him go but, prodded on by the priests, the people refused to the point where Pilate feared a full-scale riot. Consider the ironic similarity to the Jewish priests. Such a riot would make it appear as if Pilate couldn't control his territory, and that would make him look bad in Rome. The priests hated Christ because He undermined their authority and cast them in a bad light among the people. In both cases we find a political motivation. No wonder the Jews would argue, *"If you let this Man go, you are not Caesar's friend. Whoever makes himself a king speaks against Caesar."*—John 19:12. A couple of verses later Pilate asks them the hardest question of all, *"'Shall I crucify your King?'"* The Jews shouted out a fateful answer: *"We have no king but Caesar!"* (19:15.) Consider that very carefully. The Jews (for the most part)

---

[43] Although the Jews voted for Christ's execution, it was in fact purely a matter of God's will.

threw their allegiance to the ways of the earth: their religion and their politics merged (as it does today in the "Holy Land"), and that defined the difference between the two Covenants. Do you see how our governmental system does the same? As this episode illustrates, we cannot separate politics from religion, for both stem from what we take as our ultimate authority.

We find that rejection of divine authority epitomized in I Samuel 8:5 ff. The prophet had grown old and turned his judgeship over to his sons, Joel and Abiah. They did not follow his footsteps, but instead fell prey to bribes and corruption. Thus the people came to Samuel and said, *"Behold, thou are old, and thy sons walk not in thy ways: now make us a king to judge us like all the nations"*—I Samuel 8:5. Notice how that features conforming to the world in defiance of their longstanding order to remain separate from the world. Notice too how it reflects those in power as ordained by God whether we approve of them or not. We Christians are likewise commanded to separate ourselves from the world, and most of us defy that command and instead seek to fit in. (Thus the phenomenon of "social Christians"). This angered Samuel, and he consulted the Lord. God, however, made note of the fact that ever since He'd brought them out of Egypt the children of Israel had run amok, chasing after false gods and engaging in various forms of unrighteousness. Therefore He said to Samuel, *"Hearken unto the voice of the people in all that they say unto thee: for they have not rejected thee, but they have rejected Me, that I should not reign over them"*—I Samuel 8:7. Does that sound familiar? He went on to tell the prophet to warn the people of what sort of king they would have. But even after giving a rather lengthy list of reasons to reconsider, the people remained obstinate, and *". . .refused to obey the voice of Samuel; and they said, Nay; but we will have a king over us; that we may be like all the nations . . ."*—I Samuel 8:19. Both the Jews and the Christians were meant to remain exclusive and removed from the world. The Jews sought to conform to the world, and the majority of Christendom has followed suit. Our political system is our religion enacted, and both Zionist Jews and patriotic Christians share a love of the world and the belief in good vs. evil in common with every other nation in the world, including the Communists. Such a commonality should give us pause. Indeed, in order to address our title question, we must also ask one *church* under which God?

For as long as the Church emphasized the actual doctrine espoused by Christ and His apostles, it did not corrupt itself. As long as it remained united by the Holy rather than the human spirit, it remained excluded from worldly affairs. It recognized those affairs as inherently unrighteous in the same sense that we can generally equate the things of man with the things of Satan. As soon as the Church began emphasizing goodness rather than Truth—and no one knows when, why or how this occurred—and, more importantly, established a unity of the human spirit, it quickly began its inevitable move toward becoming a political entity and heir to all the corruption that implies. Think about it: every political entity on earth shares that unity. Every political entity likewise shares corruption, for politics and corruption are intimately related. In 1887, Lord Acton, formally known as John Emerich Edward Dalberg Acton, first baron of Acton (1834-1902), wrote a famous, albeit frequently misquoted, statement to Bishop Mandel Creighton: *"Power tends to corrupt, and absolute power corrupts absolutely. Great men are almost always bad men."* Notice how that parallels Christ's statement quoted earlier: *"'Ye know that the princes of the Gentiles exercise dominion over them, and they that are great exercise authority upon them. But it shall not be so among you: but whosoever will be chief among you, let him be your servant'"*—Matthew 2:25-26. That tends to make the desire for power a pagan pursuit. *"'A good tree cannot bring forth evil fruit, neither can a corrupt tree bring forth good fruit'"*—Matthew 7:17.

If you think about it, political power, formal or not, reflects the desire to control our own destinies. Thus, we can say that any entity, political or ecclesiastical, featuring self-determination is, by definition, Antichrist. Think about it: if we must in fact serve one master or the other, then a desire to control our own destinies actually reflects the Devil controlling our destinies, just as we would expect from the *Synagogue of Satan*. We've noted that, as *"synagogue"* implies, Satan's deceptions often seem righteous to the unwary, but that makes them no less deadly. Here we find an especially good example. Consider: neither the coercive power base necessary to producing the political church nor any of the other subsequent concessions resulting from it could have happened without the inversion of I Corinthians13:13: *"And now abide faith, hope and love, these three; but the greatest of these is love."* Predictably enough, elevating faith to the most important component in Christianity had a great many consequences right in line with the elevation of personal salvation to Christianity's focal point and, more immediately pertinent, to the hierarchical clerical structure characterizing the vast majority of the Christian religion. *"There is but one universal Church of the faithful, outside of which no one at all can be saved."* So declared Pope Innocent III (1160(1)-1216.) The appeal to the survival imperative as the adhesive holding the Church together is no coincidence, nor is its connection to faith. Ironically, as always, we can find a shred of Truth in this. In the end, all we have to do is to truly believe that Christ died for our sins, and was raised again from the dead. But, just as God per se is not the issue, neither is salvation per se the issue. On the contrary, making personal salvation Christianity's centerpiece has perverted that which is inherently pure into that which is diabolically deceptive, just as we would expect from translating the *mark of the beast* into spiritual terms. If we equate Anti-Truth with unrighteousness, then it has done nothing less than to turn a good part of mainstream Christianity into the *Synagogue of Satan!*

Consider: since one cannot claim to have faith without living it, and our way of life is our faith enacted, equating faith with salvation makes living in accordance with the tenets of the faith—i.e., *obedience*—the essence of salvation. Here we find the deadly mirror-image directly related to self-determination: in fact, we obey God *because we have been saved, not as an effort to gain it!* Obedience to the Law as the means to salvation belongs exclusively to the Old Covenant in what Paul refers to as the *"righteousness of the Law"* (see Romans 10:4). *"For what the Law could not do, in that it was weak through the flesh, God sending His own Son in the likeness of sinful flesh, and for sin, condemned sin in the flesh: that the righteousness of the Law might be fulfilled in us who walk, not after the flesh, but after the Spirit"*—Romans

8:3-4. Ironically, he does speak of the *"righteousness of faith"* but the key to that faith is to seek God's mercy by way of love, not His justice by way of obedience, and certainly not by way of fear. *"What shall we say then? Shall we continue in sin, that Grace may abound? God forbid. How shall we, that are dead to sin, live any longer therein? Know ye not, that so many of us as were baptized into Jesus Christ were baptized into His death? Therefore we are buried with Him by baptism into death: that like as Christ was raised up from the dead by the glory of the Father, even so we also should walk in newness of life"*—Romans 6:1-4. We obey God's Law as a result of the baptism of the Holy Spirit and the divine empowerment accompanying it. That's why the Disciples scattered like frightened animals in Gethsemane in spite of swearing to the man that they would stand by Christ come what may. They were sincere, but the human spirit without that baptism could not prevail over their natural survival instincts. In a similar sense, making obedience a prerequisite to salvation means that our obedience, and so our salvation, resides within us, manifest by my will be done and, more importantly still, by the power of the human spirit! Consider that carefully in light of the definition of blasphemy discussed above, especially the blasphemy against the Holy Spirit.

Yet, we find that at the core of the majority of the mainstream Christian denominations, and for good reason: such a belief is absolutely essential to drawing new converts in the flesh, to worshipping God in the flesh and so to maintaining the integrity of the church's political structure. Since fear, including fear of damnation, can be readily manipulated, it makes a far better coercive power base than does love which cannot be coerced at all. Thus, rather than moving love to the bottom of the triad, we eliminated it altogether and put fear in its place. Consider what this accomplished. By overemphasizing fear of Him *"who can destroy both body and soul in hell"*, we actually eliminated that fear altogether. How? Because at the same time, we deemphasized Christ's number one commandment: *that we love God with all our beings.* No wonder we've since concluded that it doesn't matter what we believe since we "all worship the same God." No wonder the church so naturally followed the secular path, and no wonder that virtually all of her protesting offspring have followed suit. Indeed, we find the roots of the oft-lamented secularization of the Christian religion right here. Given our governmental forms as our religion enacted, can we wonder that our social structures have followed suit? Taken together, doesn't that also sound like a good definition of the Great Apostasy?

Moreover, by way of excommunication and other Papal weapons, we replaced fear of God with the fear of man in another parallel to contemporary governments, that is, to paganism. No wonder the Mother Church could so expeditiously involve itself in political and military affairs while garnering unto herself the appropriate rewards. Since this unity founded on the human rather than the Holy Spirit, it could not consist of the genuine faith yielded by divine revelation implanted directly in the hearts of the congregation. Thus, we had to make it a matter of mind instead. That too served a larger purpose. Satan orchestrated Christianity's fragmentation by first insisting on a total unanimity of faith.[44] While the Church strove to impose a single faith on the world, much as we see with the Islamic radicals, self-determination ultimately led to the opposite end and the inevitable conflict that eventually led to the almost universal acceptance of religious egalitarianism. At the same time, conflict and conquest as natural adjuncts to good vs. evil seeped into the Christian character and have echoed through the ages ever since. As per Satan's plan, goodness had triumphed over Truth, and the *Synagogue of Satan* took on the mantel of Christianity. Love of the Truth took on a considerably greater importance as an integral part of the *strait and narrow way*.

By the time of the American Experiment, traditional religion had largely fallen out of fashion, especially among the intelligentsia. In many minds, the Christian religion differed very little from superstition, and again we find Anti-Truth the culprit. By incorporating demonstrable falsehoods (geocentricity, for example)[45] into its doctrine, the Church set itself up as a strawman for the growing reason movement to bowl over much

---

[44] Which we can find justified in Romans 15:16, and elsewhere.

[45] The Church long held the earth as the literal center of creation with everything else revolving around it.

as we saw prior to the Reformation. In philosophical terms, if its cosmology were so far in error, that automatically brought its other tenets into question as well. Ironically, the most basic of those tenets—good vs. evil—went unchallenged, yet it played a fundamental role in the decline of religion and the rise of reason. We had long supposed that the Church of God would produce good people, while one would expect "agnostic science" to produce evil people. Sadly, it didn't work out that way. Partly as a result of that, some brave iconoclasts began to question some of the Church's other self-evident truths, and found them equally wanting. That subtly linked reason to progress not only in the technological sense, but in the *moral* as well. That in turn casts reason, and the things of man in general, as morally superior to revelation and, by extension, to the things of God in general. That, of course, casts Satan as superior to God while casting knowledge as superior to faith. Consider the ironic inevitability: a Church trying to appeal to the *natural man*, calling him to worship God in the flesh, motivated by fear and empowered by the human spirit, yielded a mindset entirely in keeping with the *carnal mind* and, as a result, ultimately cast love of the world—*enmity towards God*—as superior to love of God! We thereby turned Christ's doctrine into a moral and ethical philosophy which we could twist to suit our own purposes.

All of this was foreseen."*And many false prophets shall rise, and shall deceive many. And because iniquity shall abound, the love of many shall wax cold*'"—Matthew 24:11-12. As our love of God waxed cold, our love of divine Truth followed, replaced by secular truths that proved far more immediately profitable. As science called into question, and then logically refuted, one "Christian" truth after another, it increasingly called the Church's moral authority into question at the same time.[46] As perhaps the biggest single question, since Christianity held that salvation was tied directly to goodness, how could any Church claim to

---

[46]   Even there we can find an object lesson concerning the Spirit War. With a few notable exceptions—the infamous Scopes Monkey Trial of 1926, for example—the Anti-Truth of science did not openly combat divine Truth, but sought to *replace it* even as light does not combat but rather seeks to replace the darkness.

have the sole means to eternal life? That held especially true when one could readily find "Christians" of less than sterling character, especially when compared to morally superior people of other faiths. Once we went that far, it proved easy to ask why salvation had to be linked solely to the Christian religion. From there we could begin to doubt whether we even needed salvation at all, and if so from what. If salvation were a matter of goodness, then all good people should be saved regardless of their beliefs. If God were good, and especially if He were All-Just, then He surely must save good people regardless of their beliefs. Once Pandora's Box had opened, we found it impossible to close it again. Iniquity began to abound, and the love of divine Truth waxed cold indeed, rapidly replaced by the self-evident truth we naturally want to believe. The essence of religious freedom is the essence of idolatry. Since it's up to us whether we believe or not, it follows that we should also decide for ourselves *what* we believe. As a result, we have literally re-created God in our own image. Yet, that is the "Christianity" we find as our spiritual roots, and what this one nation under God champions today.

"*Because strait is the gate and narrow is the way which leadeth unto life, and few there be that find it. Beware of false prophets, which come to you in sheep's clothing, but inwardly they are ravening wolves*'"—Matthew 7:14-15. That clearly associates our ability to find that narrow way with our ability to avoid the false prophets. *"False"* again implies Anti-Truth, and that's why we need the guidance of the Spirit of Truth! "*Howbeit when He, the Spirit of Truth is come, He will guide you into all Truth: for He shall not speak of Himself; but whatsoever He shall hear, that shall He speak: and He will shew you things to come*'"—John 16:13. It also clearly implies that few manage to do that because few of us rely on that Holy Spirit. That's the true fruit of the lamented secularization of society. Thus, it's hardly surprising that most of us don't seek that guidance since such reliance is absolutely essential to Thy will be done—and since we Americans so relish the diametric opposite. Accepting that Spirit comes only by total submission to the Father, and countless forces militate against that, national pride and patriotism chief among them. That also serves a divine purpose, however. *"For first of all, when ye come together in the church, I hear there be divisions among you, and I partly believe it. For there must be also heresies among you, that they which are approved may be made manifest among you"*—I Corinthians 11:18-19. The Reformation may have served that very purpose.

As mentioned earlier, long before the Reformation the Catholic Church faced a challenge to its very survival as a physical, political entity. As a result of doctrinal fragmentation, and resultant contentions, the Church came to see an absolute unanimity of faith as essential to its very survival. However, Christ quite specifically said that *He would build His church on divine revelation* (see above) from the Father Himself. *"But ye are not in the flesh, but in the Spirit, if so be that the Spirit of God dwell in you. Now if any man have not the Spirit of Christ, he is not of His"*—Romans 8:9. Notice that he equates the Holy Spirit with the Spirit of Christ, while Christ Himself calls Him the *"Spirit of Truth"* in John 14:17. It follows that the Spirit of Truth would yield a love of the Truth which means a love of the divine revelations at the foundation of the true Church as well as a love of attaining our spiritual knowledge by that method. Given that, we must take any divine "truths" not so revealed as Antichrist. What does that suggest about the entirety of doctrinal Christianity? If the true Church of Christ is founded on the Holy Spirit, then a unity of the human spirit must, by definition, be Antichrist just as the mirror image of worshipping in the flesh suggests. Yet the Church sought just such a unity as have the majority of her offspring ever since.

Since the unity it sought founded on learning, the Church hierarchy had to decide who would define Truth for the masses and, perhaps just as importantly, who would have the authority to impose it. That posed a problem: based on learning, the meaning of a single world could literally spell the difference between salvation and perdition. The Church hierarchy could not agree on such definitions however, and no one had the authority to impose one definition on the others. Ironically—or fittingly, depending on how you look at it—it was a very religious time in Rome, with nearly everyone venerating one or more gods, and most accepting divine intervention as a common daily occurrence. Constantine (272-337) was very much a man of his times, accepting both the Sun(a life god) and Mars(god of war) as his primary deities. In 305, he became co-emperor with his father, Constantius I. A general popular with his troops, his army declared him sole emperor when his father died the following year. By this time, however, the Empire had lost a good deal of its prestige, and the Emperor had lost a great deal of respect. Especially in districts distant from Rome, some provinces went so far as to elect their own emperors, and no one anywhere any longer considered him divine. Religion and politics merge: the Empire and the Church both faced a fragmentation dilemma that only unity could resolve.

Although he became the nominal emperor in 306, Constantine would have to fight rivals for another eighteen years until he finally gained sole power over the entire Empire. Some fairly amazing things happened to him during that time, and one has a very special pertinence to this work. The popular version of the story tells of him seeing a vision of the sun god in a grove of Apollo in Gaul in 310. Two years later, just prior to a battle with his Italian rival Maxentius, who commanded vastly superior forces, he dreamed that Christ spoke to him, telling him to inscribe the first two letters of His name on his troops' shields. The next day he saw a cross superimposed on the sun with the inscription, *"hoc signo Vinces"*, ("in this sign you will be the victor.") He then proceeded to defeat his rival at the Battle of Milvian Bridge near Rome, and the Senate hailed him as the Empire's savior. The reason for that belief is obvious: he delivered them from evil by way of a military operation in a clear-cut example of good overcoming evil. In spite of his obvious pagan proclivities, they hailed him as good *because* he overcame evil, his paganism notwithstanding, and that constituted a fateful compromise indeed. It re-solidified the Church's drift from emphasizing righteousness to emphasizing goodness.

As a result, divinely revealed Truth was replaced by what essentially amounted to self-evident truth. Constantine concluded that the God of that cross he'd used so effectively, the one these Christians worshiped, must be associated with the same sun god he revered. After all, those Christians had made the day of the sun the day of His worship. Thus began the hijacking of Christianity that brought the inherently heavenly crashing to the earth. We had begun to blend Jehovah God with a god of life and "Christianity" blended with the universal influence we've often noted—just as we might expect from the Universal Church. We thus began to revere life itself in spite of several exhortations to the contrary in Christ's own teachings. The connection to the survival imperative, the mark of the beast, seems too obvious to point out. Nevertheless, notice the consistency between that and elevating salvation to Christianity's focal point. Once we did that much, we had to likewise revere all that we associated with life, which made our devotion to the God Life all the more complete and extended the survival imperative to the things of the earth. Moreover, we defined that good, and so, that god, in terms of what overcame evil, which inevitably translated into what overcame both death of self and the loss of what we associate with our lives. If we define "pagan" as non-Christian, then these constitute far more fundamental concessions to paganism than all of the rites, rituals, costumes and customs taken together.

If we define life as good, and use death to preserve it, then we must call death a good. If we call death good in that context, we must likewise call *dealing* death in that context a good—and in fact we often loudly laud those who most efficiently do so in wartime, calling them "heroes". No matter how you look at it, dealing death amounts to *doing harm to ones neighbors*, but Paul defines *the love that fulfills God's Law* as the exact opposite (see Romans 13:10.) Yet, we think of ourselves a people of God any way, just as did the militaristic Popes and Protestants before us. All shared good vs. evil with good defined as that which overcomes the evil in common. Thus, we can say that America does have a religious heritage. In a speech at Bob Jones University, February 2001, John Ashcroft declared, "*Unique among the nations, America recognized the source of our character as being Godly and eternal, not being civic and temporal. And because we have understood that our source is eternal, America has been different. We have no king but Jesus.*"[47] That sense of "special purpose" or

---

[47] That last, an obvious reference to the Jews proclaiming that "We have no king but Caesar" at Christ's crucifixion was a popular

divine destiny fueled much of what Americans take as "progress", including the virtual genocide of a number of Native American nations, the aggrandizement of an entire continent, and an unparalleled lust for and acquisition of the things of the earth. If we adopt the maxim, *by their fruits so shall we know them*, does that imply Christ—or Antichrist? What does that suggest about America's religious roots?

Constantine's veneration of this new deity yielded one stunning victory after another, and again we find a parallel to American history: we long took our military successes as signs of God's approval. Those victories eventually led to the reunification of the Empire, and the restoration of much of its erstwhile glory. Those same victories also led to the unification and salvation of the political Universal Church. That helps to explain how and why the Christian and military mindsets so thoroughly blended over the centuries in exactly the kind of unanimous faith both Empire and Church had seen as vital to their physical survival. From there it's easy to blend the Christian and the patriotic, just as we found among the Jews in the Old Covenant, most dramatically at their insistence on Christ's crucifixion. The transition from Truth vs. Anti-Truth to good vs. evil had been completed, and with it a spiritual *coup* that put a pagan emperor in Christ's place as the head of the apostate Church. Not coincidentally, one of the most commonly accepted images of Christ throughout much of early Christian art is actually the image of Constantine.

That is more than symbolically important. Think about it. Which image has the majority of Christian history reflected, that of the Son of God as depicted in the New Testament, or that of a warrior emperor? Not that long ago Christ Himself had said that His Kingdom *was not now from this earth and that if it were His followers would fight* (see John 18:36.) Since Satan is called the *"prince of the world"* (see John 12:31, John 14:30, and John 16:11), what might we logically expect him to proclaim? All of our contentions ultimately come down to the very things of the earth that we are repeatedly exhorted to eschew. *"'But I say unto you which hear, Love your enemies, do good to them which hate you, bless them that curse you, and pray for them which despitefully*

---

slogan prior to and during the Revolution.

use you. And unto him that smiteth thee on the one cheek offer also the other; and him that taketh away thy cloak forbid not to take thy coat also'"—Luke 6:17-29. Notice that He again says, *"you which hear"* which applies to those who are of God (see above). That makes doing what He says essential characteristics of His followers whom God has drawn to Him, and dramatic manifestations of how we set ourselves apart. Which "Jesus" did Mr. Ashcroft have in mind? To what "principles" did Mr. McCain refer? What does Mr. Obama see as unifying us as a nation? Whom do we serve? One nation under *which* God?

As a result of the Constantine *coup,* we have adopted warrior values as Christian values. Who do we serve? Don't the false flag operations used by virtually every government, certainly including intend to feed and justify those values? Don't they serve the purpose of maintaining political power so that those in such positions can lord it over the rest of us? If we can equate the lust for such power with paganism, then must we not consider this a pagan nation no different from the world's other pagan nations? Christ equated the lusts for and concerns about physical things with pagan pursuits (see above), and this country devotes itself to just such ends. Are not the kingdoms of the world Satan's to give to whom he will? Do those kingdoms, without exception, not follow the mirror-image of Christ's every command? They have always done so of course, but now at least some of them do so in the name of God, reflective of the hijacking of Christianity by a pagan Emperor. From those imperial values we define warrior virtues as Christian virtues at diametric odds with the virtues exhibited by Christ Himself, but quite in keeping with a political church in need of coercive behavior control to maintain its power structure. Our nation of laws derived from a church of laws, both needing those laws for the same purpose. Given their diametric opposition to Christ's teachings and commands, doesn't that, by definition, make those values and virtues Antichrist? While Christ valued meekness, longsuffering, peace, honesty forgiveness, and above all, *love*, we find exactly the opposite among the virtues not only lauded, but *required* by a successful warrior in both a political and ecclesiastical context. No wonder we make "war" on every social evil: a war on poverty, a war on drugs, a war on pornography, a war on terror, etc., etc., treating those "evil doers" in much the same manner as we treat their international counterparts, and much as the Islamic extremists treat various "infidels". The Emperor reestablished much of the Rome's erstwhile glory, while decorating the capitol with numerous larger-than-life statues of himself. Take a look at Washington, D.C.. The Church followed suit, adorning itself with the wealth of the world and sponsoring some of history's great artistic masterpieces. Needless to say, that too has passed on to many of her offspring. Much of the pomp and ceremony associated with the Catholic Church, some of which seeped into those offspring, derives directly from Roman Empire court protocol as we might expect from the caeseropapism at the formal Church's foundation. Our basic concepts of justice likewise come from the Romans with direct and obvious ties to the warrior mentality. In a sense, the Roman Empire never died—it simply re-formed into a kind of invisible empire in something of a mirror image to Christ's invisible church.

The Spirit War largely rages between the human spirit and the Holy Spirit and focuses primarily on the question of whom we serve. God wants us to accept the latter, but that must come at the expense of the former, for the two are mutually antagonistic in ways going well beyond perception. *"This I say then, Walk in the Spirit, and ye shall not fulfill the lust of the flesh. For the flesh lusteth after the Spirit, and the Spirit against the flesh: and these are contrary the one to the other: so that ye cannot do the things that ye would"*—Galatians 5:16-17. The indwelling presence of the Holy Spirit is what truly distinguishes the Christian. *"And he that keepeth His commandments dwelleth in Him, and He in him. And hereby we know that He abideth in us, by the Spirit which He hath given us"*—I John 3:24. That Spirit of Truth is our only defense against the false prophets and teachers bent on our destruction. *"Perverse disputing of men of corrupt minds and destitute of Truth, supposing that gain is godliness: from such withdraw thyself."*—I Timothy 6:5. Withdrawing from such men essentially means withdrawing from an elaborate latticework commonly called "the World System."

Chapter Five

It's really quite appropriate that we bury our dead in the earth, for the things of the earth can truly prove deadly. Clearly that holds true in the physical sense, where corresponding concerns motivate us to militantly defend "our interests" collectively and individually, but it ultimately proves even more true in the spiritual sense. Rather than the *things* of the earth, we might more precisely call them the *values* of the earth. In turn we could then refer to them as the values associated with physical life. Since we derive our virtues from our values, that yields the virtues of the earth; since, by definition, what we call virtue is what we call good, that leads to an earthly definition of good. Since only God is good, that which we call good is what we call god in that it exerts predominant influence over us. Thus, by taking those values as our guiding principles, we end up taking the god of the earth as our ruling deity, and still again we find ourselves in the Synagogue of Satan. As epitomized by the Holy Land, the Old Covenant Jews had a decidedly different relationship to the things, values and virtues of the earth than do we Christians. Their religious observations founded on physical worship, their ethos defined by the minutiae of the Law. Accordingly, God would often reward the righteous fiscally, which we find reflected in our righteousness-prosperity co-equation. With Christ's advent, however, that all changed. Just as we now worship the Father in *Truth and in Spirit*, so we now eschew the things of the world and the values associated with them. Christ's earthly sojourn was something of a transitional period between the two covenants, and a difficult time for the Jews that tested their understanding.

For example, consider Christ's famous encounter with *the rich man who wanted eternal life* (Mark 10:17,) in light of one of His most famous Beatitudes found in Matthew 5:3: *"'Blessed are the poor in spirit, for theirs is the kingdom of heaven.'"* That immediately poses an apparent contradiction. If good people go to heaven, we would naturally consider poverty of spirit a severe disadvantage. Then again, who said that good people go to heaven? Notice that the man makes that very mistake right off the top when he calls Christ, *"Good master."* Christ replies, *"'Why do you call Me good? No one is good but One, that is God.'"* (Matthew 19:6.) He disavows any inherent goodness, while defining absolute goodness as God alone. As we learn in the next few verses, this man is wealthy both monetarily and spiritually, and has kept all the commandments since his youth (19:20.) Thus, by *"righteousness of the Law"* (Romans 2:26) he should have been fine. Consider Christ's observation in one of the Bible's best known verses: *"'How hardly shall they that have riches enter into the kingdom of God. For it is easier for a camel to go through a needle's eye, than for a rich man to enter the kingdom of God'"*—Luke 18:24-25. He speaks of fiscal riches of course, but also of that righteousness of the Law the Jews had come to associate with it. He essentially told the fellow to rid himself of his sense of worthiness, of his spiritual wealth (as well as its pecuniary counterparts) and follow Him in the way of meekness, forgiveness, and of course, Truth. In other words, He told him to abandon the Old Covenant and the righteousness of the Law in favor of the New and righteousness by faith. Ironically, that is more in keeping with the scion of Abraham according to Galatians 3:6-7. When we *"take up our cross"* (Matthew 10:38) to follow Him, we figuratively die to our old selves. In a very fundamental way, that reflects the difference between the two covenants. If we don't take up that cross, which largely means to abandon the world system, then by default we remain in the *Synagogue of Satan.* We've noted that the United States calling itself one nation under God but not under Christ obliges it to keep the Law in its every minute detail, as we'd expect from a *"nation of laws"*.

But this episode illustrates that America's relationship to the Old Covenant Jews goes still deeper as well. Christ, the embodiment of the New Covenant, told the man to *sell all of his possessions and give the money to the poor and to follow Him.* Notice how that parallels the *merchant seeking the pearl of great price* noted earlier. Still again, the problem lies not in our possessions themselves, including our wealth. *Joseph of Arimathaea*, in whose tomb Christ was buried, was a rich man who *"also waited for the kingdom of God"* (see Matthew 15:43 and Matthew 27:57.) Moreover, if money itself were evil, it hardly seems likely that Christ would find it righteous to give it to the poor. Christ referred to the total separation from the things of the earth that characterized the Old Covenant including the pursuit of wealth in both senses of the word. Again we encounter *"Seek and ye shall find,"* and again that applies physically (in this case, fiscally) as well as spiritually. Do we seek goodness, or do we seek righteousness? We can find many paths to goodness, and so many definitions thereof that we can surely find one that suits our fancy. Indeed, doing so is integral to religious freedom. Righteousness, on the other hand, is not nearly so broadly defined, though we can do so very succinctly: *Thy will be done.* Demonstrating that will was a primary reason for Christ's visit (see Matthew 12:18). Since we are to follow Him, it figures that doing likewise would answer our Basic Question: what is my purpose in life? The United States takes as its purpose a progressive arrogation of the world's wealth and an obsession with my will be done. Ask yourself: does that seem like Christ or Antichrist?

The rich man took pride in his fiscal wealth as a reflection of his spiritual wealth: he'd kept the Commandments since his youth. Tacitly, the United States has adopted a "divine" destiny substantiated by our wealth, and have taken that as the reason for having such a bloated opinion of our self assessed righteousness—the exact antithesis of poverty of spirit Christ cites as blessed. If we take that a step further, we find part of that root residing in the values spawned by that relationship. When Christ told him to abandon his riches and follow Him, the fellow walked away disconsolate, for he had great wealth. Consider the disciples' reaction. *"When His disciples heard it, they were exceedingly amazed, saying, 'Who then can be saved?'"* Obviously they didn't refer to rich people per se, but to the traditional connection between righteousness and material prosperity. In other words, if good people, those who appear to be rich in spirit, don't go to heaven, who does? To that, Christ responds, *"With men this is impossible; but with God all things are possible"*—Matthew 19:26. Righteousness of the Law had been superseded by the righteousness of faith.

At the same time, humility had superseded pride. Christ told him to take his self-assessed righteousness and give it to those apparently having little or none. *"For whosoever exalteth himself shall be abased; and he that humbleth himself shall be exalted"*—Luke 14:11. Note that we deal with the diametric opposite of good overcoming evil as a ticket to heaven, and find pride a definite hindrance if not an outright vice. We therefore have the diametric opposite of good overcoming evil as the definition of righteousness, with meekness the appropriate accompaniment. That follows quite consistently: pretty much by definition, the meek don't usually overcome anything in the conventional sense, at least not by force of will or arms. If we thereby do not serve the cause of righteousness by force of will and arms, what cause do we serve? Do we stand with Christ, or do we *scatter abroad?* Think about it. Whose image does force of arms more closely reflect, the Son of God portrayed in the New Testament as the Humble Servant, or the warrior emperor who essentially usurped His position by way of conquest? Which image does that reflect, quiet, reflective individuals, often invisible to normal perception, or to massively proud cathedrals enjoying international recognition and fame as well as ostentatious wealth? Which is essential to the lust for the things of the earth that preoccupies the vast majority of the global population, including political power, secular and ecclesiastical alike? *"We hold upon this earth the place of God Almighty"* declared Pope Leo XIII, one of the Emperor's successors. Holding the place of God Almighty—doesn't that pretty well define Satan's agenda? Doesn't that pretty well define self-deification? Haven't we equated self-deification with self-determination? What lies at the foundation of the world's most popular political and spiritual movements, not to mention most of our secular conflicts? We can begin to see Constantine's invisible empire taking shape, and it bears a sinister similarity to the *broad and spacious way.* The capital has moved from Rome, however.

Many have taken the idea of preordination (for which we can find a great deal of evidence) as a source of *hubris,* often characterized as a "holier than thou" attitude. The mere fact that it often finds expression in lording authority over others. the aforementioned characteristic of paganism, suggests the inherent fallacy. After all Paul, almost certainly a member of that Elect, told us *to esteem others better than ourselves.* Yet we find that attitude, epitomized by the aforementioned Ashcroft quote, reflected, albeit most often without acknowledgement, in this nation's policy makers both historical and contemporary. Notice how that matches our most basic freedom: the freedom to believe what we want. Notice too how such lording fits quite nicely with both Manifest Destiny and our tacit conviction that we have a divine duty to spread democracy and the American way to the rest of the world whether they want it of not. Notice how it corresponds to money as power and the super wealthy constituting the Elite largely responsible for that imperious policy. If we take the American Elite as God's elect we find their claim to that title firmly rooted in the Old Covenant association of spiritual and fiscal wealth: the *Synagogue of Satan!* The Jews are God's Elect; for us to so title ourselves is to call ourselves Jews when we are not. No wonder we lord it over others.

By contrast, the New Covenant Elect, cast in Christ's image, will be humble, and loving, and that doesn't even touch on their other likely qualities, all of which have a rejection of the world's values in common. Notice how that reflects the instructions Christ gave to the man cited above, and notice how our national "divine destiny" reflects the man who failed to follow those instructions, and for the same reasons. We believe ourselves to be rich in spirit, with our fiscal wealth reflecting those riches, and that yields pride that leads to hubris, and we find ourselves unable to let go of it. Rather than submitting to God, we strive to supplant Him, just as we supplanted divine Truth with self-evident truth. That self-evident truth allows us to believe that we enjoy a special relationship with God that does not necessarily involve His Son, and which allows us to ignore His teachings, commandments and examples, replacing divine wisdom with human wisdom.

All of this subtly reflects the survival imperative, and here we find one of the most insidious manifestations of its spiritual application translated into political terms. Once we accept salvation as a *fait accompli,* which, by definition, characterizes the true Elect, we can move on to more growth oriented modes, and thus gain the maturity that includes meekness and humility. That reflects one of life's great ironies: we must be empowered to be meek. Actually, that's quite consistent: after all, it takes a great deal more courage to turn the other cheek that to strike back just as it takes great strength to be genuinely gentle. Once we accept praising God for His mercy, rather than seeking our salvation by our own efforts, meekness comes a good deal more naturally and reasonably. With that comes an equally natural disinclination toward the things, values and virtues associated with the earth. Constantine came to power due to such associations, and the vast majority of the world, political and ecclesiastical alike, has followed suit, often in the name of God.

Similar to the United States and the majority of her citizens, the rich man couldn't give up his material possessions for the same reason that he could not give up his illusion of righteousness. We believe America to be "special" because we want to believe it to be special, and find ourselves very hard pressed to abandon that illusion. Well we should, for it too answers the survival imperative. Threats to our most basic sense of self constitute death-threats every bit as real as their physical counterpart, and we will normally react to them in a very similar fashion. Yet, think about it. The American version of this divine election alchemically turns patriotism into a Christian virtue, much as we'd expect from a devotion to a warrior emperor, quite consistent with the militantism we find as an ever more prominent characteristic of our global society even among "Christians". Given that money is power, can we call it coincidental that the military-industrial complex is one of the nation's most lucrative industries? Can it then surprise us that they define that American election in such terms? Can it surprise us to find the majority of the Christian community at least tacitly supporting that Elite? No wonder we call Christian sects *"denominations"*—the same term used for differing monetary amounts.

A good deal of what some call American Exceptionalism (see above) derives from the earliest explorers' efforts to "convert" the savage indigents, while robbing them blind in the process. Starting with Columbus, whose "Day" we celebrate every year, we find a very long list of cruel, greedy despots paying no vague attention to human rights (and often not even considering their victims human at all), all in the name of God or, at least, of the Church. Our Westward Expansion followed much the same pattern in a long string of broken treaties and promises to the Native Americans. Although our history usually glosses over most of these malefactions, they nevertheless leave traces of racial guilt which, rather than acknowledging, we try to justify with exaggerated estimations of our own worthiness and relationship to the Divine. All of this has the survival imperative at its root: we lie to ourselves to maintain the illusions of righteousness which have become the social adhesive holding American society together. That of course militates against the requisite humility before the Father which allows for the incongruity of claiming Christianity and "proud to be an American" in the same breath. The *Mark of the Beast* incorporates survival in the physical and the fiscal sense, and sure enough we find both well represented in our historic conquest of the continent. We likewise find them well represented in our contemporary military forays, fueled by the same sense of "divine" purpose. No wonder we've come to see that purpose as spreading the ideals of Antichrist to the world as a global ideal! Constantine's capital has been revealed, and with it the site of Babylon the Great!

A recent poll revealed that 92% of Americans believe in some sort of "higher power," usually called "God," so many at least desire to find the right path. But *false prophets and teachers* have long deluded many, and the deceived do not recognize the deception. We like to think of freedom as a blessing, and in a sense it is: no one can rightfully prohibit us from seeking the Truth for ourselves, although a great many subtle forces militate against doing so. Yet the greatest single enemy of that Truth is inherent in our very society and government: *self-determination!* As an example, only recently (late 2010) President Obama, answering his critics, maintained that he was a Christian "by choice." Those two words sum up religious freedom and the Great Apostasy at the same time. They cast self-determination—freedom of choice—as the essence of Christianity and, by extension, the essence of salvation. That casts us as the essence of salvation is about as clear an example of self-deification as one might desire. Ironically, that same freedom gives us no excuse for not seeking the Truth, and suddenly the secularization of American society takes on a considerably darker complexion as an epitomization of *economy's* two definitions. Suddenly too, the role played by diversions in our society reveal their true intent. As we've mentioned, religious freedom also reflects the freedom to ignore God's call when it comes, which, in turn, reflects our desire for the freedom to sin which we find carefully nurtured by those same subtle forces. It also helps to explain the reason behind the ever increasing appeals to both pleasures and concerns of the world that keep us so preoccupied that the Word of God gets squeezed out of our consciousness. Those blessed with the appropriate means of perception gradually come to see sin as a matter of spirit and largely a matter of our relationship to the things of the earth, both tangible and intangible. Chief among them we find patriotism, love of the world and, most of all, love of life. The first two relate directly to Constantine, the latter to the deity he venerated. Constantine remained a pagan until his death bed baptism.

We can find another link to the *Synagogue of Satan* in this warrior emperor which has likewise filtered down through the ages. The Jews proclaimed that they had *no king but Caesar*, thereby rejecting Christ as their king. Obviously we as a nation have done the same thing. At the same time, they rejected His principles and, more importantly, His re-definition of man's relationship to the Father. As a nation, we have done that as well; religious freedom allows us to define that relationship for ourselves. Most of them did so because they had expected a militant Messiah come to right wrongs and dispense justice and to overcome evil just as they had always done under God's directives and guidance. Most of the world, including the world's most prominent antagonists, the United States and her Islamic foes, seek to do the same. As epitomized by the man seeking eternal life, and as with contemporary America, the Jews in general also found it impossible to relinquish their favored traditional relationship to the Almighty. Christians adopted Constantine as their spiritual leader who fulfilled that Jewish Messianic vision, establishing good vs. evil as Christianity's primary principle. At the same time, it established justice rather than mercy as that primary principle which allowed for many paths to salvation all based on the human spirit and will. In essence, they proclaimed that they had no king but Constantine, even as we do now when we follow in his footsteps, for we can serve but one master. A warrior emperor usurping the position of the Prince of Peace: how clear a mirror-image do we need? How clear a definition of Antichrist do we need? Following in his footsteps has led to a world evermore characterized by fear and hatred. By contrast, by Christ's new definition, the Law, judgment, even justice are all wrapped up in a single word: *Love.* Think about it: if the issue were good vs. evil, and if warrior virtues were actually Christian virtues, Christ's followers would be obliged to combat Satan and his self-evident servants in a mold very similar to what the Jews expected and in much the manner as we now see in patriotic Christians obliged to battle God's enemies wherever they may find them. If we don't accept Christ as He is—the Humble Servant—and follow His lead—humility and meekness—then we'll find ourselves on the receiving end of God's wrath just as did His foes throughout the Old Testament—and just as will Satan and his angelic servants. Then we'll find out who the Conquering King is, what purpose He means to serve, and, perhaps most important of all, *when* He means to serve it. By that time, the definition of justice will revert to its original, and woe unto those who have not accepted the free gift of Grace by then. Germane to that acceptance, woe unto those who have not demonstrated that Grace, for forgiving those who trespass against us is integral to the *faith with works* James exhorts us to exhibit.

Justice relates directly to good vs. evil and, more importantly, to the Law of the Old Covenant. Yet more and more, even from within the Christian community, we hear strident calls for revenge for 9/11, including the burning or desecration of the Islamic holy book, the Koran, by alleged ministers of Christ—more accurately defined as ministers of darkness. Yet, while it's easy and very tempting to condemn such extreme examples, the rest of the Christian community is not free from fault, especially in terms of divine Truth. Think about it: while many Christian leaders deplore such actions, all that gets reported in the mainstream press are arguments over how counterproductive it would prove, and how it would damage America's war efforts and general relationship to Middle Eastern nations. Religion and politics merge still again. Indicative of just how universal the good vs. evil myth has grown both politically and ecclesiastically, nowhere, again at least not in the media, do we hear Christians decrying the fact that such hatred reflects the exact opposite of what Christ's religion is all about! By definition that makes such hatred Antichrist, but we hear not a word about that, for Truth has been devalued even among its most high profile advocates. Where is the forgiveness against those who trespassed against us? Where is the mercy? Where is the unconditional love central to Christ's teachings? A nation united by the human spirit reflects a national religion united by the human spirit. By contrast, the Spirit of Truth does not lead us to avenge ourselves. He does not lead us to combat evil any more than the embodiment of that Truth did. Neither does He approve of standing up for our rights or protecting ourselves, or our loved ones, again as exemplified by the Son of God and His chief representatives including the martyrs. All of these things are common to the *natural man*, to the pagans and reflect values and virtues shared by virtually everyone on earth. If we have truly died to our lives in the earth to find our new lives in Christ, then those values no longer matter, and we can actually see the wisdom of letting them go. Those who walk after the flesh can never hope to see that. Our way of life is our faith enacted and it is the surest sign of under which God we are truly on nation.

Even as the post-Reformation European states they'd left behind had adopted various denominations as "national religions", so the early American settlers also established their communities as mini-theocracies, often just as militantly exclusive as the states they'd left behind. We can, of course, find a Biblical precedent for that sort of thing. A good deal of evidence suggests that post-Apostolic communities were extremely exclusive, (although not militant) much as the Jews had remained largely removed from the rest of the world. There is, however, a very basic difference: an unrighteous tree cannot produce righteous fruit, and, best of intentions notwithstanding, the Puritans and their kin attempted to establish a Godly nation founded on self-determination. Although self-determination didn't start with the Reformation—and, ironically, should have been the most basic thing about the Catholic Church to be resisted—its legitimization of self-determination, with rebelliousness a divinely sanctioned tool, was its the most significant fruit, at least from the American perspective. Perhaps still more pertinent, Constantine saved both Empire and Church by defeating physical evil thereby creating a unity of belief based on military might in something of an echo of "United we stand" in the wake of 9/11.

Some make a special point of using Christ's famous *encounter with the moneychangers* (see Mark, chapter 11) as a justification for using force in the name of good. But look more closely. Christ overturned their tables and drove them from the temple, and would not allow any vessel to be carried through the it, but *that's all He did*—He neither pursued nor punished them. Why? Because they had served to make a point. *"And He taught, saying unto them, 'Is it not written, My House shall be called of all nations the house of prayer?[48] But ye have made it a den of thieves'"*—Mark 15:16. Ironically, this *"den of thieves"* actually pursued a socially accepted livelihood: selling small animals to be used in sacrificial rituals and exchanging engraved Roman coins for unadorned coins acceptable to the temple. Symbolically, therein lies the problem: they attempted to earn what must be freely given and freely accepted. After He had chased them from the temple, He alone remained—which is exactly the preferred state of our introcosmic body temples, for He is the ultimate sacrifice which we do not and cannot earn or buy. *"Verily, verily, I say unto you, he that entereth not by the door into the sheepfold, but climbeth up some other way, the same is a thief and a robber'"*—John 10:1.

---

[48] Ironically enough, that's exactly what the word "mosque" means.

He goes on to describe Himself as the Good Shepherd, and as the gate to the sheepfold. Perhaps as importantly, He also describes Himself as the voice to whom His sheep respond—and that *they flee from any other voice.*

Again, that defines the evil we should fear as Anti-Truth. Which voice did the American colonists heed? They sought to deliver themselves from the evils of poverty and the religious persecution running rampant in Europe. As we'll see a bit later, it's no coincidence that the two meanings of *economy* merged in this nation's nascence. For now, consider that their flight from evil mirrored their endeavors to worship God, and still made them subject to the real evil of Anti-Truth. Worshipping God in the flesh left that worship open to political control which meant that no one could worship God without the political freedom to do so. We find this echoed all over the world today, and again we can find an important differentiation between true Christianity and most other faiths. The vast majority of the world's religions require some sort of physical freedom, and that makes them subject to political control and repression. By contrast, true Christianity is an internal religion, where we worship God in our *hearts*, regardless of where we find our bodies. This religious internalization frees us from political constraints, threats and oppressions, just as we'd expect from a religion exhorting us to eschew the physical in general. Consider the subtle double-reverse involved. We thus made eternal salvation subject to political control in much the same way as did the caeseropapism instituted by Constantine and continued by the Papacy. No wonder political freedom has grown into such a holy issue more and more liberally comingled with religion! In essence, salvation becomes at least as much a political issue as a spiritual issue, just as the cessation of Christian persecution and the eventual acceptance of Christianity as Rome's state religion had been. Due to that, the backlash created by his authoritarianism (and that of both Church and state thereafter), ultimately lent a pseudo divine sanction to both freedoms and, in the process, made defying Christ's commands a virtue. Self-determination came to full fruition, with freedom of choice at the focal point.

Since we thus saw self-determination as a major influence spiritually, can we wonder that we likewise saw it as an appropriate form of government? Our governmental form is our religion enacted. Our efforts to deliver ourselves from evil ended up delivering us to it instead, but few of us noticed, and fewer still cared. The deceived do not recognize the deception, especially when they seek to believe what they want to believe. Yet, the deception is really rather obvious. We've noted that democracy is a very strange governmental form to come from those looking to nature as their guide since social animals usually follow a very rigid hierarchy. We did however take one important element from our natural cynosure. Those hierarchies are always determined by strength which we translated into "right makes might". But, since we believe that good always eventually wins out over evil, we have since reversed that to *might makes right*—exactly the attitude social animals would take were they capable of it. We humans are different in one significant way, however. We noted earlier, however, that animals are incapable of breaking the First Commandment. Consistently, we humans have long since realized that true earthly power resides not in arms but in lucre. *"Whoever controls the volume of money in any country,"* James A. Garfield observed, *"is absolute master of all industry and commerce."* We can then conclude that right makes rich—the foundation for our prosperity-righteousness co-equation, and a reflection of the Jewish tradition reflected in the rich man cited above. Again we find a connection to the *Synagogue of Satan.* That also adds a pseudo-divine justification for the empowerment of the wealthy Elite on the assumption of their inherent moral superiority, leading America from democracy to plutocracy in the name of good vs. evil while simultaneously making duplicity an inherent part of our national identity. We end up linking LOM to righteousness, and it is largely on that basis that we assume ourselves the moral guardians of the earth. *"'Ye are of your father the devil, and the lust of your father ye will do'"*—John 8:44. We believe what we want to believe and end up serving the god of the earth.

While the Civil War officially unified the nation—only after the War did we commonly refer to the United States in the singular—what kept America from splintering into a European-style patchwork in the first place? If it wasn't Christianity that unified the colonies, and, indeed, Christianity was largely responsible for the initial fragmentation, then what did? More pertinent to our title question, if our governmental form is our religion enacted, and if that unity didn't found on Christianity as many like to believe, then on which god did it found? Here we find the most self-evident answer to our title question. For, in spite of considerable rancor over doctrinal differences (especially between Protestants and Catholics), the colonies saw no problem with *trading* with each other. While at first each colony had its own script, which meant that they took "trading" quite literally, the Colonies' eventual issuance of their own money was a major factor in American unification, and England's denial of that right a major reason for the Revolution. Consider that carefully. The two meanings of economy merge in this nation's very foundation. That makes *the things of the earth*, with money per se one of the most major of those things, what actually united us in spite of the overt spirituality involved in our inception. Think about it. Given the competing doctrines characterizing it, that overt spirituality was defined by the same kind of value addition that we find in LOM's more conventional applications. Each sect had derived its doctrine in the same manner: it added value to certain spiritual precepts, took it away from others until it created a blend that suited it.[49] We see that same pattern repeated today: we will trade with pretty nearly anyone promising a sufficiently lucrative market, regardless of considerations we normally use to maintain our aura of moral superiority, including the most all-inclusive: human rights. Again we find that hypocrisy characteristic of the Pharisees an inherent element of our national character.

"A mere lover of silver will not be satisfied with silver, neither any lover of wealth with income"—Ecclesiastes 5:10. As does power, wealth always seeks to enhance itself. The two definitions of economy merge again in that we also largely measure our

---

[49]   We don't mean to be flippant about it. No doubt those devising doctrine thought they were doing God's will—and may have been. *All things work for the good to those called to God's purposes.*

progress in terms of our self-assessed efficacy, including our power to create wealth. *"But thou shalt remembereth the Lord thy God: for it is He that giveth thee power to get wealth, that He may establish His covenant which He sware unto thy fathers, as it is this day.*—Deuteronomy 8:18. Paul refrains essentially the same sentiment in I Timothy 6:17: *"Charge them that are rich in this world that they should be not highminded, nor trust in uncertain riches, but in the living God, who giveth us richly all things to enjoy."* In direct contrast, we commonly maintain that man's *reason* has enabled us to acquire our wealth even as it has elevated us above the other creatures. But we take the apostasy a step further. We conclude that reason alone cannot account for either that wealth or for what we take as human progress. We have also *freed the human spirit* to soar as high as the individual can take it, in service to none but its own interests. Just as we seek freedom from God's authority and from the Truth embodied in His Son, so we seek freedom from the Holy Spirit, replacing Him with our own.

We are indeed one nation under god, but that god is *Mammon*. Think about it. That revolution we so gaily celebrate every July 4th—inevitably accompanied by a wide variety of "sales events"—reflects the dichotomy between the things of heaven and the things of the earth at this nation's very foundation. Our whole revolution against Great Britain, and so against God, focused on the riches this new land had to offer. Those same riches also provided us with the impetus to enact the Monroe Doctrine, and our Destiny soon Manifested itself in the arrogation of whatever lands suited our lust for worldly things regardless of the moral cost or the human rights of those already occupying them. What else might we expect from the human spirit dedicated to Nature's God and the belief that might makes right? That Destiny continues to Manifest itself in our military presence in well over one hundred nations worldwide, all geared toward essentially the same goal, now on a global rather than continental scale. Our governmental form is our religion enacted. Rather than the change in nature central to Christianity, Nature's God mandates that we act in accordance *with* our basic natures, and that natural impulse drives us to conquer and dominate, while my will be done forces us to try to mold the world to fit our own image. Since the *natural man* can't please God, we seldom even give it any thought, and seek to please ourselves instead. Ironic, isn't it. That same freeing of the human spirit that we so loudly laud has created a plutocratic Elite that simply continues to aggrandize more of the nation's wealth and more authority by the year. Moreover, it has done so largely by emphasizing that aforementioned dichotomy of *fearing man rather than fearing God*—i.e., by way of appealing directly to the survival imperative. Again, the two meanings of economy merge, and we should seriously ponder whose spiritual economy we follow as a nation. To whom do we all but universally react, the Son of God as presented in the New Testament, or a warrior emperor elevated to His position as the precursor to His "Vicar"? No wonder the President could so comfortably praise the Pope.

To accept Christ's Truth and to thereby become Christian, ultimately means that we divorce ourselves from the concerns of the earth, and set our hearts, minds, and lives on the pursuit of heavenly things, although even the most pious among us choose in favor earthly things far more often than we should. Still, we find ourselves with an increasing desire for heavenly things as we mature in our knowledge, understanding of and lives in the Truth. *"But godliness with contentment is great gain. For we brought nothing into this world, and it is certain that we carry nothing out. And having food and raiment let us be therewith content"*—I Timothy 6:6-8. Does that sound like something that would appeal to the average American? What does that suggest about our whole notion of progress? Take that a step further. Given our dependence on consumption, would we not have to consider such an attitude not only unpatriotic, but as a threat to the national security? Think about it: our entire global economy, not to mention our most basic perception of progress, founds on *discontent*, and the commensurate desire for products—the things of the earth—to satisfy it. In short, we have made covetousness and deliberately manufactured discontent essential to our social and economic survival in response to economic laws that no one fully understands, no one mandates, no one can control but from which no one can escape. What does that suggest about the concepts of freedom and self-determination?

We find a very similar discontent at the roots of our Revolution. Much of that discontent could and should rightfully have been aimed at the colonial Elite, but they managed to refocus it on the British. Fittingly, we find elitism in this nation's more formal foundation as well. A small handful of Eastern Seaboard intellectuals, all from the upper class, all well schooled in the classics and far removed from the people they set out to rule, assiduously studied numerous political philosophies, both modern and arcane, in their efforts to distill American democracy. They made no bones about this country being founded on reason and man's wisdom: as we've noted, they actively disclaimed any "interviews with the gods" or "inspiration from heaven". Even at that, we do not mean to vilify or demean them. Indeed, in a scholarly sense we can find much to admire about them. From their point of view, they did the best they could to free mankind from the shackles of superstition and fear that had dominated the world for countless centuries. In other words, they did their best to deliver mankind from their vision of evil, and therein lies the point. As held true for the Reformation, and presented in far clearer terms here, turning from an overt evil does not necessarily mean that we've turned toward God. In our case it didn't even mean that we intended to turn toward God. Sometimes, again as in America's case, it can mean the opposite. We may turn toward relative goodness, but that doesn't mean that we've turned toward righteousness, but the *natural man* can never hope to understand that, or to even care. Still, we may judge by fruits.

For example: despite the respect due the Founding Fathers' scholarship, it's hard to overlook the duplicity inherent in the formation process itself. Consider: while the Founders studied, most Americans had no knowledge of or relationship to the esoteric thinkers who would guide their lives and those of their children. Dare we deem it coincidental that this relationship is an exact mirror-image of a country of, by and for the people? But has that description ever reflected reality? In fact, hasn't the government actually reflected those elitist roots ever since?

As held true for Constantine, however, it's hard to argue with success. For more than a century America has enjoyed an unprecedented international prestige, and for over twenty years has likewise adopted the mantle of the world's only true superpower. But, observe that our government continues to find deception increasingly necessary to maintain our way of life, and that applies as much domestically as internationally. Does it seem consistent with a foundation of divine Truth such as taking Christianity as our spiritual basis implies? Didn't Christ say, *"But let your communication be Yea, yea, Nay, nay: for whatsoever is more than these cometh of evil [the evil one]"*—Matthew 5:37? If we associate deception with our survival, that makes skillful lying a good, just as we see in our entertainment industry. We *call evil good* just as the prophet foresaw (see above). Perhaps we should seriously consider those deceptions a diversion.

A diversion from what? Let us again pose our Basic Question, who do we serve, bearing in mind that our political system is our religion enacted. Largely as a result, how many of us consider *absolute truth* even ascertainable, much less vital—or give it any thought at all? Science doesn't claim to have it, and most scientists would doubtlessly claim it impossible to ever attain, if it even exists, the ever elusive "quantum theory" notwithstanding. If we don't think it's possible to ascertain it, wonder about its applicability to life, and even doubt its very existence, we won't likely seek it, and that's exactly what Satan counts on. Complacency, a close relative to indifference (see above), is one of his chief allies, and one of our deadliest enemies. Think about it. One characteristic underlies virtually all of Christ's teachings and those of His Apostles: *Passion!* Just as a casual "belief in God" will prove inadequate, so a lukewarm devotion to Christ proves likewise futile. Thus, a lukewarm devotion to His Truth avails nothing. Consider Revelations 3;15-18 and how it applies to contemporary America: *"I know thy works, that thou art neither cold nor hot: I would thou wert cold or hot. So then because thou art lukewarm, and neither cold nor hot, I will spue thee out of My mouth. Because thou sayest, I am rich, and increased with goods, and have need of nothing; and knowest not that thou art wretched, and miserable, and poor, and blind, and naked: I counsel thee to buy of me gold tried in the fire that thou mayest be rich; and which raiment, that thou mayest be clothed, and that the shame of thy nakedness do not appear; and anoint thin eyes with eyesalve, that thou mayest see."'*

We must bear in mind always that in our unchanged states, not only do we have no inherent love of the Truth, but have a commensurate love of (and desire for) Anti-Truth, and herein we find one of Satan's most subtle and successful deceptions. A lukewarm love reflects the "Christianity by choice" Mr. Obama alluded to above, which reflects those *"having a form of Godliness, but denying the power thereof"* (II Timothy 3:5)—from whom he emphatically exhorts us to *"turn away."* Since Christ is both the *Truth* and the *Life*, that in turn implies a commensurate love of and desire for *death.* Think about that very carefully. In our unchanged state, we naturally desire damnation![50] Christianity is not confined to Sunday mornings or a specific set of rituals, rites and incantations. It's quite literally a way of life. Since to *be carnally minded is death*, we can equate carnal mindedness with Anti-Truth. Carnal mindedness is therefore something against which we must guard—bear in mind that the Spirit War is an *internal* conflict, with the heart and mind the battleground. Suddenly, our complacent obsession with worldly concerns takes on a considerably darker and more deceptive shade since we can no longer limit it to the tangible. Even as LOM concerns money but is not limited to it, so worldly concerns include materialism, but also go beyond them. For one thing, it also subsumes physical perception and the conclusions we draw from it. "Nature's God" teaches that we can learn all things by way of a close study of nature. Consider that carefully. That means that virtually all that the modern world holds as true stems from perception characteristic of the *carnally minded* who cannot please God! That means that we almost universally take that perception as our foundation for truth.

A diversion is worthless unless it's realistic. As a nation, we substituted self-evident truth for divine Truth, and we can

---

[50]   We tell ourselves as much all the time. When showing amazement at some unexpected occurrence, we'll often say, "Well I'll be damned!"

readily take all the techno-wonders we've created since as evidence of its veracity. But, consider: we attain those wonders by overcoming nature in the technical sense just as we attain it socially by overcoming the "superstitions" contained in the Bible. But even that's only the surface. For, along with overcoming those superstitious Biblical truths, we must likewise take secrets that we reveal for ourselves as superior to secrets revealed by the Almighty. Do you see the parallel between divine revelation and excogitated doctrine? Isn't that a logical consequence of wishing to overcome God's authority, the true but unstated end of self-determination? Christ *established His church on divine revelation* (see above); we have established our nation on the exact opposite just as have the vast majority of Christian denominations. Doesn't that, by definition, make both the foundation and the structure Antichrist? Consider what this means: apostate religion and agnostic science lead to the same goal: overthrowing God's Truth—or, more specifically, a passionate love of a Truth that often cannot be proven or empirically demonstrated. In other words, it attacks love and faith at the same time. It likewise seeks to overthrow the authority derived from divinely revealed Truth and granting the resultant authority to ourselves. Doesn't that describe a spiritual *coup* with the intention of replacing God with ourselves? Yet, in the most fundamental sense, that's how we define progress, with countless signs to support our conclusion and so to support the illusion of human wisdom! We can say the same ecclesiastically: man-derived doctrine which allows people to "come unto the Lord" based on secrets we reveal for ourselves largely accounts for Christianity's burgeoning ranks. Talk about *strong delusions!*

Arbitrary efforts notwithstanding, we cannot truly separate the physical from the spiritual, for every physical act has a spiritual root: we must serve one master or the other, and while we're in the world that service will reflect in the world. Thus, our quest to overcome physical nature, with the obvious goal of eventually learning all of nature's secrets thereby transcending its power, has a spiritual correlative. Think about it: just as we seek to transcend nature's dominion, so we seek to transcend God's constraints placed on salvation, thereby freeing ourselves from

His dominion as well. But it goes further than that. By holding my will be done as our ideal, we seek not only to transcend God, but to *replace* Him, just as Satan has sought to do all along. Doesn't that therefore cast *self-deification* as the unstated goal of our "progress"? Isn't to be *"as gods"* one of the primary sales pitches the Serpent used on Eve? (See Genesis 3:5). In a similar sense, by believing that we can save others and ourselves, by replacing the Holy Spirit with the human spirit, we will eventually attain the godhead itself. Isn't that also what Satan has long yearned to do? Doesn't that sound like a pretty accurate definition of blasphemy? Isn't that the spiritual foundation of this one nation under God?

If we claim ourselves one nation under God or, worse still, claim that we accept "Jesus" as our king as per the Ashcroft quote, and at the same time advocate religious freedom that, by definition, allows for other gods, does that not qualify as hypocrisy? Christianity is not Christianity without Christ: a "belief in God" does not suffice! *"'Thou shalt worship the Lord thy God, and Him only shalt thou serve'"*—Luke 4:8. Given that Christ also said, *"'Put up thy sword into his place: for all that take the sword shall perish with the sword'"* in Matthew 26:52, we may safely assume that we do not serve Him or His Father by way of warfare or any other kind of physical conflict. By contrast, given LOM at this nation's roots, it's no coincidence that the military-industrial complex exerts predominant influence over our national decisions. Nor is it coincidental that warfare proves enormously profitable. The two economies merge: our beloved national security ultimately comes down to a matter of dollars and cents. According to Reuters, 10/02/10, while the United States has only about 5% of the world's population, it spends 46.5% of the global expenditure on defense. By the time we figure in the number of people employed in related industries we find this nation, purportedly dedicated to peace, is in fact utterly dependent on war. We were born of war; what other fruit could we logically expect to harvest? Still, it poses the question of which "Jesus" Mr. Ashcroft had in mind. *"Peace I leave with you, My peace I give unto you: not as the world giveth give I unto you. Let your heart not be troubled, neither let it be afraid'"*—John 14:27.

But more tellingly, the master deceiver has changed this into a matter of desire just as he did with Eve in the Garden! As with WWII, we chose to see our Revolutionary victory as an example of God's approval of our course, and our successes over the next century or so offered no reason to believe otherwise. Do you see the parallel to Constantine and the Church's reasons for elevating him to its head? No wonder we share the same virtues. Notice the role played by unity, and political survival in each case. We can find more parallels as well, especially in the Church's subsequent aggrandizement of lands and peoples in its pseudo righteous efforts to bring the globe into the Catholic fold. As early as 1823, James Monroe had come up with his *Monroe Doctrine*, stating that he saw American dominion over North America as a divine mandate. In 1845, a journalist named John Louis O'Sullivan writing in the *Democratic Review*, advocating the annexation of Texas, called it, "... *the fulfillment of our manifest destiny to overspread the continent allotted by Providence for the free development of our yearly multiplying millions."* The term caught on, and soon we used it to validate many other shows of strength and avarice far removed from the Southwest. Note that "Providence" when capitalized means, "God perceived as a caring force guiding humanity"—conveniently differing from the detached Prime Mover held by deism, and just as conveniently removed from any mention of Christ or His examples, teachings and commandments. Given that, we must pose some disturbing questions. Which god would sanction the slaughter of the Native Americans, the arrogation (theft) of their lands, the wanton decimation of their food supply, the destruction of their way of life, and their deracination to land so barren that no one else wanted it, followed by sending them missionaries to teach them the gospel of love? *"Yea, a man may say, Thou hast faith and I have works: shew me thy faith without thy works, and I will shew thee my faith by my works"*—James 2:18. Our way of life is our faith enacted. What faith did our actions enact?

For nearly two centuries we believed what we wanted to believe thinking that we pleased God. In retrospect it can prove difficult to accept that we could so delude ourselves and still call ourselves Christian. Yet it can prove difficult to believe that the German people were so deluded by Hitler too, but it happened. Might we not expect a similar force involved in both instances?

Chapter Six

We have noted a number of mirror-images throughout this work. Consider an especially ironic one directly related to our way of life as our faith enacted. Christians are called upon to act as the *light of the world,* which is just what the Statue of Liberty is supposed to symbolize. Indeed, the statue's official name is "Lady Enlightening the World." However, in spite of America's "Christian" origins, she sheds the "anti-light" of freedom from Christ, His teachings His examples and, ultimately, His Father. *"Who is a liar but he that denieth that Jesus is the Christ? He is antichrist, that denieth the Father and the Son"*—I John 2:22. Do not countless millions see her as a symbol of religious freedom granting them the liberty to do just that? She also symbolizes delivering ourselves from evil in that millions have visualized her as their goal of escaping persecution, dominance, poverty and so forth. Most of all, she symbolizes the essence of democracy and of unrighteousness: my will vs. Thy will be done. Given what we've discussed, especially including the quoted verse, doesn't that quite literally make her a symbol of *Antichrist?* Think about it: does she represent the *Truth that Christ said would make us free* in John 8:32? Doesn't she instead quite specifically represent "truths we hold as self-evident"? Does she represent the *Way* that Christ embodied? Or does she represent a way of life devoted to the things of the earth and the lusts of the flesh? Does she symbolize the all-consuming love of God that fulfills His Law, or does she symbolize LOM? Our political system is our religion enacted.

If Satan can get us to serve two masters, he's won, and that is just what he has accomplished in this one nation under God. We try to serve both God and Mammon, glorying in our material prosperity and constantly seeking to enhance it as our national purpose in life while still paying lip service to the broadest possible definition of "God." Freedom from God's authority initiates a concatenation of consequences both political and ecclesiastical that begins and ends in freedom from the divine Truth embodied in His Son. It automatically subsumes freedom from His Son's authority, and so freedom from the Grace His sacrifice yielded. No wonder we spend so much time, effort, and money of endeavors to deliver ourselves from evil. Again by definition, that puts us in the *Synagogue of Satan*, fully subject to the Law in its minutest detail. *"For whosoever shall keep the whole Law, and yet offend in one point, he is guilty of all"*—James 2;10. Accepting that Grace and God's authority embodied in Christ comprise the same deal: we cannot accept the one without the other. Strictly speaking we are not saved by Christ's sacrifice itself but by the reason for it: we are saved as a result of God's will that mandated that sacrifice just as we, like Christ, are saved by God's mercy manifested in that will. If you think about it, God's mercy saving us from perdition and that same mercy delivering us from evil have a great deal in common. Yet accepting that is in diametric opposition to the whole concept of self-determination which the Lady in New York Harbor symbolizes.

By the mid-19th Century, the vast majority of new immigrants came to the Northern states where they thought they could most realistically hope to find a better life. For most, it didn't work out that way. Far from streets paved with gold they'd imagined, most newcomers found streets lined with tenements. Many found squalid conditions, and blatant exploitation not greatly superior to what they'd fled in their homelands. Especially Italians and Irish, but including pretty nearly everyone at one time or another, they likewise found a good deal of prejudice and bigotry. As a result, rather than a "melting pot," the country quickly resolved into a patchwork quilt of ethnic types clustering together in specific geographic areas for mutual support and comfort. The Industrial Revolution, a key element in that golden illusion, rather than making life easier, accelerated this trend as it displaced former farm workers, and country dwellers and crammed them into cities ill-equipped to deal with such an influx. At the same time, the country rapidly moved from an agrarian to an industrial base, and this too had many repercussions not immediately self-evident. But, of all the self-evident issues involved in the American Civil War—saving the Union itself, abolishing slavery, issues over states' rights and so on—the most important remains virtually unnoted. For it was during this conflict that America clearly identified the deity under whom it would henceforth unabashedly unite, and which would unequivocally guide its national destiny from that point on. The seeds planted at our national nascence came to fruition.

Arguments still rage over just why we fought that bloody conflict but, as important as the other issues may have been, at least in the common perception, the issue of slavery gave the war its deep moral aura. The North, the "good" in most people's minds at least in retrospect, found the abandonment of slavery relatively painless largely because it never had nearly the financial investment in it that the South had. Instead, it had the aforementioned influx of migrant workers who could be treated as slaves with only a modest expenditure, much of which it recouped by way of "Company Towns" and suchlike. The Confederacy, on the other hand, fought for a familiar reason: to protect its way of life. Again we deal in generalities. In fact, the South had its Elite just as did the North, while the majority consisted of "poor whites" often not much better off than the black slaves. Indeed, the two groups would sometimes try to help each other. Efforts to keep them separated largely accounted for the tradition of segregation extending well into the next century.

To pretty nearly any but a Southern mind, slavery cast those Elite as evil, especially by contrast to the rest of the world, nearly all of which had already outlawed it. But despite that, we must bear in mind that Confederates, even including the cruelest slave masters, were nevertheless patriots. For that matter, so were the Nazis, the Viet Cong, the Taliban and servants of any other "rogue nation" you might like to mention. Good vs. evil inevitably leads to conflict, for we make ourselves the good by overcoming the evil. Yet in order to believe in self-determination, we must believe not only in relative goodness but also in man's ultimate perfectibility as a destination striven for, but never to be reached. In a similar sense, if we ever attained such perfection we could no longer define progress and, since a living thing cannot remain static but must either grow or wither, that presents a kind of death threat to our basic sense of racial identity. That of course brings up the question of the vehicle of that perfectibility. As noted earlier, science largely attributes human survival and progress to our reason, but reason cannot fully function without freedom.

Thus, freedom vs. slavery, the classic Civil War dichotomy, had a considerably deeper and more universal moral side than most of us acknowledge, directly related to the survival imperative. Indeed, given our governmental form as our religion enacted, the War between the States literally amounted to a holy war. Think about it. It's not uncommon among those believing in a "higher power" to define that power as *divine intelligence*. It's also not hard to see how that parallels the deistic definition of God, but it goes further than that. As holds true for our introcosmic cosmology, our internal theology—our essential concept of God and our relationship to Him—has enormous influence over our most basic self-image. If we take self-determination, aka self-deification, as our introcosmic base, then certain other beliefs and consequences must necessarily follow. Case in point. In order for us to live by good vs. evil, we must judge everything; in order to judge everything, we must *know* everything. That automatically links knowledge, and its relative, intelligence, to our most basic concepts of morality, of goodness, and, so, of God. Consistently enough, most of us believe that, as we have progressed technologically and scientifically, we have also made moral progress. It logically figures that we would conclude that. If man can determine ultimate truth for himself by way of Reason, then we should be able to devise ultimate morality by the same means. If we equate morality with goodness, and goodness with righteousness, then we can (and must) likewise attain righteousness by the same means. Suddenly we again find knowledge the key to righteousness and, so, to salvation, just as many mainstream churches maintain. That casts knowledge as the good, ignorance as the evil which helps to explain our ever increasing reliance on and demand for "intelligence" on virtually everyone and everything. Intelligence and knowledge save us politically, physically and spiritually. Thus we create a holy whole of goodness, righteousness and morality all based on reason, all ascertainable by the human mind, all attainable by the human will, all summed up in the doctrine of self-determination, and all requiring freedom as the ultimate catalyst. No wonder we believe we have a divine destiny! Thus, freedom becomes an indispensible part of our quest to replace God, just as freedom from His authority suggests, and just as Satan has yearned to do all along. One nation under *which* God?

We must believe that we move in a moral direction to give any legitimacy to our basic definition of progress, lest we see it for what it really is. But what if we dare look at it in the light of the reality expressed by the Son of God and His representatives? More and more that progress is characterized by a lust for the things of the earth utterly bereft of any semblance of the divine culminating in a progressive departure from the true God and His Truth. We seek not the God of the Bible, but the Freedom God of our own device, not divine Truth, but self-evident truth that will set us free from God's authority. It's the *Golden Calf* all over again! (See Exodus, chapter 32). Again consider Ephesians 4:17-18:*"This I say therefore, and testify in the Lord, that ye henceforth walk not as other Gentiles walk, in the vanity of their mind, having the understanding darkened, being alienated from the life of God through the ignorance that is in them, because of the blindness of their heart"*. What would we expect from "anti-light" but darkness of understanding? What else might we expect from the anti-light of freedom from God's authority symbolized by the sculptor's mistress enshrined in New York Harbor replete with numerous pagan symbols? In a symbolic and literal sense, it stands for unfaithfulness, quite appropriate to the covetousness of the nation it represents.[51]

In a way, the intellectual Founders themselves embodied the deity defined as divine intelligence they envisioned. Consider: by the academic manner in which they derived our governmental system, we could rightfully refer to that Creator as Reason, and Reason dictated that we cannot have justice for some without justice for all. Much of our national legislation had fallen very short in that regard, but rather than holding Reason per se to

---

[51] To be fair, some sources cite the model as actually two: the sculptor's mistress and his mother.

blame, we could attribute a good deal of that failure to erroneous assumptions, i.e., faulty intelligence. Upon their initial discovery, for example, theological arguments arose over whether "Indians" were human at all, and for many years doubts remained as to whether they qualified as God's children. In a similar sense, slaves were not regarded as human. For that reason, they remained outside the law's protection and could expect no justice. Legislators of conscience could not avoid seeing this as a blatant contradiction to the principles the nation's Founders had envisioned. Notice, however, the subtle sleight of hand. We reacted not to Biblical God nor to His Son, but to the Goddess Reason, and our own inherent goodness. Goodness emphasizes what we obey; righteousness emphasizes *whom* we obey, and that which we obey reflects that which we take as our paramount authority. By definition, that which we take as that authority is that which we take as our deity. Self-determination amounts to self-deification, with human reason the deity in question.

We had good reason to believe so. Especially in the North, Reason had already shown her industrious side, but with the freeing of the slaves, she showed an unanticipated moral side as well. On the basis of physical perception we had more than adequate evidence to conclude that reason combined with freedom was both beneficent, and moral and, especially given the connection between righteousness and prosperity, the decades following the War gave us little reason to believe otherwise. Between the War's conclusion and the end of the century, for example, we issued more patents than in the rest of our history up to that point put together, and that pace simply continued to accelerate. As if to demonstrate what the freed human spirit could accomplish, America quickly became the global focal point of innovation and invention, and great wealth inevitably followed. Given that, how could anyone of the *carnal mind* seriously question that we had found the right means, the right path to final human perfection as a process rather than a destination led by the holy tandem of Liberty and Reason? As her official title implied, Lady Liberty's light stood not only for freedom but for enlightenment: the veritable definition of the way that seems right. Ironically, to *enlighten* means to "teach religious beliefs to an unbeliever" (Encarta). Yet, in a very real sense that's just what she did. Think about it. How could we not take the Freedom God, and its newly discovered favorite daughter, the Goddess Reason, as *the* God in essentially the same manner as had Constantine and his advocates? Had Reason not unified the nation and brought to it glory unknown since the Roman Empire? How could we not see the spread of this blended political and religious doctrine to the rest of the world as a Godly thing to do much as had the Church? If that were the case, why limit *Manifest Destiny* to just North America? How could we not take this "terrible swift sword" and use it in God's name wherever we found His enemies? Appropriate to a sense of divine destiny, America cast herself as a kind of secular Moses, seeking to set free those in shackles wherever she found them. After all, if God blessed us with our freedom, then His enemies had to be those who withheld or resisted that freedom. To be against America was to be against God! The American national identity defined in the Revolution had fully crystallized; LOM had superseded love of God and our military-industrial complex had found a divine justification.

While that complex found its place in the Spanish American War and WWI, World War II was the planet's first fully mechanized conflict, and it was then that Reason came into full bloom. For, along with our own reason we leaned ever more heavily on our own wisdom, the two of them constituting the truths we take as self-evident, with life itself the most self-evident of all. In light of that, let us again pose a previous question: if the death of *das Fuehrer* could have prevented the multiple millions who would die as a result of his egomania, not to mention the other millions of lives that would be horribly disrupted, not to mention the billions of dollars worth of damage, could we not justify it on those grounds alone? Human wisdom founded on good vs. evil makes the choice self-evident to virtually everyone, but *that which is held in high esteem by man is abomination to God* (Luke 16:15). The Christian's choice is difficult but clear: we embrace physical life, or we embrace everlasting life; we can't do both, and numbers mean nothing. *"Whosoever shall seek to save his life shall lose it; and whosoever shall lose his life shall preserve it'''*—Luke 17:33, is an absolute statement just as Paul intimates in Romans 8:36: *"For Thy sake we are killed all the day long; we are accounted as sheep for the slaughter."* Again that directly links delivering ourselves from evil to defiance of the most basic Truth of them all: we are saved by God's mercy and *that alone*, and that applies equally to those evils encountered during our lives. This "Christian nation" justified that war (as with all conflicts) with survival, delivering ourselves from the self-evident evil of death, just as do our adversaries; moreover, we threaten them with death just as they do to us. Given that commonality, how do we differ ourselves from them? Given what Christ has told us, do we not thereby justify ourselves before men, being unable to do so before God? Given the virtually universal acceptance of such justifications, doesn't that still again reflect the influence of the entity having the world's kingdoms to give to whom he will? If we must serve one master or the other, and if the Founders were not under the influence of heaven during our inception, who did influence them?

Let us again pose our Basic Question: who did we serve by combating the Axis, the God of the New Covenant, or the God Life? Given our political system as our religion enacted, we could pose the same question about mainstream Christianity with its emphasis on spiritual survival attained by overcoming the evils of divers temptations, and which more often than not supports its nations' military agendas against self-defined evil-doers. The underlying principle remains the same: *the mark of the beast.* We found the same with Constantine's elevation to head of church and state, implying a direct connection between the caeseropapism coming out of that elevation, apostate Christianity's fall from divine Truth, and the religion of self-evident truth underlying America's form of government. That in turn implies a common *coup d'esprit*, with a warrior emperor taking the place of the Son of God, just as our desire for freedom from God's authority manifest in both political and ecclesiastical self-determination, as well as the bloody history of the Christian religion both suggest. That again takes us back to the *Synagogue of Satan* which pretty well answers the question of influence. Think about it. Good vs. evil belongs to the Old Covenant; as they were obliged to combat evil, we Christians are obliged to *tolerate it* just as Christ did! *"Who, when He was reviled, reviled not again; when He suffered, He threatened not; but committed Himself to Him that judgeth righteously"*—I Peter 2:23. He also says that *". . . even hereunto were ye called . . ."* (21). Consider also Luke 6:29: *"And unto him that smiteth thee on the one cheek offer also the other; and him that taketh away thy cloak forbid not to take thy coat also'".* Attacks on our persons, our sense of dignity, or our possessions all demand the same tolerant forbearance. Nowhere in the New Testament do we find anything even vaguely resembling a qualifier to those statements much less a call to arms, and for a very consistent reason. Just as we are saved by God's mercy rather than by our good deeds or obedience, so we must *show* that mercy on those who offend us. That's how we act as *the light of the world. "'Bless them that curse you, and pray for them which despitefully use you'"*—Luke 6:28. Have you ever heard of anyone praying for Adolph Hitler? How about Osama bin Laden? Saddam Hussein? How about Mahmoud Ahmadinejad?

How seriously we take such commands distinguishes the serious Christian from the social Christian. Thus, for all the complexities involved, a very simple question comes out of all this: *do we believe Him or not?* Given that the survival imperative lies at the root of all our conflicts, and given that it subsumes not only life itself but all that we associate with it, including our cherished liberties, we find ourselves facing a very basic package-deal. We pursue the things of earth or the things of heaven—*there can be no middle ground.* Choosing the middle ground amounts to trying to serve two masters and that plays right into Satan's hands by participating in his deceptions under the name of God. False teachers need not be limited to the theological. That ultimately means that we pursue the things applicable to physical life or the things applicable to eternal life, and again, there is no middle ground. That's what makes the survival imperative so significant. That's why we must abandon the flesh *and all of its concerns* in favor of heavenly pursuits if we expect our righteousness to exceed that of the Pharisees. *We worship God with our lips, but our hearts remain far from Him.*

In our natural state, we believe what we want to believe, which largely explains the appeal of self-evident truth. Although sharing the glory with our allies, much as we saw with Constantine, the resounding victory over the Axis Powers pushed America to the status of global superpower. Her self-evident truth then marched on in defiance of Christ's expressed examples and teachings, consolidating her power and glory by equating freedom with righteousness in a global effort to deliver the world from the evils of despotism. Again, dare to look beneath the surface. If we define that freedom as self-determination and religious egalitarianism, must we not define it as freedom from divine Truth and the absolute authority derived therefrom? *"He that is not with Me is against Me; and he that gathereth not with Me scatttereth abroad'"*—Matthew 12:30.Doesn't that cast us as Christ's enemies? Isn't that, by definition, Antichrist? Which do we do by way of religious freedom's acceptance of all creeds and deities? Which master do we acknowledge by demanding the right to guide our own destinies? Do we not then fight *in favor of unrighteousness*, just as we fight for a way of life centered on pursuing the things of the earth? Do we not then take Antichrist as our cause, his religion that which underpins our governmental form? If *Christ disclaims an earthly kingdom while saying that if He had one, then His followers would fight,*(John 18:36), what should we logically expect from His mirror-image? If we do fight, how do we show ourselves as subjects of that kingdom? Given the definition of those outside Christ's church as pagans, doesn't that make good vs. evil per se a primary characteristic of paganism and so of ungodliness? If we accept good vs. evil as truth, how do we Christians set ourselves apart from those pagans? The *entire world is under the sway of the Evil One*, and the entire world takes the conflict of good vs. evil as its most basic truth. Dare we deem that a coincidence? How *"highly esteemed among men"* do we want? Doesn't that define such contentions and the reasons for them as *abominations in God's sight?* Do not those engaging in such conflicts devotionally dedicate themselves to the same deity, implying the universal influence we've noted throughout this work? Doesn't the *"prince of this world,"* the *one who has the world under his influence*, the *one who has the kingdoms of the world to give to whomsoever he desires* qualify as such an influence? We either value the things of heaven or those of earth, and which we truly value will determine what we take as our virtues, and so as our basic definition of goodness. We must "live our faith" one way or the other; we must also die by it, and that applies physically and spiritually.

Ever since the Constantine *coup*, we have progressively incorporated warrior values and virtues into the Christian character in defiance of Christ's every teaching and example. Ironic, isn't it: good vs. evil is the very evil we must resist! Yet aren't those the religious roots of this country? Doesn't that also reflect the Christ Mr. Ashcroft had in mind? What virtues has this pseudo-Christianity spawned? War, retaliation, even self-defense, all require *aggression*, while Christ tells us quite specifically that *the meek shall inherit the earth.* That meekness subsumes an absolute submission to God's authority and power, even that reflected in those in power ordained by God, but the *natural man* finds that impossible to do. Perhaps the most difficult lesson to learn, the one most clearly defying human wisdom and flying in the face of the survival imperative, is that to deliver ourselves from evil *is in itself evil*, for it defies God's will.

Consider Daniel, chapter three. Three of the more famous names in the Bible, *Shadrach, Meshach, and Abednego*, face off with King Nebuchadnezzar over the issue of worshipping false gods. Nebuchadnezzar warns them that if they don't toe the line, they'll be case into a fiery furnace, and *"who is that God that shall deliver you out of my hands?"* (Daniel: 3:15). Their answer is quite pertinent to our current discussion. *"If it be so, our God whom we serve is able to deliver us from the burning fiery furnace, and he will deliver us out of thine hand, O king. But if not, be it known unto thee, O King, that we will not serve thy gods, nor worship the golden image which thou has set up"*—Daniel 3:17-18. Notice how they equate fearlessly putting their lives on the line with serving God and, more importantly, how that service is absolutely exclusive. Consider how that mirrors the martyrs who came long after them facing similar fates. Notice too how they did not so much as reproach the king, in spite of his obviously evil intentions and overt paganism, but defied him while still showing him due respect.

There's an important reason for that. God established Nebuchadnezzar just as he established Pharaoh—and just as He established Hitler, all for essentially the same reason: to force us to answer our Basic Question: who do we serve? While we might well deliver ourselves from a physical evil, we inevitably deliver ourselves to a far more serious spiritual evil in the process, and again we touch on the issue of fruits. Remember that Revelations 12:7-9 describes Satan's heavenly revolution, and identifies him as the one *who deceived the nations*. That of course poses questions about the nature of that deception. If life as the highest good is taken as a virtually universal truism, can we not expect the deception of the nations to involve it? Do not all of those deceived nations take survival as their common good? Look again at Revelations 12:11: *"And they overcame him by the blood of the Lamb, and by the word of their testimony; and they loved not their lives unto the death."* By referring to Satan as the deceiver, that means that they overcame his deceptions—his Anti-Truth—by the word of their testimony—i.e., with the Truth, even if doing so meant their physical deaths. Bear in mind that this allusion refers to the Second Death, aka perdition. Thus, they did not so love their physical lives that they forfeited their eternal lives. *He who would save his life shall lose it.* That is repeated in four separate contexts which strongly implies the survival imperative as one of Satan's major deceptions and so as a major evil defined as Anti-Truth. In case after case throughout Christian history, we see the meek allowing themselves to be subjugated, dominated, even annihilated by the powerful. Why? Because they held meekness as an integral part of a Truth for which they were willing to die. But, if we take the conflict as good vs. evil, and define the good as that which overcomes the evil—if we take Constantine as our Lord, and adopt warrior virtues as integral to the Christian character—then we must likewise define meekness as a *vice*, just as we would expect from a mirror-image. Who do we serve?

The *"Pax Americana"* following World War II didn't last very long. The guns hadn't much more than quit firing when

Winston Churchill announced the descent of an "Iron Curtain" across Europe, officially casting our erstwhile allies as our new adversaries. America quickly lost her monopoly on The Bomb as well, as the Soviets acquired one of their own by decade's end. Ironically, perhaps at no time in our history, with the probable exception of today, did fear of man play a more prominent role than in the years to follow. Even as we today hear fears that America has "lost its greatness", so that fear permeated the 'Fifties as well. The Soviets' acquisition of the Bomb combined with our stalemate in Korea greatly eroded our confidence in our right granting us our might. As a result, some began asking questions, and some began to find some disturbing answers. Admittedly we still enjoyed the highest standard of living in the world, but at what price? Even as we inserted "one nation under God" into the Pledge of Allegiance, our title question began posing itself with increasing insistence. A growing sense of nihilism, epitomized in the fashionable belief that "God is dead," began creeping through America's social fabric. Perhaps still worse, for those of us who dared to look, we could find more similarities than differences between the U.S. and the Soviet Union. Those suspicions proved true, although even now very few of us care to acknowledge it.

As the most immediate example, although unknown at the time, the Soviets had acquired the Bomb by the same means that the Americans maintained their nuclear supremacy: by raiding the Nazi stockpile of weapons experts and experimental data (see *"Operation Paperclip"*). That proved at least equally true of the associated ICBM delivery systems, and largely accounted for the subsequent missile superiority NATO held over the Warsaw Pact. Consider that commonality carefully: in both countries men who under other circumstances could well have been convicted of war crimes, instead enjoyed privileged immunity because they could successfully answer the question, "What can you do for me?"—or, more specifically, "What can you do to my enemy?" Those questions maintain a very fluid definition of good and evil based on that all-too-familiar principle of expediency. But that also suggests expediency as a profounder philosophical principle than we might have imagined. Think about it. Isn't it funny how two nations with such sharply divergent ideologies could so commonly resort to the same means to reach the same objectives? But look more deeply and find the spiritual commonality. Both shared the same desire for independence from God's authority, as suggested by the fact that both had started with delivering themselves from evil by way of a revolution against God's ordained rulers. Ideas do not and cannot remain confined to their initial context. If we desire to deliver ourselves from evil, we must constantly seek the *power* to do so. Thus, we must take power per se as a primary good, with any means that facilitate its acquisition as commensurate goods. That follows one of our most basic market axioms and most fundamental definitions of progress: more is better.

By contrast, in 1630 John Winthrop, Governor of the Massachusetts Bay Colony, stated that if America kept its "pact with God," then, *"we shall find that the God of Israel is among us, when tens of us shall be able to resist a thousand of our enemies . . . ."* Consider well that phrase, "when ten of us shall be able to resist a thousand," for it reflects the Old Testament Jews' military successes: *"And five of you shall chase an hundred, and an hundred of you shall put ten thousand to flight: and your enemies shall fall before you by the sword"*—Leviticus 26:8. Apparently we didn't keep that pact even as early as the Revolution. It's commonly known that America could not have won her independence without the aid of both the French, whose motivation had nothing to do with American independence (she wanted to weaken England, her chief rival), and of Hessian mercenaries whose motivation was self-evident. Similarly, the North won the Civil War due to huge advantages in both personnel and material—it had entire armies that never even saw combat. In a very similar vein, in February, 1945, the "Big Three", Churchill, FDR and Joseph Stalin, met at Yalta where Stalin proposed a toast. He rightfully attributed the War's successful conclusion to America's industrial might: the Allies had quite literally buried the Axis under an avalanche of men and material. But his statement also went further than virtually anyone noticed, for we had finalized another mirror-image. We had gone from believing that *right makes might* to *might makes right* which legitimized the expediency and militantism that remain our essential guiding principles today. We have answered our Basic Question: we worship and serve the God of War, just as did Constantine, for with a mindset of good vs. evil, how can we avoid it? The Emperor's ghost haunts us still again, pointing an empty sleeve toward a broad and spacious path that leads to destruction both figuratively and literally, and that virtually the entire world blindly follows in the name of the mark of the beast.

For a generation we essentially defined good and evil in terms of Democracy and Communism, and saw the world as a huge, often silent, battlefield between the two. For a time, as one nation after another fell under its "sphere of influence", it appeared that the Godless Commies just might win that conflict, and that engendered doubts of our moral superiority even as we hear today that America has lost the "moral high ground". To this nation given to self-determination, such a threat can prove the greatest fear of all, for it strikes at the very heart of our national identity. In order to determine our own destinies, we must be able to control them which means that we must control all of the circumstances affecting them. Thus, loss of status, or especially power, can act as a kind of death threat even though physical survival is not necessarily involved. As a case in point, those two fears came into exceptionally sharp focus when our Cuban neighbor, Fidel Castro, officially embraced the Soviet Union in the late 'Fifties. Now we had a Communist dictatorship in what should rightfully be *our* sphere of influence, and the Soviets could readily turn it into a military base that could threaten our homeland.

At least that's what general opinion held. In reality, America and her allies had little to fear militarily from the Communist bloc. NATO held such a huge missile advantage over the Warsaw Pact that any nuclear strike against it would have amounted to suicide regardless of from where that strike originated. In fact, the American public's fear of Castro was deliberately fomented for political ends largely geared toward ousting the newly elected Democratic President, John F. Kennedy. Far from an absolute dictator, Soviet Premier Nikita Khrushchev had to answer to many critics both internal and external. That forced him to maintain national prestige as a major consideration directly associated with his political survival, and that prestige translated directly into military power. That often compelled him to do things he'd rather not do. He was an avid Communist, and honestly believed that the Soviet Union would "bury" America. However, true to the Communist ideology, he saw that victory in the marketplace rather than on the battlefield, and that was where he would rather have focused his efforts. To help in preventing him from being pressured into military exploits not in the best interest of anyone, both sides had tacitly agreed not to publicly announce the missile gap, lest the Soviet leader find himself forced to take face-saving steps. Exactly who breeched that contract no one seems to know for sure, but we can say with certainty that is was done for the same essential reason: as a matter of political expediency.

It too had a number of unforeseeable consequences, the most major of which was the Cuban Missile Crisis of 1962, a prime example of what the Premier should not have done, and possibly would not have done under other circumstances. Convinced after the Bay of Pigs disaster (1961) that he could bully the young American President, and embarrassed by the reports of Soviet missile disparity, Khrushchev hit upon the idea of establishing a Soviet military base on the very doorstep of the Leader of the Free World which would equally embarrass Kennedy. Obviously Cuba, only ninety miles from America's southern shores, would make an ideal site for such a base. The Premier also realized that nuclear war wasn't an option, but that didn't really matter. The political prestige and propaganda value associated with such a presence in America's sphere of influence was a far larger consideration on both sides of the Iron Curtain.

Although when he came to power Castro maintained that his *coup* had nothing to do with Communism, U.S. interests shuddered when he began nationalizing foreign holdings, and with good reason: by the end of 1958 the U.S. owned over one billion dollars worth of Cuban assets. America has long retained the aforementioned *moral high ground* by its advocacy of human rights and self-determination. However, as she learned the hard way during the Bay of Pigs disaster, Castro was much more popular among his own people than U.S. intelligence had thought. They had expected their forces to be welcomed as liberators; instead, they were resisted as invaders. If Cuban missiles could not pose a significant threat to American soil, and if liberating the Cuban people wasn't what the Cuban people wanted, then what justified our invasion? Castro's rebellion, which enjoyed a good deal of popular support, had ousted Fulgencio Batista who had also been a dictator, but one friendly to the U.S. That, too, has a familiar ring to it. A brief and not especially comprehensive review of America's Twentieth Century foreign policy reveals a number of similar associations. This one was especially significant in one specific way, however. America's *amigo*, had allowed organized crime to run several gambling establishments worth multiple millions, while Castro almost immediately evicted them. Well substantiated reports maintain that the Mob played a very active role in subsequent attempts sponsored by the U.S. government to eliminate the Beard. Let's get this straight: Castro ousted organized crime, and America sought to *reinstate* it and partnered with organized crime to that end?

That's what happens when illegal activities originate in the department responsible for law enforcement, but the illegalities don't stop with such superficials. We can easily forget, and even more easily gloss over the significance of the fact that two very prominent Americans, John F. Kennedy and Richard Nixon, both tried to assassinate a foreign leader not as a matter of national security but as a matter of personal political gain. While Vice President, Nixon had inaugurated a number of covert assassination plans, some with the complicity of the Mob, to dispose of Castro so as to assure himself the Presidency in 1960. Kennedy too wanted to oust him both to assure himself of reelection in 1964 and to stifle critics calling him "soft of Communism". Consider what that means. In spite of what a court of law would call attempted premeditated murder, we still refer to Kennedy as "America's brightest and best", and elected both him and Nixon as the Leader of the Free World. Again we must pose our question, *freedom from what*, and again must consider our religious underpinning as reflective of a very specific deity.

"'He was a murderer from the beginning, and does not stand in the truth, because there is no truth in him.'" Do we dare take that classic satanic combination of murder and deception so essential to both our national security and to our very identity as coincidental? If fruit must follow the pattern of its seed, what else might we expect? After all, this country was founded by traitors to the British crown. How can we expect the resultant system not to produce more of the same?

Just as we've broken our Christian covenant with God by substituting my will be done for Thy will be done, so the Elite have broken their constitutional covenant with the people who in name constitute the government. We've seen numerous examples of that same lawbreaking mindset from Watergate through all the "gates" since. In each instance, the perpetrators were also guilty of treason, which the *Dictionary.com* defines as *"the betrayal of a trust or confidence."* That confidence is summarized in the Presidential Oath of Office in which the newly elected swears (or affirms) to " . . . *faithfully execute the office of President of the United States, and will to the best of my ability, protect and defend the Constitution of the United States."* Each instance of executive constitutional malfeasance violates that trust, which amplifies the crime from a matter of misconduct to a matter that is theoretically punishable by death! We don't mean to vilify either Nixon or Kennedy any more than we mean to vilify the government or the Church. Rather, we mean to illustrate a point: we are not the nation we claim to be which makes duplicity an inherent part of our national definition just as the ever increasing emphasis on government secrecy implies. While Castro was the first high profile example, most of us now take "Black Ops" for granted, and even play video games based on them. Especially with the advent of the wars in Iraq and Afghanistan, we've come to know that this one nation under God has attempted and completed assassinations and other international illegalities as part of our foreign policy. Yet rather than feeling moral outrage at such a thing being done in our name—or, in the case of the Christian, in Christ's name—most of us either ignore it or applaud it as necessary toward the end of national security and survival. If you think about it, isn't that in itself a pretty good definition of the Great Apostasy?

Ideas, as with thoughts, do not and cannot remain confined to their initial context. If we can justify murdering the leader of a foreign sovereign state in the name of national security, but in fact do so as a matter of personal political and/or financial gain, how much of a leap does it require to justify the murder of a domestic leader for similar reasons? We could, of course, argue that political assassination, both domestic and foreign, has been used as political expedients for centuries. But if that's the case, in what way can we claim to have improved? In what way can the U.S. claim the moral high ground? In what way can we claim ourselves a nation of laws when our country's leaders, or *their* leaders, quite systematically and consistently place themselves above the law? If we use murder as a tool to further political careers, to protect, enhance and consolidate power within our political system, so as to enable the Elite to lord that power over the rest of us, should we not expect to find pagan seeds at the foundation of that system? Can it then surprise us that we so commonly use vicarious murders to promote entertainment careers while making those engaged in them wealthy as well? Can it surprise us to find ourselves seeking to "make a killing" in the marketplace, illegalities be damned? Should it surprise us to find financial interests behind many if not all of the government's illegal activities, and so most probably the focal point of the power consolidation? Should it surprise us to find the Profit Motive as our holy of holies, with the sale and the profits derived therefrom overwhelming any sense of humanity much less godliness? Should it surprise us to find aggression in the marketplace, in entertainments, in everyday life as well as in our military adventures evermore commonly taken as a prime virtue? If we value being "number one" more than anything else, we must likewise value "looking out for number one" more than anything else. What does that do to the very concept of humility, and *esteeming other better than ourselves?* Clearly this is not what the original settlers, the Founding Fathers, or what any specific group had in mind, which illustrates a basic Truth: we serve only one spiritual master, but one way or the other, we *must* serve!

Unless we consciously serve God and the Truth embodied in His Son, we inevitably end up serving His rival by default. More importantly, we end up doing so as a matter of conscious choice and active desire.

In one of the great ironies of modern times, government secrets are not secret these days; quite the contrary, although the contents remain hidden (Wikileaks notwithstanding), the fact of their existence is very widely known. But, when you think about it, which is more shocking, the fact that this sort of thing happens in a supposedly Godly nation, or the fact that knowing about it causes hardly a stir amongst the electorate, including the Christian community? Indeed, some of the participants in those secret activities consider themselves part of that community, while others vocally approve of and support them. Of course it is not for the Christian to condemn, but it does bring up one of the hardest questions of all. Although we are proscribed from actively resisting it, how can the Christian in good conscience support or participate in such a government acting in our name? We speak not of specific leaders but to the larger issue of the *governmental form itself.* We've repeatedly mentioned that the essence of democracy, my will be done, is at diametric odds with the essence of righteousness, *Thy will be done.* Going beyond that, given Christ as the Truth, and given what He and His Apostles said throughout the New Testament, how can we possibly take prevarication, deception and murder in defense of earthly values such as self-determination, materialism, religious freedom and survival as reflections of God's will as expressed by His Son? If they're not in accordance with Christ, must we not consider them Antichrist? *"I am crucified with Christ: nevertheless I live; yet not I, but Christ liveth in me: and the life which I now live in the flesh I live by the faith of the Son of God, who loved me, and who gave Himself for me"*—Galatians 2:20. Do we believe that or not? Do we love Him in return, or do we make a mockery of that sacrifice?

We cannot have faith without trust, for in many ways they mean the same thing. Thus we find the juncture between faith and love, for we cannot love without trust either. We must truly believe that Christ loves us and has our best interests at heart, even when His commands fly in the face of conventional wisdom or human norms. As a primary example, we must trust Him when He tells us *not to resist evil* (Matthew 5:39). Why? *"'Ye are My friends if ye do whatsoever I command you'"*—John 15:14. He says that just after saying, *"Greater love hath no man than this, that a man lay down his life for his friends'"*—John 15:13. He gave His life for those who do whatsoever He commands. That, my friend, is justification by faith. We must be willing to do the same both literally and figuratively: we must be willing to put on lives and all that we associate with them behind that trust, and to lose them if necessary. Just as did the martyrs, we must not only live our faith, we must also be willing to die for it just as we figuratively die to our old selves.

Given that, and given Satan as the *deceiver*, consider the role played by lies and deception in defense of way of life. Freedom itself is a deception, a falsehood, an Anti-Truth: *who do we serve* is an unavoidable question we each must and will answer. If we don't consciously serve God, then we serve His usurper by default. That explains why we find so many exhortations throughout the New Testament to remaining vigilant and avoiding unwitting service to the Lord's mirror-image. *"And every spirit that confesseth not that Jesus Christ is come in the flesh is not of God: and this is the spirit of antichrist, whereof ye have heard that it should come; and even now already is it in the world"*—I John 4:2. Which spirit would urge service that defies *Thy will be done?* Yet, which spirit has ascendency in this one nation under God? Think about it carefully. The Christian's entire purpose in life begins and ends with adhering to the First Commandment. If we break it, if we have any gods or values above or instead of our Heavenly Father, then our most valiant efforts to keep the other Commandments will avail us absolutely nothing. Yet that is exactly what religious freedom not only allows but *encourages*, and is what this one nation under God advocates, defends, and spreads to the world as the spiritual ideal! We do indeed seek self-destruction as our unstated goal. We must: in our unchanged state divine concepts, even eternal survival, have no appeal. In that state, we substitute physical life, for eternal life and run the risk of finding our eternal home in the Lake of Fire. *"And the smoke of their torment ascendeth up for ever and ever: and they have no rest day or night, who worship the beast and his image, and whosoever receiveth the mark of his name"*—Revelations 14:11. If we don't actively refuse that mark, we receive it by default. *Strive* to find the strait and narrow way!

Willingly or not, wittingly or not, we must serve one master or the other just as we must experience one posthumous destiny or the other. Which does the American government reflect as a matter of national policy? Political "game-playing" has become one of Washington's worst-kept secrets. By now pretty nearly all of us at least marginally realize that if you don't toe the line you have no chance of even being heard, much less of making a difference in the Federal Government. At the same time however, no one can say just who originated those unstated rules by whom all must play, nor who enforces them. But, perhaps still more disturbing, we find increasing evidence the even the President must play by those rules. Who's really in charge here? As an especially dramatic contemporary example, in spite of President Obama's promises to close Guantanamo and other "black bases", to end "enhanced interrogation methods" and to bring justice to the terror-related detainees, nothing of the sort has happened. Guantanamo remains open which at least implies that the world's other black bases also remain active and there seems nothing the Commander-in-Chief can do about it. This gives rise to speculations about shadowy groups such as the *Club of Rome*, *The Bilderbergers*, and especially the *Illuminati* who supposedly even decide who global leaders will be. True or not (and most probably not,) our elitist roots have in fact produced an elitist government with everything from legislation, to law enforcement, to judicial renderings reflecting the interests of the ruling class—business (including banking) and industry for the most part—often at the expense of those who in name constitute our government. Who uses conventional economics as his method of interacting with the world?

Of course, any discussion of secret cabals, conspiracies, and especially assassinations must include JFK. Even now, forty-seven years later, his murder still ranks as the nation's number one mystery, and for good reason: questions just go on and on. Why, for example, do over one thousand files on Lee Harvey Oswald remain classified under the cloak of national security? How can a "nobody" like him, a "lone nut assassin," still pose a threat to the world's most powerful country so many years after his death? That's a more important question than initially seems self-evident, for in a way, he does pose a threat. While important in itself if only because of the dignity due a human being and American citizen, Lee Harvey Oswald is much more important in another sense. Indeed, given that the current Presidency rests on this case, it poses the question of what this nation truly values, and that offers many clues as to our nation's spiritual underpinnings. Even more than that, if our way of life is in fact our faith enacted, then it has a great deal to say about the officially manifested national faith underlying our current form of government. More specifically still, it poses the question of whether this nation of law actually seeks justice and, if so, then for whom we seek it and what definition we ascribe to it. Think about it. If fruit must follow the pattern of its seeds, and if this country was born of rebellion, treason and sedition, then what must we suspect? If those seeds were planted and nurtured by an Elite at our inception, can we not logically expect to find a similar Elite nurturing the resultant crops? If that proves the case, what does that suggest about our whole concept of law and justice?

For example, we are supposed to believe Lee Harvey Oswald guilty due, not to the legal process guaranteed to each citizen, but to the conclusions reached by the Warren Commission—by definition, an elite body and so, not just different from those Constitutional guarantees but *diametrically* different, just as darkness is the diametric opposite of light. Isn't that essentially the same as the prosecuting attorney selecting the jury? In some peoples' eyes, it's more like the *guilty* selecting the jury. Doesn't organized crime have a reputation for doing that sort of thing? Hasn't the intelligence community, particularly the CIA (OSS), shared a long and cozy relationship with the Mob ever since WWII? Don't both the CIA and the Mob commonly use murder as a tool? (Though the extent remains in question, the CIA had been intimately involved in the assassinations of Vietnamese president Ngo Dinh Diem and his brother/adviser Ngo Dinh Nhu only three weeks before Kennedy's death.) The number of mysterious deaths of people involved in the Kennedy case, called natural or accidental, but which could easily have been murder, far exceeds what would prove statistically plausible.

Then there's the motive for creating the Committee in the first place. A good deal of evidence points to Johnson forming the Warren Commission in order to forestall a similar Congressional investigation, as well as to quell conspiracy rumors that had already begun to surface. At the same time, some maintain that LBJ had a hand in the assassination, and we can find evidence, albeit circumstantial, for that too. For example, it's no big secret that Kennedy and Johnson didn't like each other, nor that Kennedy had seriously considered dumping him for another running mate in the '64 election. What would that have done to his political career? Given that he knew about these rumors, which he almost certainly did, and given his general dislike of the man, in spite of his new position as Chief Executive, does he really qualify to select a truly objective board to review Kennedy's death? Again consider the fruits. For example, since Kennedy had recently fired him as director of the CIA in response to the embarrassing Bay of Pigs fiasco, and considering that the event had created a good deal of ill-concealed bad feelings throughout the intelligence community, (where some labeled the President a "traitor" and others a "communist"), Andrew Dulles seems a rather odd choice to head the committee. Given the bitterness and resentment he and some of his cronies had openly voiced against Kennedy, one has to wonder if a more objective selection process would have included him at all.

The Commission's research methods won't win them any prizes either. Beginning with the presumption of Oswald's guilt, the committee then built its case accordingly, quite systematically eliminating or marginalizing contradictory evidence and testimony.[52] While that contradictory evidence doesn't prove Oswald's innocence, under the American legal system it doesn't

---

[52]   Perhaps the most significant testimony comes from the Parkland Hospital staff where *all* of the participants in the original autopsy cited the President's fatal wound as coming from the front.

have to. Even with that marginalizing, enough leaked into the Report to create the "shadow of a doubt" necessary to acquit a murderer, and a good deal more has been added since. Consistently, the Dallas law enforcement community (which was ordered by the FBI to suspend its own investigation), came to the same pre-trial conclusion, while involving similar unorthodox methods in its initial investigation. Even more curious, however, the Federal Government's investigators quickly discounted even the possibility of a conspiracy while at the same time going out of their way to paint Oswald as a Castro supporter and a Communist. At the same time, they went to equal lengths to distance any related groups from the assassination in what some have called a "benign cover-up", intended to keep the popular passion from demanding a nuclear response against the Communist bloc. That seems possible but not plausible. On the contrary, associating them would have given J. Edgar Hoover the license to investigate organizations with whom he'd been obsessed for years, and which both the FBI and the CIA saw as legitimate threats to the national security. That in itself suggests that the President's murder involved national security by a definition that didn't necessarily have anything to do the nation as a whole, with due process, or even the law itself. But again, Oswald's innocence or guilt per se is not the issue. The point is that the current Presidency rests on a murder case that was resolved in a most unconventional (and one could argue, unconstitutional) manner. Given our stated reverence for justice, particularly since we take it as our justification for the War on Terror, this again casts duplicity as the cornerstone not only of our country in theory, but of its most powerful office *in practice.* Who's really in charge here?

We cannot have justice without truth, yet the truth about this one nation under God has long been systematically distorted, hidden and withheld from the populace, always with the same justification: national security. Popular awareness of that fact began right here, and with it began a gradual erosion of confidence in our government, our governmental system and, ultimately, in our ability to govern ourselves. We can see that reflected in a growing frustration with both political parties among the electorate; we vote the rascals out only to vote new rascals back in again. But there's also a deeper issue involved. To take something as truth is absolutely vital to our ability to function cohesively, yet our chief authority source, the government, has proven not only unreliable, but prone to deliberately distorting or covering up the truth. Again, religion and politics merge: the profusion of religious options accomplishes the same purpose. Politically and spiritually, we find ourselves entering a void where truth is a matter of opinion, and fragmentation is an inevitable result. Reflective of that, we more and more commonly hear cries for effective leadership not only domestically but internationally which we could readily see as a precursor to global leadership. Given that what we take as truth is what we take as our highest authority, and given that, by definition, such an authority is what we take as our deity, Lee Harvey Oswald epitomizes this one nation under God not only politically but spiritually and answers the question of who is really in charge here.

The truth of his guilt(or even of his participation) in the assassination is far from fully demonstrated, and certainly not fully enough to convict him in a court of law even without a formalized defense. Yet the government adamantly holds the case as closed, reluctantly releasing a small handful of pertinent documents, often highly redacted, only after great efforts and legal maneuvering. Why? Consider: if we take America as elitist in its inception, and if fruit must follow the pattern of it seed, must we not logically expect an elitist government to follow? With the notable exceptions of Andrew Jackson and Abraham Lincoln, hasn't virtually every President been far, far removed socially and economically from the common man even as were the Founding Fathers? Can we not at least entertain the notion that Kennedy threatened not the security of the nation itself, but of those Elite, especially if we define them as the super-wealthy? For example, his stated desires to end the Cold War in favor of cooperation with the Soviets (and thus end the very lucrative arms race) and to withdraw American troops from Vietnam[53] (thus curtailing another very lucrative source of revenue) labeled him

---

[53] In all fairness, although conspiracy advocates point to such a withdrawal as a primary motivation for Kennedy's death, proof

as "soft on Communism," but in fact threatened the pocketbooks of select powerful individuals. Don't we see a parallel to that in the fomenting of the American Revolution where economics and the promise of a land of virtually unlimited wealth played instrumental if not decisive roles? If the United States was born of the Love of Money, can we not expect to define the Elite in those terms? If America is in fact ruled by a shadowy, largely anonymous Elite, and if power, like money, never voluntarily relinquishes itself but seeks to preserve and enhance itself instead, can we not logically expect to find that Elite at the bottom not only of this murder but of all the similar unsavory aspects of American foreign policy for the past half century? In spite of the secrecy invoked, haven't we seen military intervention or black ops time and time again throughout Latin America including Guatemala, Chile and even Cuba used to modify foreign sovereign states to suit American corporate interests? If those anonymous forces do so internationally, how can we imagine them incapable of doing so domestically? Does that not help to explain the secrecy surrounding not only the President's murder, including Oswald's participation, but around virtually everything that has happened in Washington ever since? Given the roles played by LOM and the survival imperative, must we answer our title question?

We can pose further disturbing questions. How did President Johnson manage to get Chief Justice Earl Warren involved in this investigation (cover-up)? Most concede that Johnson, a well-known "arm-twister", almost certainly used some variation on the fear that if Oswald were found to be working as a Soviet agent sent to kill Camelot's king, then an outraged American public might very well demand a powerful (i.e., nuclear) response which could have precipitated WWIII. We thus begin to answer the question of how we define justice, for in order to define justice, we must first define the law to which we demand obedience. Assuming that to be true, then we clearly reveal our every administration since and quite possibly before Kennedy founded on *the mark of the beast*, just as national security implies, with the satanic combination of deception and murder

---

that he actually intended to withdraw all troops proves difficult to authenticate.

so intimately associated with it as to be taken as indispensible. With that as the accepted "law of the land" anything that facilitates that survival must be taken as both good and just. That largely explains the aforementioned loss of the moral high ground, as expediency has subsumed all other considerations. We find ourselves mouthing high sounding platitudes about human rights and dignity only to abandon those principles whenever we feel sufficiently threatened. If security requires secrecy, then we can legitimately wonder whose security we have in mind. The answer to that question largely answers the question of what principles we actually hold. That in turn answers the question of whom we actually serve.

By definition, a "nation of law" is a nation of the powerful which, again by definition, makes it a nation ruled by the Elite who hold that power. As we mentioned earlier, in at least some pre-Revolutionary colonies, we found a very sharp distinction between the rich and the poor, with the former having both the military and law enforcement on their sides. Superficial appearance notwithstanding, very little has changed since. Power never voluntarily relinquishes itself and seeks to enhance itself instead. In this context, the only way to do that is to manufacture still more laws—and the U.S. has passed an average of about three hundred new laws each year ever since the '70s, and that doesn't count state, county and local edicts. Albert Einstein observed, *"Nothing is more destructive of respect for the government and the law of the land than passing laws that cannot be enforced."* Many of those laws are in fact unenforceable, with laws against drug (especially marijuana) use the most prominent examples. Can we call it coincidental that accompanying this avalanche of laws we have also experienced a sharp decline in respect for law itself? Again, who does this benefit? That question gains considerable importance when we realize that instead of benefitting the Elite, it will eventually lead to their downfall: they too seek self-destruction. Already we hear clamors to reign in corruption and abuse of power in virtually every part of the world as the invisible rule of the Elite gradually enters the popular consciousness, and comes under ever-greater scrutiny. Again we see the familiar divide and conquer motif. Think about it: rather that producing a law-abiding citizenry as would seem our self-evident intent, we instead produce a nation of lawbreakers, right in line with our origins, and the more laws we have, the more lawbreakers we create. That in turn legitimizes still more laws which creates still more lawbreakers in a never ending cycle. Speaking of the scribes and Pharisees, Christ said, *"'For they bind heavy burdens and grievous to be borne, and lay them on men's shoulders; but they themselves will not move them with one of their fingers'"*—Matthew 23:4. Doesn't that smack of leaders who consider themselves above their own laws? That adds to a frustrated discontent and an adversarial relationship between the governed and the governors; if they don't follow the rules, why should we? Still more importantly, unenforceable and "stupid" laws invite and eventually beg a free people to defy them, which makes us lawbreakers as a matter of conscious choice and active desire—again, right in line with our origins. Those factors taken together partly account for the frustrated rage fueling the rise of the Tea Party, Islamaphobia and other contemporary phenomena that have already made a number of international observers regard America as a land of hatred. Therein we reveal who this actually benefits while reflecting our national spiritual origins manifest in our break with God's absolute authority. We will *love the one Master and hate the other.* The true God stresses unconditional love for all, most certainly including our enemies; Love of Money squires defensiveness, aggression, intolerance and, ultimately, hatred. No wonder religion and politics so freely comingle, and no wonder we hear cries to return to God, with many of those cries motivated by rancor, bigotry, and fear.

That brings up perhaps the most pertinent question of all regarding the JFK assassination as it relates to the Elite power structure. In the Oliver Stone film, *JFK*, Jim Garrison meets with a mystery man who identifies himself as *"X"*. During their conversation, "X" points out that the who and the how of the assassination act to distract the public, *"like some sort of parlor game,"* and keep them from asking the most important question: why? In many minds we can answer "X's" question in a single word: Vietnam. No doubt it is the most dramatic result of the *coup*, and has implications going well beyond the political.

Indeed, the staggering financial cost, and the still greater cost in human suffering pale against the unforeseeable long term consequences of this pivotal period of the 20th Century—and, one could argue, of human history. The Vietnam Era re-defined our nation and, by extension, the rest of the world, in terms of our relationship to authority per se, to our government, our peers, and our God.

As a primary example that may prove difficult to conceive for some born since then, prior to Vietnam most Americans believed virtually everything the government told them; now most of us believe virtually nothing it tells us. Furthermore, consider how much of what we take as modern America either began or gained social acceptability during this period, including: co-habitation, fornication, adultery, divorce (including "no fault divorce",) single parenthood, pornography, homosexuality, abortion, birth control, sex and violence in the media, greater government involvement in individual lives, greater dependence on government entitlement programs, greater secrecy of government activities, proliferation of government agencies, greater toleration of profanity in mainstream media, drug usage, etc., etc.. That's by no means a comprehensive list, and you can probably add other examples of your own. At the same time, as a backlash to the "materialism" some saw rampant in America and the "immorality" of the Vietnam War, supported by most of the mainstream Churches (at least initially), many turned to other forms of "spirituality" in search of a morality more in keeping with their desires and contemporary moral standards. Most of the elements now associated with the New Age Movement, including crystal power, pyramid power, occult sciences, mystic philosophies, and Eastern religions, all found their entree into the American mainstream, and found general acceptance and respectability either during or as a result of this time. Yet, for all that has been written, most of us have taken the wrong lesson from the Vietnam Era.

While we can readily point to the financial rewards some of the Elite reaped from the conflict, that too was a distraction, albeit a revealing one. Ask yourself, in addition to using conventional economics as his means of relating to the world, who has a vested interest in seeing us as a nation of idolaters, blasphemers and workers of iniquity? That was the true point of the Vietnam War, and it succeeded very, very well. Indeed, perhaps most blatantly manifest in the "free love" characteristic of that era, especially pertinent when we remember that fornication also means idolatry, nowhere in our history did we more clearly see our desire for liberty as a desire for sin. Since we saw that freedom as good, and since we co-equate goodness with righteousness, we therefore had to equate freedom of expression with righteousness just as we had long done by taking religious freedom as a legitimate means to salvation. "Speaking of ourselves" became a virtue, just as the First Amendment suggests. Freedom comes about due to rebellion, as had both the Protestant religion, and this one nation under God, so we had to come to see rebellion itself as righteous. That rapidly degenerated into rebellion against authority per se, and we return again to our roots. *An evil man seeks only rebellion;* perhaps we were intended to protest the Vietnam War even as we are meant to protest the current conflicts in Afghanistan.

But why? Fittingly, that was probably the single question that best epitomized the Vietnam War, and aside from some vague references to "halting Soviet expansion" and preventing the dreaded "domino effect," the government never gave us an answer. That seems quite strange. Propaganda plays an indispensable role in warfare, and a big part of that role is to provide us with a moral justification for enduring the hardships, dangers, sacrifices, and pain associated with the conflict. Reflective of that, not long before his death Kennedy had said in a nationally televised interview with Walter Cronkite that we'd have a great deal of trouble winning the war unless we did a much better job of selling it to the American people. We never did so. How is it that we have in place the world's most effective Propaganda Machine, daily selling us everything from soap flakes to senators, and yet we saw no concerted effort whatsoever to sell the Vietnam War? Odder still, we saw the exact opposite. Rather than rousing slogans and patriotic rhetoric, all we got were nightly "body counts," and images of an enemy that remained distressingly human—and sometimes pre-pubescent. Just to make things worse, even the Vietnamese themselves seemed indifferent, not seeming to care who won the conflict so long as they could be left in peace. That, together with the images of dead bodies and occasional tales of American atrocities, constituted a kind of anti-propaganda appropriate to an ideological conflict fought, not in Southeast Asia, but in American minds and hearts, with an objective that had nothing to do with Soviets or dominoes. We must wonder if perhaps protesting the Vietnam War was really its point.

Again we return to that divide and conquer motif, this time with its satanic elements much more clearly revealed. Consider the nature of the conquest. The seeds of doubt planted by the Warren Commission Report and nurtured by Watergate and the scandals to follow, in addition to the governmental prevarication concerning virtually everything from Vietnam to our current Mideastern conflicts, cause many to automatically deride governmental proclamations in general as "a pack of lies" at best, and as expletives best deleted at worst. Consider what this means given our governmental form as our religion enacted. If we mistrust our leaders, that must have a corresponding effect on our trust in our deity. True to the myth of its Christian roots, America has undergone a number of "reawakenings" that resulted to a resurgence in traditional religion. Not coincidentally, from the nihilistic disbelief of the '50s, we have rebounded to the point where an overwhelming majority of Americans "believe in God". In a sense that establishes the kind of unanimity the Mother Church, the very personification of traditional religion, sought and achieved due to the Constantine coup as a matter of survival as a physical, political entity. Our motivation is much the same. Yet, while "God bless America" has come back into vogue as a result of 9/11, consider what this means. A rebellion against our own government is a rebellion against our own god—the self-deification inherent in self-determination is proving harder than it looked. This reawakening is more revealing than previous ones, however. Consider: we cannot disparage our leaders without reproaching the One ordaining them, yet we find just such reproaching central to our entire electoral process and overall government functioning. Moreover, in spite of religion's resurgence, rather than decreasing we find it sharply *increasing* over the past decade or so. What if we ask whose purpose we serve by such criticism as we have seen in both the Bush and Obama administrations. If our governmental form is in fact our religion enacted, then we simultaneously pose the same question in both a political and ecclesiastical context. Again we find a decline in our belief in our ability to govern ourselves, and the myth of freedom begins to reveal itself as a trap. Think about it. We cannot escape our need for authority; but if we reject God as that authority, and lose confidence in our own authority, whose authority remains? If we reject divine Truth, what truth remains? The two amount to essentially the same question. Furthermore, in the chaos caused by such a huge and essential void, such an authority will prove necessary to our survival. Who are we describing? The seditious seeds planted at our inception sprang into unanticipated flower during the Vietnam Era, and have flourished ever since as an extension of the Constantine *coup*. At no time, not even during the Revolution, did we more clearly see the true nature of our desire for freedom, nor of the role played by good vs. evil in that desire.

To a large extent, we turned that criticism on the country itself, and that has not abated. For example, in addition to the war, we could readily find a whole raft of unaddressed domestic social evils ranging from racial inequalities to environmental issues. We find similar criticisms now during a prolonged financial crisis while multiple billions are spent on foreign entanglements and what many believe to be unwinnable wars. Beneath the surface, the more astute began to ask some deep and disturbing questions similar in nature to those posed today about America's declining global influence. We had long assumed that right makes might, and that our long string of military successes had reflected our national righteousness. That no longer seemed nearly so sure. Maybe we'd somehow broken that "pact with God", or had in some manner fallen from His Grace. We find that sentiment implied in "One nation under God," "God Bless America," and in the very existence of the Tea Party. Vietnam badly tarnished America's international reputation, and the *Wikileaks* documents dealing with the War in Iraq have accomplished much the same. But

Vietnam was different in a very fundamental way. By the time you add some highly questionable examples of how the war itself was conducted—fighter-bombers going on dangerous bombing missions with only one bomb, for example—and the tremendous wealth that certain war merchants and suchlike accrued—by replacing downed fighter bombers, for example—it's no wonder that the war fell out of favor. Indeed, you almost get the impression that it was *supposed* to fall out of favor in the same sense that perhaps the JFK cover up was *supposed* to be found.

Maybe that's not as far-fetched as it seems. For example, in the Kennedy case the entire media, electronic and print alike, portrayed the President's demise as a major tragedy, emphasizing a "nation united in mourning" when in fact some segments of the population actually *celebrated* it. We find the media not reporting facts but endeavoring to manipulate our responses to carefully crafted stories and partial truths. To that end the entire media, print and electronic alike, very quickly acted in unanimous accord with the government's line, in some cases even retracting or denying previous stories (including eye witness accounts) contradicting it. All of this has ended up strengthening popular opinion that we the people do not know the whole truth. That poses another, much more important question. Forgetting the "why" for the moment, what power could so expeditiously either bribe or coerce what many consider one of the nation's most powerful agencies into such universal compliance? The News Industry is like any other: it exists to make a profit. If any one of them could "blow the lid" off the Kennedy case they would assure themselves of astronomical profits in increased circulation or viewership. Yet, in defiance of the clearly manifested public desire for such, as well as defying the axiom of giving the customer what they want, no major medium has dared to even seriously reinvestigate the case. Quite the contrary, the major outlets, especially the electronic, have aired a number of presentations supposedly either debunking the conspiracy theory as a whole or upholding the Warren Commission's report. Again we find an example of a segment of the Elite working against its own best interests. As has happened with the government itself, this has eroded public confidence in the news media as sources of factual truth. Notice the parallel to Christianity's fragmentation and the common questions: if we really seek the Truth, where do we look and who do we believe? Those in turn pose the unavoidable question of authority: who's really in charge here?

We saw what initially appears the exact opposite in Vietnam, yet it served essentially the same purpose. In addition to the aforementioned body counts, the nightly news reported seemingly uncountable demonstrations conducted by an indecipherable alphabet soup mix of protest organizations that appeared to threaten the very fabric of the country. In fact, the media, especially the electronic, greatly exaggerated the protests. Oh they happened, and a good deal of property was damaged, a good many people arrested, some people hurt, a very few even killed. Still, to listen to the news you'd think the whole country was ready to explode when, in reality, very large sections remained entirely unaffected by and far removed from such protests, although not nearly so far removed from the media's coverage of them. Many parts of the country had only a vague notion of what a "hippie" even looked like, and a protest was some teen-ager refusing to eat her vegetables.

That epitomizes a problem long recognized. Deceptive exaggeration is inherent in television for the simple reason that most of us take something as especially important *because* it shows up on television, and that was far more true then than now. To a slightly lesser extent, the same holds true for other news media. Thus, deliberately or not, the media managed to send a message to the entire country that there was something basically wrong with the government, and something valiant about the protesters. No, it didn't look that way when we initially saw it on the screen. At first glance, all we saw was a bunch of unkempt trouble-makers out getting their drug-induced kicks. At the same time however, there was an air of "freedom" about them in sharp contrast to the conformity still dominating most of middle-class post-McCarthy America. Somehow, in spite of their shortcomings, the "jeans" seemed more all-American than the "suits," and even their detractors had to reluctantly admit to similarities to the Sons of Liberty. (Some "straight" people would sometimes rent wigs and the appropriate garb and masquerade as "week end hippies.") In actuality, we had established battle lines between the government and the governed, and those lines have sharpened ever since.

The Federal Government, especially the Administrative Branch, played an active role. Aside from some rather vitriolic denunciations by Vice President Spiro Agnew, instead of addressing the protesters' grievances the government simply looked the other way, apparently hoping they would disappear. In many minds, that hurt more than anything: not only were their grievances not addressed, they weren't even taken seriously. The violent police reactions (overreactions?) to the protesters helped to establish the government as cruelly despotic, and we suddenly start to see a familiar pattern emerging. Its indifference defined it as far removed from the will of the people it was supposed to serve, and at sharp odds with our traditional ideal of rugged individualism. Notice how that reflects the indifference to individuals characteristic of Mother Nature (see above) as opposed to the intimately individual relationship between the Christian and both Father and Son. Much as held true of the pre-Reformation Church, which set itself up as a cruel and despotic tyrant whose demise "good" people could rightfully applaud, our government set itself up as a bastion of demagoguery, a strawman for the protesters to bowl over in a righteous rebellion to the plaudits of freedom lovers everywhere. Did any human actually orchestrate this end? Probably not. But, as with the aforementioned rules by which American politicians must play, it came to pass nevertheless. Who's really in charge here? Notice again how that question fits nicely with the eroding confidence in our ability to govern ourselves. Satan demands our service as a matter of active *desire*. That is an essential step to installing himself in the temple of our hearts. That too was an objective of the war.

Do not underestimate the significance or the scale of the role played by the *mark of the beast*. Survival, the most universal of self-evident goods, gives rise to "false flag" operations now taken as vital to maintaining political power, and the *Gulf of Tonkin incident* (August, 1964) makes a very good example.

Much as we saw in the wake of 9/11, it resulted in a Resolution granting President Johnson virtual *carte blanche* to do whatever he deemed necessary to protect American forces in Southeast Asia. However, it has since been officially determined that there had been no naval engagement at all, that the entire incident was fabricated, and that the President and his staff knew it. That means that the entire Vietnam War founded on a lie in much the same way that the Presidency itself founds on a series of lies. Do we not see the same in our war with Iraq (and, by extension, Afghanistan) over WMD which were known not to exist? Given that fruit must follow the pattern of its seed, we must ask, who is the *"father of lies"* (see John 8:44)? Given the growing necessity to the survival of this nation, we must then ask, who is the spiritual father of our country?*"Who is a liar but he that denieth that Jesus is the Christ? He is antichrist, that denieth the Father and the Son"*—I John 2:22. Isn't that just what we did by substituting self-evident truth for divine Truth? Isn't that what the entire doctrine of religious egalitarianism maintains? Isn't that essentially what President Obama set as a matter of national policy?

More immediately pertinent, that means that the aforementioned global redefinition is also based on Anti-Truth in accordance with the champion thereof. All of a sudden, America as the *"mother of abominations"* doesn't seem quite so out of the question. We made self-determination the global ideal, and ideas cannot and do not remain confined to their initial context. That had to begin a chain of consequences no human could have foreseen, yet which in retrospect we can see as inevitable. As the most immediately pertinent example, we've noted that if one takes protection of citizens as a government's primary function, then that government can do virtually anything it pleases in the name of that protection. Perhaps more importantly, especially when coupled with the secrecy deemed essential to that end, it can use virtually any pretense as a justification for its actions, thereby establishing the on-going lack of accountability necessary to continued arrogation of authority. Not coincidentally, that essentially defines the ruling Elite, most of whom remain safely anonymous: not only do the electorate not vote for the nation's true leaders, we are deliberately and systematically kept unaware of their very existence. That ties those sorts of activities directly to power, and power never voluntarily relinquishes itself but seeks to enhance itself instead. Since money is power, we can readily find the Profit Motive and those most successfully embracing it reaping the benefits, and again the two definitions of economy merge. With both its own survival and the continued arrogation of power as its motive, such a government will only very reluctantly give up its secrets and will seek to keep more instead, with who actually benefits from its actions chief among them. One can readily make the argument that certain things must be kept secret from the populace to facilitate government functioning, especially in time of war. But does the conflict between good and evil ever end? If not, does the necessity of secrets, lies and deception ever end? Again, just as we'd suspect from the role played by LOM, we find the survival imperative as our motivation in diametric opposition to the teachings and examples of the nominal head of this "Christian" country. Think about it. Who benefits from prevarication, and who benefits from Truth? Who seeks to save their lives, and who will lose them? Within those questions we find the answer to our title question.

We have noted that good vs. evil is inherently deceptive. As that implies, turning from overt evil does not necessarily mean that we've turned toward God, though good vs. evil would have us believe so. As a case in point, consider what appeared to have been accomplished during the Vietnam Era, contrasted to what was really accomplished. Given that the era's victories over social evils came about due to the government's concessions to the protesters, we could believe that power had been restored to the people. But think about it. Despite that self-evident return of power, since the Vietnam Era we've seen a steady *increase* in the Federal Government's influence over our lives as well as in the information it conceals from us. Consider too that every aspect of that increase invokes national security; again we find fear of man and man's law in an unholy blend and, as we found in pre-Revolutionary America, those laws benefit the Elite in ways profound and subtle, and that applies as much ecclesiastically as politically. For example, we've noted that when we define good as that which overcomes evil we allow the one defining evil to also define good. In practical terms, if someone else does the watching, they will also do the warning, which means they define what constitutes a threat as well as defining the steps necessary to deal with it. Again we establish an Elite defined as experts, and that's especially pertinent to the Christian depending on a doctrinal theology. As the term *seek* implies, it is the Christian's duty to remain vigilant and alert for ourselves, and again we see the difference between religion as a matter of Sunday morning rituals and as a way of life. Consider again I Thessalonians 5:2-6: *"Ye are all the children of light, and the children of the day: we are not of the night, nor of darkness. Therefore, let us not sleep, as do others, but let us watch and be sober."* Of all the translations of "sleep" given in various texts, *to live thoughtlessly* seems the most appropriate. That applies to each of us individually; ultimately no one can take that responsibility for another. Notice too that, in spite of the ancient and arbitrary dichotomy between them, faith and reason are meant to work in concert with each other.

Thus we find the well documented and oft lamented "dumbing down of America" to have a spiritual component as well. As George Orwell noted in his novel, *"1984"*, those who control the past exert an extreme amount of influence on the future, and the American government quite deliberately controls the past as taught in our schools. But the problem is not only with what is taught, but with *how*. Still again, we find an effort to deliver ourselves from evil delivering us to it instead. For example, the whole idea of *political correctness*, which greatly influences the nation's education, supposedly aims at fairness and the elimination of stereotyping. Instead, it really comes down to a very subtle and very effective form of mind control. Words are ideas: control the words one can and cannot use, and you control the thoughts one can and cannot think. Consider the parallel to *capturing every thought into the obedience of Christ*, and the fact that we seldom even hear His name outside a religious context. That grows considerably more important when we bear in mind that righteousness lies not in what we obey, but in whom.

Again too we find LOM and the Profit Motive involved. Because the U.S. textbook market is dominated by just four companies—Pearson, Vivendi, Reed Elsevier and McGraw Hill—and because they don't want their titles dropped over some tiny tidbit that some buyer might consider offensive, the whole educational system is effectively hijacked by an essentially anonymous force very similar to that controlling the rules Congress must obey. At one extreme, textbooks cannot make reference to dinosaurs (which might be considered an implicit recognition of the evolutionary theory), while neither can they refer to God, Satan, Christ or any other holy personage for fear of showing a religious preference. They cannot refer to black people who are petty criminals or on food stamps, or to Asian Americans who work hard (both of which would pander to racial stereotyping); nor can they deal with old people who are frail, or women who stay home to raise their children (age/gender stereotyping) in addition to other restrictions. Again we encounter that vexing question: why? *"The secret of superiority of state over private education,"* wrote pioneering American sociologist Lester Frank in 1897, *"lies in the fact that in the former the teacher is responsible to society. The result desired by the state is wholly different from that desired by parents, guardians, and pupils."* Note how that equates "society" with the "state" while casting the state in an adversarial relationship to pupils, parents and guardians, thereby implying the state as having a very separate agenda. There's nothing new about this: every totalitarian government ever to exist has tightly controlled education in still another variation on national security. In those cases as in America's, national security came down to the security of the ruling Elite.

How? The result of such control, wittingly or not, is to create a hermetic seal around the learning environment almost entirely lacking in international perspective, largely unaware of American history, especially it more unsavory aspects, and, most of all, isolated from any kind of critical thinking. How does this serve the security of the Elite? Consider: as a result, people who cannot think about complex issues, not necessarily because they lack the mental capacity but because they've never been taught the importance, or even the possibility of doing so, often tend to take out their resulting frustrations irrationally, and even violently. Indeed, those displays often tend toward the petulantly childish, right in line with the racial dematuration we've noted. This leads to demands for more laws, hence more power to the Elite who commonly ignore or circumvent such laws, while making the rest of us more subject to their arbitrary authority. But still more importantly, this results in still more "stupid laws" against which most of us rebel, again making us lawbreakers as a matter of conscious choice and active desire. Whose agenda have we just described? Who is the prince of the world? Beware: many of his *"ministers of righteousness"* have gone out into a world eager to embrace them, and they find an especially warm welcome in this one nation under God.

Knowledge and truth mean essentially the same thing. If we have defined reality in terms of self-evident truth, it follows that we define progress in similar terms. Since we have essentially equated self-evident truth with Anti-Truth, that in itself implies that we commonly define progress not only as movement away from divine Truth, just as freedom from God's authority suggests, but *toward* Anti-Truth, just as service to one master or the other suggests. We see this most obviously in measuring social progress in terms of overcoming restrictions of a Biblical origin. As a result of this progress, we hold *materialism* as the most fundamental of our self-evident truths manifest in our almost universal acceptance of science as the fountainhead of knowledge. Common usage notwithstanding, *materialism* refers to more than an absorption with physical things such as wealth and acquisitions. Rather, acknowledged or not, it is a philosophy maintaining the material universe as the totality of reality. Isn't that just what we would expect from Nature's God? Isn't that just what the *natural man* would desire? Isn't that the exact kind of perception the beasts utilize, and would they not reach similar conclusions were they capable of it? Doesn't that again cast those adopting that philosophy in the image of the beast? Doesn't that fit right in with Satan, the master of deception, using conventional economics as his means of interacting with and ruling the world? Ironic, isn't it: even our "free market economy", which we've demonstrated as both deceptive and duplicitous, amounts to freedom from God's authority.

In a similarly ironic sense, our increasing reliance on experts "frees" us for more mundane activities, such as deciding which of those conglomerates' products we will buy, right in line with taking the pursuit of happiness as our guiding principle, and consumerism as our philosophy of life. Such a proliferation of products and the associated choices add to the illusion of controlling our own destinies. Yet, that sometimes simultaneously creates a sense of hopelessness and confusion which generally grows more pronounced as we age and supposedly gain wisdom. Deliberate or not, that too serves a purpose. The fact that we must make so many trivial decisions coupled with our education squired disinclination to think critically leaves us with little energy and even less desire to delve into increasingly complex physical issues such as politics, economics, and international relations. More importantly, that holds still more true for spiritual matters, which explains the inherent appeal of the clergy/laity distinction. Rather than forming an intimate, personal relationship to Father and Son implicit in the very idea of a *walk with God*, most church-going Christians end up with a vague sense of affiliation not with the divine but with their denomination. More insidiously, this intensified need for spiritual experts opens the door for false messiahs, prophets and teachers who do the seeking for their patrons just as a worship "service" implies. Rather than an association emphasizing service to God, we have been long conditioned to take personal salvation as Christianity's crux, while largely leaving the service to the clergy. Inspired by the survival imperative rather than the Holy Spirit of Truth, that leaves us vulnerable to whichever of those teachers can best sell us his product. It's not coincidental that Christian religionists have long been called *merchants of hope*. Given that, consider Revelations 18:13 where an inventory of Babylon's merchandise includes *"the souls of men."* Maybe we've been sold a bill of goods which sounds hauntingly similar to our Bill of Rights. Then again, that Bill establishes our atmosphere of religious egalitarianism which leads us to believe that it really doesn't matter what we believe because we all worship the same god. Indeed we do, but *which* God?

While the serious Christian's duty is to grow in the knowledge of the Truth, we cannot divorce what we learn from how we learn it: Christ's church is founded on divine revelation and the indwelling Holy Spirit. Forgetting that is how we fall prey to those *unstable souls who wrest the scriptures to their own ends* (II Peter 3:16). As do any merchants, they endeavor to sell us what we want, and in our unchanged states we have no desire for divine Truth, but instead want to believe in the efficacy of the human spirit to deliver us from eternal evil. We've noted that efforts to deliver ourselves from evil inevitably deliver us to it instead. More often than not those evils involve the survival imperative, including that imperative translated into spiritual terms, and here we find an excellent case in point. Those doing such wresting try to teach inherently spiritual matters to those of the carnal mind toward the self-evident good of saving souls whom the Father has not called. As a result, rather than leading them to the *strait and narrow way*, they end up adding to the ranks of the *broad and spacious way* instead. That largely accounts for Christianity's burgeoning membership. *"Let us not therefore judge one another any more: but judge this rather, that no man put a stumbling block or an occasion to fall in his brother's way"*—Romans 14:13. Such huge numbers of physical converts establishes such worship as the Christian paradigm and that constitutes an enormous stumblingblock. In a still more fundamental and disastrous sense, it casts self-determination, *my will be done*, as that paradigm: we are saved because we decide to worship God in the manner prescribed by other men. No wonder democracy and religious freedom sweep the world as a holy tandem! Yet, consider what this ultimately means. We are led to replace the Holy Spirit with the human spirit—the unforgivable blasphemy against the Spirit discussed above—*as the Christian norm!* Given that Christ said that our Father must be worshiped *in Truth and in Spirit*, and given that He likewise said that *the flesh profits nothing* (John 6:63), must we not consider such contrary actions Antichrist in spite of their self-evident good appearances? Doesn't that make the majority of the mainstream

Christian religion Antichrist? Perhaps America has "Christian" roots after all.

The Mother Church demanded dependency on theological experts to just that end, and if we are to take Mother Teresa seriously (see above), we still need those experts to *"put Jesus there for us."* But far more fundamentally, the whole idea of a "religious service" involving the clergy/laity distinction in most cases presumes the necessity of a similar ecclesiastical expert for a similar purpose. Who has ordained them? What empowers them? If our Father has done so, we would expect them to confine their teachings to the Truth. Yet in many, many cases we find them *teaching the commandments of men as doctrine,* as often as not more concerned with form than with essence. Like a sorcerer's apprentice, they frequently must learn the proper incantations, rituals, movements, vestments and other fleshly manifestations deemed necessary to propitiate a God who must in fact be worshipped *in Truth and in Spirit.* In complete accord with religion as a "Sunday thing," many teach the physical "house of worship" as the proper place to do so, when in fact *we* are the temple of God. *"What? Know ye not that your body is the temple of the Holy Ghost which is in you, which ye have of God, and that ye are not your own?"*—I Corinthians 6:19. Our bodies, specifically our hearts, are where we truly worship God regardless of where we may be physically. If we don't worship Him there, we don't worship Him—*period.*

To worship God is to love Him. We noted Constantine's invisible empire and the divide and conquer motif. Let's forget the *conquer* and ask how we characterize the *divide* part. In the most basic sense, we see it in the dichotomy between the things of the earth and the things of heaven, especially when we take into account that *we cannot serve both God and Mammon.* That means that the division itself is not only the source of the conquest, it's the *objective* of the conquest! The whole idea is to divide our loyalties between God and something else, and the something else doesn't really matter just as specific "stuff" doesn't really matter in our consumerist philosophy. Patriotism, nationalism, love of family, false religion, love of money, good guys, bad guys, and many other divisions can accomplish that purpose which again epitomizes the idea of *striving* for *the strait and narrow gate*, and of doing so to the virtual exclusion of all other considerations. *To love God with all of our hearts, minds and beings*, the love that fulfills the Law, implies undivided devotion, and that essentially defines faithfulness. Suddenly, the idea of a worship service, where someone else essentially loves God for us, is shown as an utter absurdity. As with a good and devoted wife, the Christian is not true to the Lord some of the time. Indeed, as with sin per se, faithlessness is spiritual in nature, and comes down to heartfelt desire—i.e., what we truly desire, in spite of what we tell others or even ourselves. That concept will likely seem meaningless to the pagan, but to the Christian to whom this work is dedicated, that constitutes a sincere exhortation. We must remain focused on what really matters, and not allow the mundane concerns of daily life distract us regardless of their self-evident importance. Yet, our entire culture, American and global alike, considers such concerns the highest values, worthy of our attention, devotion, and even our very lives! That poses still another question we must all eventually face: we all must die; for what are we willing to do so? Look again at John 15:13: *"'Greater love hath no man than this, that a man lay down his life for his friends.'"* Then combine that with James 4:4: *"...know ye not that the friendship of the world is enmity with God? Whosoever therefore will be a friend of the world is the enemy of God."* Most of the world takes dying in the cause of enmity toward God as a high virtue! Doesn't that pretty well describe *the broad and spacious way leading to destruction?* The vast, vast majority of humanity unites under the God Life, and adopts the appropriate values and virtues, all of which conform to the world, all of which relate to good vs. evil defined by the world system, all of which seem wise to the *natural man*, and all of which constitute enmity toward God! If God is love, then love is god: that which we love exerts paramount influence over us. Thus, we could rightfully say that the world unites under love of life, at least in terms of what we most highly value and most ardently seek to preserve. Still again we find a mirror-image. *"He that loveth his life shall lose it; and he that hateth his life in this world shall keep it unto life eternal'"*—John 12:25.

It's really not hard to see how LOM and love of life go together since the wealthy have greater access to the pleasures money can bring. Then again, we should bear in mind that Christ mentioned the *"deceitfulness of riches"* in Matthew 13:22 as what *chokes the word*. Consistently, in a very fundamental sense, money is the key to controlling our destinies and the more money we have, the more control we can exercise. That casts economic freedom as the foundation of self-determination, just as we might expect by now. No wonder money plays such a preponderant part in our political system. Enough money amounts to power over others and such power is essential to controlling our own destinies. If taken far enough, money amounts to power over literally everyone on earth toward that end. Thus, control over the entire earth is the logically inevitable goal toward which both LOM and self-determination lead. Suddenly, America's desire for global hegemony makes a good deal more sense, while going a long ways toward answering our title question. Think about it: who *has the kingdoms of the earth to give to whomsoever he will?* What price did he demand? Our leaders are ordained of God, but they too must answer our Basic Questions, and they too can readily fall prey to the machinations of the Adversary. Yet, while the Elite may most dramatically manifest it, rich or poor, in our unchanged state we all share the same basic survival instinct, and the same inherent desire to preserve our way of life, regardless of how modest. Thus, love of life includes the love of our way of life, and the specifics or scale don't really matter just as the actual amount of money has nothing to do with LOM. We either love our lives in this world or we don't; there is no middle ground.

That love can take on some very subtle manifestations, many of which seem right, but in each case we find worldly values at the root. For example, fleshly worship requires political freedom which makes piety subject to the political control that LOM seeks. Think about that: not only is salvation subject to physical evil, but LOM can prove the ultimate savior from that evil. No wonder we throw money at every social ill. Thus, in order to attain salvation, we must overcome that evil and in the process, religion, economics, and politics intimately intertwine. If political or economic oppressors threaten our eternal survival, sooner or later we must take them as a great enough evil to rebel against and seek to overthrow. Good vs. evil blends with the survival imperative, and the Mark of the Beast wins out over the Truth embodied in our Savior. Once we take that step, it requires very little to take the same attitude about lesser oppressions that affect the other goods of our lives, and we soon find ourselves sucked into the world system of lies and deception thinking ourselves good for doing so. Our *garments thus spotted by the flesh*, we begin to justify ourselves with redefinitions of piety that accommodate our actions and we find self-evident truth replacing the far more difficult divine Truth that will actually save us.

With our break from England, we likewise broke with virtually everything English. That created an unanticipated social void that had to be filled. A nation (or any other group based on the human spirit) must have something to act as a social adhesive in order to remain unified. Traditionally, the Church would fill that need, but America's credo of separation of church and state made such a function impossible, at least formally. But if our governmental form is really our religion enacted, then we could not actually avoid that adhesive, but could only delude ourselves about it: one way or the other, we *must* serve. Sure enough, the very force that unified this nation even before the Revolution mandated that we take the things of the earth as our social unifier. Thus was American consumerism born, as both an economic and a philosophical principle, inspired by the mark of the beast in service to the god of this world. No wonder we take threats to our economic interests so seriously: just as individuals take challenges to their most deeply held beliefs as a kind of death threat, so America takes such threats to those interests as threats to its very foundation. Our educational system has long promoted the appropriate values by creating endless generations of mindless consumer robots, geared to fit into both the production and consumption of goods, goods and more goods. But again, there's a deeper issue involved.

Please remember that we do not mean to vilify the government or anyone in it. Quite the contrary, while powerful and largely anonymous Elites do undoubtedly exist, very probably exert unknown influence over government, and may even have nefarious agendas in mind, for the most part our leaders act to the best of their abilities. Moreover, Churchill was probably right: democracy, for all its faults, is most likely the best form of government man has yet to devise. Therein lies the problem, however. An inherently unclean tree cannot produce clean fruit. Goodness depends on what we obey; righteousness depends upon *whom* we obey. A stand for democracy is a stand for unrighteousness, for self-determination and all that they entail which, by definition, makes it Antichrist whether we intend that end or not. That strongly suggests democracy as a major part of the oft-mentioned *strong delusion*, a love for it the love of *the lie* that Paul mentioned. Consider again, dear Christian: unless we *actively* serve God, we serve His usurper by default, and we can't serve God without serving His Son; unless we *actively* serve God, we find ourselves enmeshed in the things of the world, with the survival imperative the most basic of them all, in direct opposition to the teachings and examples of that Son. The *whole world is under the sway of the evil one*, superficial differences notwithstanding, and that includes this one nation under God.

Given that America was born of rebellion against God's authority and Truth in favor of our own authority and self-evident truth, it shouldn't surprise us to find her having little interest in spiritual wisdom in favor of the pragmatic. We have repeatedly noted how the serious Christian relies on God's empowerment; secularists have their counterpart. There can be no doubt that wealth empowers us to do things we couldn't do otherwise—sort of the unholy Spirit of '76. Since it also facilitates the control of our own destinies, it seems inevitable that LOM and self-determination would walk hand-in-hand. If that's true, then we can reasonably surmise the Elite to be empowered by great wealth; that's how money can work to control the circumstances surrounding those possessing it. Thus, as we can say of LOM itself, we can also extend that to say that *the love of power* is the root of all sorts of evil, even as the connection to paganism cited above would suggest. Consider the irony: this nation dedicated to self-determination is ruled by those seeking power over others. Again, "hegemony" comes to mind. Given that, we can further extend that to say that the love of self-determination is the root of all kinds of evil since that is the primary reason for seeking wealth in the first place. Seeking wealth and serving Mammon come down to the same thing, and we cannot serve two masters. Again, we find the survival imperative's influence, for that Elite combination of wealth and power is what ultimately holds this nation together. For example, the wealthy, defined as those earning over $207,000 per year (single), while constituting a very small percentage of the population, contribute about 14% of the spending that keeps the economy rolling (Associated Press, 8/1/2010). Doesn't that put LOM at the heart of our social and political structure just as we'd expect from the role it played in our inception? No wonder we spend so much on national security.

That national security takes on some very subtle manifestations, some of which again pose the question of whose security we have in mind. We noted that there is actually little difference between educating and conditioning. For example, while obvious in the case of advertising and media programming, we are also conditioned to accept LOM and the consumerist philosophy all through our primary education, often including high school and even college. Think about it: since we more and more rely on experts, it follows that a lucrative career comes to those who provide that expertise. Here advertising and education merge. For the most part, we define the "good life" as having a good (lucrative) job (career) that allows for good times—the pursuit of happiness defined in material (consumerist) terms. But it doesn't stop with material consumption. We also see that increasing emphasis on specialization at the cost of a broader awareness. Does that have a somewhat sinister ring to it? Whose purpose does this serve? Consider: especially in lower grades, but often including high school, questions concerning the purpose of life and human destiny are banned, with the consumerist/materialist philosophy filling the void by default. Although they do so for a familiar reason—fairness—by doing so, public schools end up restricting the use of reason itself to the material world (hence the emphasis on math, physics, chemistry, and other natural sciences.) In that subtle manner, they propagate the philosophy that best suits the Elite: fulfillment through consumption. We deliberately create and assiduously foster an never ending lust for the things of the earth that Christ proscribes and which add to the power of the Elite. Moreover, unless we encounter it in our churches—many of whom have long since fallen prey to the same mindset—we never even think of questioning the fundamental philosophy that rules our lives, and call ourselves Christian anyway. Do you see the parallel to the intellectual Founders and those they would govern? (See above.) Who do we serve? That reemphasizes our natural disinclination to even seek much less abide by spiritual truths while tacitly promoting a materialist viewpoint to the exclusion of any other—our governmental form is our religion enacted whether we acknowledge it not. It essentially maintains us as *natural men* given to the *carnal mind* by conferring upon those who conform all the advantages and benefits the world has to offer in still another echo of Satan's final temptation of Christ.

We could argue that our elitist roots made government control of education inevitable from the beginning. As noted above, with our break from England and everything English, we found ourselves without a common unifier. As the Catholic Church before us had realized, and as held true for all her protesting offspring, the integrity of a political structure founded on the human spirit demands a set of common beliefs to hold it together. In America's case, in order to justify our very existence, we had to consider ourselves the good who had overcome evil throughout our history which meant to ignore a good many facts that the Elite would just as soon the general populace didn't know. Notice how that establishes the motif of keeping secrets from the people as necessary to national security. More fundamentally, we find good vs. evil at the cost of divine Truth common to both church and state. Protestantism had to take on essentially the same attitude to justify its violent break with Catholicism. Catholicism had to maintain that attitude to justify its numerous military campaigns and other opprobrious malefactions. As that required doctrine in the case of the churches, in our government's case it required the creation of national myths, legends and standards: we believe what we want to believe. In this case, however, we believe what someone else wants us to believe. Isn't the essential purpose of propaganda? Isn't that entirely inconsistent with the very idea of self-determination? Yet, isn't that the very essence of advertising which is absolutely essential to our consumerist lifestyle and so to our entire social structure? Who do we serve? Think about it: this nation dedicated to self-determination must resort to a series of deliberately manufactured lies that someone wants us to believe in order to maintain its national integrity and social cohesion just as we find it increasingly necessary to maintain our national security. That holds true in politics, in advertising ("truth in advertising" laws notwithstanding) and in education. Doesn't that seem an odd end for a nation nominally dedicated to self-evident truth? What does it suggest about how much we value truth even as a concept? The Church and its offspring incorporated pagan beliefs and symbols into their doctrines for much the same reason, suggesting both a common lack of divine Truth, and a common dedication to expediency. *"For the time will come when they will not endure sound doctrine; but after their own lusts shall they heap to themselves teachers, having itching ears; and they shall turn away their ears from the Truth, and shall be turned unto fables"*—II Timothy 4:3-4. The deadening of our critical thinking function keeps us inured to the fallacy of our myths even as they fall apart around us in the same way that a church service keeps us from seeking God's Truth for ourselves. The deceived do not recognize the deception, and never will without divine intervention. Yet, our whole society, indeed the very concept of self-determination, militates against even thinking in those terms. Who do we serve? Who is the master of deception, *the father of lies?* If we serve deception, do we not thereby likewise serve its master? If we teach lies as truth, do we not thereby avow our allegiance to *the father of lies?* Yet, think about it: given that we justify our very existence in terms of our goodness overcoming innumerable evils, if our true history were taught—the genocidal proclivity of Christopher Columbus, for example, or the cruel racism of Andrew Jackson—it would prove far more difficult to maintain the necessary myths that hold our social structure together. What does that imply about that social structure? Moreover, if we can't have justice without truth, what does that imply about how much we really value justice? If we don't value justice, how can we claim ourselves a nation of law? Suddenly, we begin to reveal the law that really matters to us: the law of survival. We seek self-destruction after all.

If Christ is "the Life," then His mirror-image is "The Death." That adds considerable import to our recurring question: who's really in charge here? We've noted that one must play certain games in Washington if one wishes to get anything done, but no one can say who originated those games nor who enforces the rules. That offers an intriguing possibility. What if the answer is *no one?* We build our metaphorical "house"—our lives—either on *the Rock or on the shifting sands* (see Matthew 7:24-27.) Christ defines those options as those hearing His words and doing them, or not doing them. On which have we built this nation? Haven't we largely defined our social progress as transcending outdated restrictions, often of a Biblical origin? Isn't the elimination of Christ and the divine Truth He embodies one of the major hallmarks of the religious freedom we take as emblematic of our national greatness? What we once held as good we now hold as evil: doesn't that define relativity not only in terms of good and evil but in terms of truth and even of reality itself? Don't redefining reality and distorting history mean essentially the same thing? Do we not base our entire sense of national greatness on relative goodness, the definition of which continues to change with the expediency of the moment? (Waterboarding and other torture techniques are "good" if they produce "actionable information" that helps to ensure our security.) We have no choice. If we base our national identity on such a fabrication, challenges to it constitute a death threat, one powerful enough to inspire automatic defense mechanisms sometimes referred to as the "fight or flight" response. While we normally hear that term used in a physical context, the same holds true psychologically and is equally involuntary: a significant enough threat causes us to either run from it or fight against it. What if the web of fabricated reality has grown so huge and elaborate, with the individual strands so interdependent that to seriously challenge one is to seriously threaten the entire structure—our entire sense of reality—with collapse? What if that structure has taken on a life of its own and also obeys the survival imperative while forcing us to follow suit? Think about it. In the absence of absolutes only relativity remains; in the absence of absolute good, only relative good remains, and relative good has no meaning without relative evil with which to contrast itself. If we take the good as that which overcomes the evil, then our relative goodness as well as our national identity *requires* evil, and it thus obeys the survival imperative quite independent of our wishes, determination, or even awareness. If we wish to consider ourselves a good nation we must cast ourselves as one that consistently overcomes evil: that becomes the focal point of our national survival imperative. We've eliminated the other social adhesives, so the lie is quite literally all that remains to keep us from falling apart. In short, we are held together socially by a number of carefully crafted and maintained falsehoods and myths that have redefined reality in our own image even as we have redefined Christianity to suit our own purposes.

In a very real sense, the "Great Experiment" of self-government has long since failed, but the illusions associated with it are too well developed for most of us to realize it. For example, we supposedly live in a representative democracy, but to what extent can we honestly say that our representatives act on the will of either the people in general, or even of their specific constituents? But the problem goes much deeper than that. If we accept the idea that the state's proper role is to protect the people, and that it must maintain secrecy in order to do so, then we must conclude that it cannot act as a government of and by the people and still maintain our security. In short, it has *failed.* To reiterate a point already made, to whatever extent the government acts without either the consent or the knowledge of the people it supposedly represents, especially when that includes those peoples' representatives, to that same extent it cannot be considered a government of or by the people. Moreover, especially given that the people's representatives usually are not informed, that defines the Administrative Branch as an Elite that arbitrarily decides what's best *for* the people, including what knowledge the people should have. Consider too that this in itself hints at an uncommonly acknowledged shift in the balance of power between the administrative and legislative branches—a shift characteristic of *fascism*. If we combine that with the well known and poorly hidden influence of corporate America, suddenly the aforementioned similarities to Nazi Germany and to Hitler don't seem quite so far-fetched. *"Fascism should rightly be called corporatism as it is a merge of corporate and state power"*—Benito Mussolini. He ought to know; he's the one who popularized the term.

But the parallels between corporatism and fascism go beyond superficial politics and economics, and again strike at the idea that our governmental form is our religion enacted. We've noted that the most chilling parallel to Hitler, a very probable Antichrist, doesn't lie in his politics per se, but in his maniacal devotion to my will be done. We have also noted that nothing on earth can more directly reify my will be done as does money. Taken together, that strongly suggests the American combination of self-rule and corporatism as the economy of the Antichrist. Bear in mind too that the Soviets declared themselves atheist, thereby adopting my will be done by default. Suddenly the similarities between the United States and both fascist Germany and the erstwhile Soviet Union don't seem so far-fetched. Indeed, the arbitrary political and economic divisions between us manifest the invisible empire's drive to divide in political terms in order to conquer in spiritual terms. Like it or not, we live in an absolute existence: we live as part of the kingdom of God, which has yet to visibly manifest itself on the earth, but which exists in the hearts of its constituents, or we live as part of the king of the earth, plainly visible to physical perception, but which will one day be swept away. We cannot do both, but efforts to get us to do both lie at the heart of the Spirit War. We've also noted that relative goodness has no meaning without relative evil to which to contrast itself. By declaring the Soviet Union atheist, Satan was able to make America look righteous by contrast while serving his agenda more fully than did the self-evident bad guys. The same holds true for WWII: self-rule must have seemed godly indeed contrasted to the blatant cruelties of the Axis, yet that "godliness" amounted to the essence of unrighteousness. The same also holds true for our current wars against terror. Idolatry, aka religious freedom, seems good by contrast to what the terrorists seem bent on imposing on the world. In fact, however, Christ's kingdom will feature only one religion, one universal belief, and one God who demands and will receive total, undivided devotion. Religion and politics merge: in essence, while we make war physically on such an imposition in the name of freedom, spiritually we make war on the concept of religious exclusivity at the heart of Christendom. We shall have **NO** other gods besides Him.

Serious Christians must look beneath the surface and seek the Truth for ourselves by way of humble petitional prayer! We must challenge the preconceptions hammered into our minds since our youth from school, Washington, the media, our entertainments, our peers, and even the pulpit. Thus we find the importance of the critical thinking we alluded to earlier, for in spite of the ancient and utterly arbitrary dichotomy between them, given the proper premise, faith and reason can and should work in harmony. For example, if we accept the premise of unknown and unknowable influence exercised over us by invisible forces within our government, virtually all of which involve huge sums of money, and given the necessity of the lies, deception, duplicity, and murder characteristic of the devil not only to our national survival but as inherent parts of our national policy, can we afford to discount Satan as one of those forces? More than that, given that these reflect the larger motif of freedom from divine authority, and given democracy's diametric opposition to the very concept of *Thy will be done*, the essence of righteousness, and its willing embrace and encouragement of idolatry guised as religious freedom, can we dare to dismiss the possibility of Satan at the core not of our government but of our *governmental system?* Given that we eliminated Christ from our national documents just as we replaced divine Truth with self-evident truth, can we doubt Satan and his Anti-Truth as our foundation? If we don't believe Christ, we believe His mirror-image instead, for we must serve one master or the other, and we take the one we serve as our ultimate definition of truth. If we're not under the influence of heaven, what influence remains? Who exercises deital-like influence over the entire world?

When the day comes when we must *take the literal mark of the beast* (see Revelations 13:16-17) *in order to survive,* people will ask: how can you refuse when it means that your children will suffer and possibly die? *What kind of parents are you?* Holding "innocent children" hostage is one of Satan's oldest and favorite tricks and constitutes one of the severest tests of our faith. Yet, it's not enough to believe in God; we must ask ourselves if we love and trust Him enough to put our lives and all that we associate with them on the line, including not only our own lives but those of our loved ones as well. Abraham did, and it was *"accounted to him for righteousness"*—Galatians 3:6. He was willing to sacrifice his only son, whom he loved very dearly, with no questions asked simply because God demanded it. The martyrs did likewise. Bear in mind that not only did they face the prospect of very unpleasant deaths, but they had to subject their loved ones, including their children, to the same threat. So will the martyrs of those end days: *"Fear none of those things which thou shalt suffer: behold, the devil shall cast some of you into prison that ye may be tried; and ye shall have tribulation ten days: be thou faithful unto death, and I will give thee a crown of life"*—Revelations 2:10. Do we believe that or not?

By contrast, those taking the mark in order to preserve their lives and the lives of their loved ones in those days will be seen as the good and the wise by everyone not gifted with spiritual perception. But while superficial circumstances differ, serious Christians confront that situation now in the face of criticism, ridicule, and thousands of subtle pressures which, in a way, makes the commitment harder. Political freedom guarantees that we don't have anyone threatening our physical lives if we refuse to conform to the world but, ironically, that makes it all the more tempting to do so, for sometimes it can prove easier to die for our beliefs than to live by them. Under those circumstances, the only threat we have to accept is the very real but intangible threat of the *Second Death* which, fittingly enough, relates to the gratification deferment we've mentioned. It makes avoiding those compromises a matter of faith summarized in the nearly forgotten virtue of *patience.* Patience can prove not only a very effective means of defense, but also an extremely potent offensive weapon. Satan is well aware of that.

We called the Constantine *coup* the hijacking of Christianity, and now we see why. By replacing Truth vs. Anti-Truth with good vs. evil, and so justice deferred with immediate retribution, we simultaneously replaced the Humble Servant with the Conquering King *and made ourselves subject to an idol of our own device!* We literally re-created Christ in our own image to suit our own purposes just as we see in America's "divine destiny:" we have *wrested the Scriptures to our destruction* (see II Peter 3:16.) Think about it: *not even Christ Himself knows the time of His return* (see Matthew 24:36,) and so the time of His transition from Humble Servant to Conquering King. When that identity changes, our relationship to Him will change accordingly, *but not until then.* It is obviously the idolatrous image of Jesus the premature Conquering King that Mr. Ashcroft and the American Revolutionaries had in mind (see above,) which demonstrates that the idolatry at this nation's foundation is still alive and well. Why not? It's the Jesus that most of mainstream Christianity has in mind, and has taught for hundreds of years! That is the Christ of good vs. evil—or, more accurately, the *Antichrist* of good vs. evil.

Think about it. Even the term *Conquering King* suggests righteousness as that which overcomes evil—which, ironically enough, it eventually will. Satan can't actually *create* anything, not even an original lie. All he can do is to twist and distort our perception of divine reality even as he does with self-evident truth. Case in point: that "righteousness," that self-evident divine approval, manifested in the very things of the earth that initially united thirteen highly disparate colonies into a single nation and which Christ and His representatives have long exhorted us to eschew. Doesn't that, by definition, make that unity Antichrist? We can find other signs of the *Synagogue of Satan* in our national history. As a primary example, some saw our startling victory over Britain, at the time the world's foremost superpower, as a sure sign of God's divine intervention and, indirectly, a divine sanction of liberty and self-rule. Yet, consider the fruits. We took that precedent as a divine mandate to run roughshod over the entire continent, taking whatever we wanted with no concern for the rights of those who possessed it. When you think about it, that is a fairly accurate definition of covetousness, but then our entire economy is based on just that which makes covetousness the foundation of our nation just as we'd expect from a unity based on LOM. *"Mortify therefore your members which are upon the earth; fornication, uncleanness, inordinate affection, evil concupiscence, and covetousness which is idolatry"*—Colossians 3:5. For a good many people, we can say that such an intense desire for the things of the earth essentially answers their Basic Questions, and that includes a great many professing Christianity. Thievery is bad enough, and is common to every political state in the world. America, however, did so with a pseudo-divine sanction, and that makes a world of difference. Consider the echo of God's commands to the Jews when taking possession of their Promised Land inherent in that sanction. Doesn't that imply the same kind of relationship? Doesn't that classify us as *those who call themselves Jews and are not Jews?* Isn't that clearly abiding by the Old Covenant which makes us fully subject to the Law and God's vengeance for those who break it? Quite the contrary, lying, cheating, stealing, even murder held true not only for the Native Americans and the Mexicans, but often for our fellows as well. *"I tremble for my country when I reflect that God is just; that His justice cannot sleep forever"*—Thomas Jefferson. A word to the wise: many of us believe that slumber is coming to an end. For those who have demanded justice, justice will be demanded of them. To those who have shown no mercy or forgiveness, none will be shown. Perhaps most of all, remember II Thessalonians 2:11-12: *"And for this cause God shall send them strong delusion, that they should believe a lie: that they all might be damned who believed not the Truth, but had pleasure in unrighteousness."* Verse 10 equates not the Truth itself but our *love of* the Truth with righteousness and those not accepting that love as both the unrighteous and the damned. Just as we must serve one master or the other, so we must abide by one truth or the other. Notice too that he says *"received"* not the love of the truth which makes us passive recipients, quite incompatible with the very notion of self-determination. By definition, a "strong delusion" is very difficult to detect, and in our unchanged states constitutes what we want to believe. Given that, a strong delusion and self-evident truth have a great deal in common, and that applies equally to the political and the ecclesiastical. If that's true, and we think this work has made a good case for it, then this nation is founded on just such a delusion.

Case in point. What an objective source would take as hypocrisy insinuated itself into our most basic national definition now clearly manifest in Iraq, Afghanistan, and in the more than 150 nations where America has established a military presence, often covertly. Again we can find a parallel to Constantine. America has succeeded where the others failed; our conquests stay conquered, and have never seriously challenged us. Spain, Portugal, France, even Great Britain, all had their colonies and the riches derived from them, yet all gradually declined, eclipsed by the New World. That seemed reconfirmed by our ideological victory over the Soviet Union, leaving America the world's only true superpower. How can we not see it as a logical conclusion to that divine Destiny Manifest so long ago? After so many decades of defining the Cold War in terms of good vs. evil, how could we not see this as a major victory for global good? But don't overlook the import of the fact that America won an *ideological* victory. That not only Manifested America's Destiny but helped to specifically define it in economic terms! That which initially united us had now defeated our greatest adversary, the "evil empire," and now seemed destined to bring prosperity and happiness to everyone on earth. No wonder we've so long equated our material prosperity with God's approval, and no wonder we had such good reason to believe it: this represented the quintessence of self-evident truth. *"Set your affection on things above, not on things on the earth"*—Colossians 3:2. We serious Christians can no longer ignore the question associated with that: *do we believe it or not?* If we do, then we had better start acting accordingly; if we don't, then we've answered our title question. Those things of the earth are not necessarily confined to the tangible.

Religion and politics merge in a cryptic statement that, taken out of context, could be used to justify violence in Christ's name.

Matthew 10:34: *"'Think not that I am come to send peace on earth: I came not to send peace but a sword.'"* We spoke earlier of the futility of seeking external peace, and that we should seek the internal peace Christ promises instead. Here's why:*"And when ye shall hear of wars and rumors of wars, be ye not troubled: for such things must needs be; but the end shall not be yet'"*—Mark 13:7. External conflicts, major or minor, individual or collective, are all destined to come to pass, and, as with evil in general, they act to pose the question of whether or not we believe Christ's Truth. Simply consider how many conflicts we have engaged in with the stated purpose of establishing peace on earth, yet rather than coming closer to attaining it, it forever seems all the more elusive. As long as we cling to good vs. evil with good defined as that which overcomes the evil, we shall never know external peace, for the survival imperative cannot allow it. Thus, battle lines have in fact been drawn, as Christ's subsequent statements clearly imply, and the reason is explicitly clear. We must love Father and Son more than anything else on earth, including parents, family, possessions, lives, and most certainly our country. aqui

The natural man and those given to the carnal mind can never understand that. By taking nature as our cynosure we can find plenty of self-evident reasons to engage in violence. Indeed, violence and territorial conflict seem inextricably woven into the very fabric of physical existence. We've touched on the "struggle for survival" characteristic of the animate world, including the floral, but consider as what an incredibly violent a place science portrays even inanimate nature. The stars, for example, don't really burn in the conventional sense, but instead detonate countless megatons of nuclear energy every second. Yet, if it were not for those explosions on the sun's surface, life on earth could not exist. As if that were not enough, some of the larger stars eventually explode into unimaginable bursts of destructiveness, and yet science calls the remnants of these explosions the stuff of life itself. We arise from destruction only to end in destruction (see above): it would seem that we seek self-destructiveness after all as an inherent part of our natures. In a similar vein, we find weather patterns, also essential to life on earth, portrayed as conflicts between different kinds of air masses trying to occupy the same space at the same time. We even cite the fact of tectonic movements that create the violence of earthquakes, tsunamis, and volcanic eruptions as evidence of our "living earth" which, in a fundamental sense, makes conflict what differs ours from a "dead" planet such as the moon or Mars. Given that all of these are aspects of Nature's God, and the natural world we've taken as our paradigm, can we wonder that violence and conflict play such an integral part in our lives? Given what Paul says, can it surprise us to find these as the pursuits and concerns of the *natural man?*

"He that believeth on the Son hath everlasting life: and he that believeth not the Son shall not see life; but the wrath of God abideth on him"—John 3:36. That encompasses a good deal more than simply accepting Christ's existence, even if we intellectually accept Him as the Son of God. It must also include believing what He said, what He taught, and what example He put forth, including walking in *"the meekness of wisdom"* (James 3:13). We summarize that wisdom as a devotion to God's will as the Humble Servant, offering no defense of any physical value even including His physical life. By contrast, our every conflict has to do with some physical value, beginning with basic survival and extending to all that we associate with it. We can safely say that after Christ's advent, *not one battle has been fought in the name of the true Son of God.* Nor will there be until the advent of the Conquering King. Do we believe that or not? How we answer that question answers our title question.

Epilogue

We call ourselves the *land of the free,* yet we have more restrictions on individual freedom than any nation in history, and add more restrictions by the year. There's nothing especially revelatory about that; indeed, it's relatively common knowledge, yet very few seem to care about the inherent contradiction nor explore its implications. Nor do many seem inclined to explore the implications of the fact that those same restrictions actually make us freer and more prone to break God's law and that we champion that fact both as moral progress and as the global ideal. Instead of standing firm in the name of Christ's Truth, much of mainstream Christianity aligns itself with the Freedom God in the name of toleration, and fairness yet, at the same time it embroils itself in sometimes violent controversies over issues of good vs. evil in defiance of Christ's commandments. We have replaced a brotherhood of Christ with the brotherhood of man as our ideal just as we have replaced serving and pleasing God with serving and pleasing ourselves. If we do so and still call ourselves Christian, how does our hypocrisy differ from the Pharisees? If it does not, how do we expect to inherit the kingdom of heaven? That should be the Christian's ideal, the purpose to our lives, but many of us have likewise long since traded the things of the earth for the things of heaven. That's the one essential characteristic of America that it fights and kills to defend.

If our political system is our religion enacted, and if we can demonstrate that this country is not what it says it is politically, and is instead Antichrist, can we not at least suspect the same about the national religion of which that government is a reflection? More specifically, although many claim this a Christian nation at least in its origins, based on the fruits resulting from those roots, must we not see that claim as spurious? If we broaden that question, again judging by its works, must we not take a great

290

deal of the worldwide Christian religion as equally apostate? If that's the case, can we not see that religion as a major element of the Great Apostasy, just as we'd expect from the Deceiver and his legions of false prophets and *wolves in sheep's clothing* masquerading as *ministers of righteousness?* The Antichrist will lead both politically and ecclesiastically. Given that, can we not expect to find the Great Apostasy reflected in politics as well as in religion? Can we not see the Great Apostasy unfolding before our very eyes? Can we not trace it back to the Constantine coup nearly two thousand years ago?

Constantine gained *de facto* control over both the Roman Empire and the Roman Church, thereby inextricably blending religion and politics. He did so by establishing himself as the good by overcoming evil just as we consider ourselves a great nation for essentially the same reason. As a result, the Mother Church spent many centuries and countless lives trying to subject the globe to its vision of goodness in the name of the Son who promises us *"peace, not as the world giveth"* and, much more importantly, told us that *no one comes unto Him unless our Heavenly Father so calls him.* Every combatant considers itself the good, its adversary the evil, so in a very basic sense the Church conformed to the world's standards and made itself one with the pagans in a grand example of masquerading as a minister of righteousness. Very little has changed. Consider again a question already posed: taken as a whole, which does the mainstream Christian religion more closely resemble, the Son of God teaching peace and meekness, or a warrior emperor emphasizing strength, guile, and conquest? Which does this nation manifest as evidence of its greatness?

Look beneath the surface! Beneath those warrior attributes we find deception, guile, and murder—characteristics intimately associated with he *who was a murderer from the beginning*—in the exact combination we find increasingly evident in our global battles for national security! Even as we once fought in defense of the faith, we now fight in defense of our way of life. *There is no difference*, for our way of life is our faith enacted. Self-evident faith and true Faith each squire diametrically different ways of life. For what does a physical warrior fight if not for the survival imperative, if not of self then of cause or nation? For what do we fight? What do most seek when they go to church? Consider what this means. That means that deception and murder in both the literal and spiritual senses have moved beyond a means to the end of maintaining national security and have become the *essence of* the nation we seek to secure even as they have long since become the essence of most of mainstream Christianity! We find the *mark of the beast* at the foundation of both!

If we come to Church seeking salvation, we come to Church with the intention of saving ourselves in response to the survival imperative just as would the beasts were they capable of it! Fear, fear of death above all, rules the animal kingdom, but *love* fulfills the Law. *"There is no fear in love; but perfect love casteth out fear: because fear hath torment. He that feareth is not made perfect in love"*—I John 4:18. That fear certainly applies to the fear of perdition which the false prophets use to herd huge numbers of "believers" onto the *broad and spacious way.* Ironically, they thereby manifest a divine Truth in spite of themselves: efforts to deliver ourselves from evil inevitably deliver us to it instead. Their ultimate appeal lies in the idea of saving ourselves, just as the Church has long tacitly taught. Thus we find the dénouement of self-determination defined as Antichrist, yet carefully nurtured in mainstream Christianity and finally coming to full political fruition in this one nation under God. No wonder we had to substitute self-evident truth for divine Truth just as man-derived doctrine does. We believe what we want to believe, but in our unchanged states we have no interest in nor desire for divine Truth, and readily accept the suave Anti-Truths put forth by the Adversary. *The desires of our father the devil we want to do*, and the things of the devil and the things of man are essentially the same things. This country, as with every country, devotes itself to just those things, making them not only their purpose in existing but, for all practical purposes, making them their very definition! Shake off the politically correct propaganda and consider—*seriously* consider—what we have done. We have come to believe that we can worship any deity we chose in any manner we chose, to any extent we chose and still reasonably expect to inherit God's kingdom! Who do we serve? Which

"Jesus" did the revolutionaries and Mr. Ashcroft have in mind? How can we claim a foundation on the One telling us *to love our enemies*, and yet find ourselves bent on destroying our enemies by annually spending more on the tools of war than the rest of the world *combined?*

Is this the walk in the Spirit that Paul describes? Consider Luke, chapter nine. Christ and His Apostles approach a Samaritan village while on their way to Jerusalem. The Samaritans do not receive them and, *"When His Disciples James and John saw this, they said, Lord, wilt thou that we command fire to come down from heaven, and consume them, even as Elias did? But He turned, and rebuked them, and said, 'Ye know not what manner of spirit ye are of. For the Son of Man is not come to destroy men's lives, but to save them'"*—Luke 9:54-56. We save lives—presumably American lives—by *destroying* the lives of other men—not to mention women and children. This, too, is the "Jesus" Mr. Ashcroft had in mind. Isn't that, by definition, Antichrist? Think about it. Where does Christ or any of His Apostles tell us to do that? Noble embellishments notwithstanding, that still reflects the survival imperative and the God Life. Moreover, given the ties between national interests and national security, that also reflects LOM and plutocratic Elite that actually run this country. When you think about it, it figures that the God Life would stress the survival imperative, and it figures that those with the highest investments in the world system would rank among its staunchest supporters. Thus we reveal the God Life's true identity.

Again we find religion and politics merging in the person of Constantine, for he garnered both glory and riches for his empire. If we accept the premise that he usurped Christ's role as the head of His Church, as the political Church's subsequent actions strongly suggest, then by definition we must cast him as Antichrist. If that's the case, then we must likewise cast the religion—or *religions*—growing from that usurpation as Antichrist. That casts the followers of those religions as those *"who went out from us"* (I John 2:19.) If we find our own government in that same mold, how can we avoid the same conclusion about it? If we accept our political system as our religion enacted, then we must ask some difficult questions. Who would prompt us to seek freedom from both Father and Son, and then pat ourselves on the back for our great wisdom? Who stresses lies, deceptions, and murder as his major means of operation? Who is the *prince of this world, and who offered Christ its kingdoms in return for an act of veneration?* How did Christ respond? Most of all, who stresses *my will be done*, and whom do we serve by doing so?

Our way of life is our faith enacted. Christians are called to devote themselves to the Truth, but how many of us actually do so? We spoke at some length about how our history teaches us the necessary American myth often far removed from the truth. Parents routinely do the same sort of thing, resorting to fictions such as the Bogyman, Santa Claus and so forth in order to elicit desired behavior from their children. That commonality suggests a broader and still more disturbing fact. What subtle message gets imparted later when we learn the truth, especially when we learn that those telling us those lies knew the truth all along? To put it another way, what basic element of both good citizenship and overall good behavior gets imparted? The idea that it's OK for important authority figures to lie to us in order to achieve a "good" cause. We forget about the Bogyman, and usually don't care about Ben Franklin's womanizing, but the truth that it's OK to lie gets firmly embedded and remains as one of our most fundamental lessons and as one of the most fundamental aspects of our good citizenship. In that same fundamental manner, we find lies—America's "divine destiny" comes to mind—at the very foundation of our entire society as the essential glue holding the nation together. Suddenly the devaluation of absolute Truth as a concept gains considerable import. Consider again Matthew 5:37: *"'But let your "Yes" be "Yes." and your "No" be "No." For whatever is more than these is from the evil one.'"* Consider also Revelations 21:8, where the Lamb says that *"all liars"* will *"...have their part in the lake which burneth with fire and brimstone: which is the second death."* Come out from them, dear friend, and be separate.

Again we mean this not as an indictment but as a *warning.* Ironically, in many cases the fault lies not in the Messiah they've chosen but in the manner in which they follow Him. In some ways it comes down to the fact that we don't take Him seriously when He says that He is *the way*, and that the Father must be *worshipped in Truth and in Spirit.* Think about it. Worshipping God in *Truth and in Spirit* and pursuing the things of heaven have so much in common as to be virtually synonymous. So do worshipping God in the flesh and pursuing the things of the earth. To which is good vs. evil more appropriate, and to which is Truth vs. Anti-Truth? Again we pose our title question. John Foster Dulles pretty well summarized the official American view: *"For us, there are two sorts of people in the world: there are those who are Christians and support free enterprise, and there are the others."* Talk about believing what you want to believe! Read the New Testament and then ask yourself if you can see the Son of God depicted therein as an advocate of our rabid devotion to the free market. The vast majority of Americans try to serve two masters, and that cannot happen. We cannot follow the true Son of God and derive our values and virtues from the world-system, so again we pose our title question. Think about it: which has a greater general appeal, Christ's way of asceticism or the "he-who-dies-with-the-most-toys-wins" attitude common to consumerism? On which have we founded this "Christian" nation? One nation under *which* God?

When we dethroned King George III, the power behind the throne went with him, and we declared our allegiance to quite a different deity. *"An evil man seeketh only rebellion: therefore a cruel messenger shall be sent against him"*—Proverbs 17:11. Throughout both Testaments, *"an evil man"* refers to Satan. Look who we find as that evil man's chief agent on earth guised as ministers of self-righteousness! We've defined our entire sense of progress as rebellion of one sort or another, certainly including an ongoing rebellion against God's authority. But for all that, there is a bit of truth to the American myth. Although clearly rebellions and such antedated the United States, no other country has achieved the same kind of mystic aura as a result. Consider again both the Ashcroft quote and the John Foster Dulles quote above, not as individuals but as representative of the general American character, and then again consider: *"For such are false apostles, deceitful workers, transforming themselves into the apostles of Christ. And no marvel; for Satan himself is transformed into an angel of light. Therefore it is no great thing if his ministers also be transformed as the ministers of righteousness; whose ends shall be according to their works"*—II Corinthians 11:13-15. That could very well prove to be America's actual divine destiny.

By their fruits may we judge. Our entire national government revolves around necessary lies, necessary evils, necessary murders, necessary deception, all deemed necessary to the self-evident good of survival both physical and fiscal, with the latter frequently superseding the former. If we grow up believing that it's acceptable for an authority source to lie to us for a good cause, can we wonder that our government believes it as well? Given that such a situation makes a government of the people and by the people impossible, that means that we in this country quite literally live a lie politically even as those who do not walk in the Spirit literally live a lie spiritually. Doesn't that seem an appropriate fruit to come from seeds of self-evident truth and a foundation of the human spirit applied first to religion and then to politics? At the same time, doesn't that seem a very appropriate end to following the prince of Anti-Truth? What does that make of self-determination? If fruit must follow its seed, who does that cast as the author of self-determination? Who does it cast as the father of our country? If we must serve one master or the other, then we must accept self-determination itself as a lie, and with it freedom from absolute authority. If we don't accept that we must serve one master or the other, then we call Christ a liar. Think about it: the issue of self-determination itself constitutes not only an on-going rebellion against God's authority but also an effort to put ourselves in His place. Do we not attribute most if not all of our progress, especially our moral progress, to rebellion? Haven't many if not most of those rebellions been against restrictions with a religious (Biblical) origin? If our march toward "goodness" has led us away from God's Truth, whom have we been following—and toward what end? At what price have we sold our national soul?

Fear and love are the two greatest motivators in the human experience. Although the difference between human love and divine love can prove difficult to see superficially, we can find a very significant difference. Human love engenders fear of loss thereby provoking fear of those who can harm or kill the body and the resultant defensiveness which cancels out meekness, forgiveness and, ultimately, the unconditional love central to Christianity. By contrast, divine love eliminates fear: once we accept Thy will be done as our guiding principle, we realize that there is quite literally nothing to worry about, for *"we know that all things work together for good to them that love God, to them who are the called according to His purpose"*—Romans 8:28. Note the operative term: *all*. Here too we find a sharp contrast. Every secular conflict revolves around human love and the associated fear of loss, but now it's gone further than that.

As we've noted, contemporary political bodies more and more lean on fear as the source of their power. Still, not all fears are deliberately manufactured. Wars, violent crime, rumors (and evidence) of government malfeasance, global warming, pandemics, and other elements have begun to collide, yielding the sense that the world, and maybe even the universe is beginning to spin out of control. For a great many years we took the lack of divine chastisement as evidence that God approved of our course and, so, took seeking His Truth as of little importance. Now however, energized by the fear generated by 9/11, we find religion and politics blending in ever increasing transparency and, with it, ever more frequent calls for a return to the values that established this nation, not realizing that we now endure the inevitable harvest of those values. Many others have taken to reading spiritual mentors of innumerable schools in a desperate effort to find an inner peace that their erstwhile spiritual beliefs can't provide. At the same time, a great many have turned to traditional Christianity in all its multitudinous variations, but many find both of the above wanting. The old lies no longer work, and we've begun to realize that believing what we want to believe is ultimately a dead end as well. Most of us, however, have yet to realize that fear does not fulfill any law but that of survival, and so we find the spiritual connection to the mark of the beast. Many flock to churches and temples in frantic efforts to find peace and salvation, yet most find none.

We thus find ourselves left with a void aching to be filled, and find self-determination inadequate to the task. *"When your fear comes as desolation, and your destruction comes as a whirlwind; when distress and anguish come upon you. Then they shall call upon Me, but I will not answer; they shall seek Me early, but they shall not find Me"*—Proverbs 1:27-8. But that aching void serves a sinister purpose indeed. For one day—one day soon, many of us believe—one will arise who will offer hope to the fearful, salvation to the masses, and the mark of the beast to all. Then will come the final fruition of divine revelation, for those lacking it will not survive.

The mainstream Christian religion counts on learning as its means to salvation. Ironically, we will indeed learn a great deal when the *Day of the Lord* finally arrives. Self-determination, the essence of both democracy and of the mainstream Christian religion featuring that kind of salvation, will begin to reap its ultimate harvest as many fail to recognize the difference between learned doctrine and the *implanted Word of God*. Thus we will finally come to realize the full value of divine Truth and the futile folly of striving for goodness. Think about it: if God is good, then good is god. Thus, to strive to be good is to strive to be God—Satan's objective all along! That's why the Truth of a single word makes all the difference: **ONLY** God is good! In a very similar manner, they will fail to see the difference between the empowerment of the Holy Spirit and that of the human spirit. *"There is therefore no condemnation to them which are in Christ Jesus, who walk not after the flesh but after the Spirit"*—Romans 8:1. Walking after the flesh and worshipping God in the flesh lead to the same condemnation. Perhaps most importantly of all, many of us will come to realize that Christ did not die in order to save us! In actuality, He fervently prayed in Gethsemane that: *"'Father, if it is Your will, remove this cup from Me; nevertheless not My will, but Yours, be done.'"* (Luke 22:42.) Given the context, we could call that brief statement the essence of the Grace Economy and so of salvation. How can we reconcile that with *my will be done*, the essence of this democratic government that we evangelically spread to the world? How can we reconcile that with "coming to Jesus" as the essence of personal salvation as

Christianity's proper centerpiece? Only then will we recognize the mark of the beast in its true spiritual context. We will learn that our efforts to deliver ourselves from God's authority have delivered us to His judgment, and to the extent that we have demanded justice be done upon those who have offended us, a similar demand for justice will be laid upon us. In human understanding, mercy and justice are diametric opposites, but God's mercy *is* the Law, and so the *definition of justice*. Thus, to fail to accept that mercy is to fail to keep the Law, and to therefore be subject to the appropriate dispensation of more traditional justice. How can we reconcile that with our innumerable forays in search of justice or vengeance in defense of our "homeland"? Judgment, especially when defined as condemnation, is an absolutely essential element of good vs. evil; thus again, we see both as primary characteristics of the *Synagogue of Satan*.

Consider an episode occurring in Luke, chapter 12. While the scribes and Pharisees sought a way to contradict Christ, a huge crowd gathered around Him *". . .insomuch that they trode one upon another . . ."* (Luke 12:1.) Note that carefully: they quite literally tried to come unto Him in the flesh, just as Judas tried to follow Him in the flesh (see above). Yet Christ did not warn this huge gathering of the hypocrisy of the Pharisees, but only His inner circle of twelve. *"Beware ye of the leaven of the Pharisees, which is hypocrisy'"*—Luke 12:1. Why did He chose this particular moment to do so? Based on what He'd said earlier, we may intuit that only these would be able to hear His words, but there's more to it than that. Consider the commonality between that crowd and the Pharisees. The crowd put on a *show* of piety in trying to come to Christ which, considering the fact that they trampled one another, we cannot take as genuinely motivated by divine love. On the contrary, that conjures up an image of people stampeding in a panic from fear of a threat to their lives or wellbeing—i.e., motivated by the survival imperative. Do you see the parallel to those coming to church in a frightened effort to save their eternal skins? Even as that was happening, Christ was telling His disciples, *"For there is nothing covered that will not be revealed, nor hidden that will not be known.'"* (12:2.) That statement, of course, implies divine revelation. More than that, however, it also implies a different kind of perception. Obviously He didn't speak of crowd's actions, for they were plainly visible to anyone with eyes. What remained to be revealed was their *motivation,* which was quite different from what it appeared. Consider that huge crowd as described, all united in their efforts to come to Christ in what could be taken as an evangelical model, yet clearly not united in love—sadly, also often reflective of evangelical congregations. In essence, they were all united in their belief that this Man was worth reaching in terms of spiritual survival, just as we find in most mainstream Churches today. What will be known is that those actions reflected the hypocritical pseudo-piety of the Pharisees.

We have posed some serious questions for your consideration. Let us add a few more. Each of us will face the Judge alone, and will be judged according to criteria that we can't begin to comprehend. One thing we can and *must* understand is that Christ, the Truth incarnate, will testify either for or against us. By definition, that makes divine Truth the foundation for that testimony. What do you want Him to say about you? Perhaps more pertinently, what can you legitimately *expect* Him to say about you? Do you expect Christ to confess to His Father that you're a good person and therefore *deserve* salvation? If so, then do you also expect Him to confess that His sacrifice was in vain and that His Father's plan for our salvation was flawed if not entirely unnecessary? In short, you found your claim to salvation on a rebuke of the One judging you. That doesn't sound like an especially strong opening argument, yet in myriad forms a great many religions do just that, summarized in the sentiment that "good people go to heaven." We fail to remember the *"sword with two edges"* mentioned above, and that such a sword describes our Lord reflecting the judgment of His Father. Christ warned us to *fear Him who can destroy body and soul in hell,* but most of us paid no attention. Nope, we wanted to believe in self-determination, and self-evident truth which means that we ultimately put all our hopes in our own goodness and wisdom. No matter how you slice it, claiming goodness whether defined as obedience or as inherent, comes down to *deserving* salvation, and even a novice Christian can tell you that such is entirely contrary to the whole idea of Grace. To put it a bit more intellectually, that is contrary to God's will and, so, to righteousness, which makes *unrighteousness* our claim to deserving salvation. Doesn't that sound just a wee tad like Antichrist? Wouldn't' we logically expect "anti-salvation" from such a belief? Christ Himself disclaimed any inherent goodness (see above), but even if we ignore that, consider: *Christ perfectly kept the Law and died any way.* That summarizes the biggest single difference between the Old and the New Covenant: *even obeying the law does not keep it*, for God has reinterpreted it. God's mercy is the law, and the only way we can fulfill that law is to depend entirely on that mercy, for *"Mercy triumphs over judgment"* (James 2:13.) Any claim to goodness founded on obedience, regardless of how justifiable, reflects unrighteousness, and still reaps the appropriate rewards.

Consider some further questions germane to much of orthodox Christian doctrine. Do you want the Son of God to confess to His Father that you fought against evil your whole life when He told you to *resist not an evil person and to turn the other cheek?* Do you want Him to confess that you did so because you considered yourself a loyal American (Dane, Scot, Russian, Spaniard, etc.,) even though James warned *that friendship to the world is enmity toward God* or that Paul says that *our citizenship is in heaven* (Philippians 3:20)? Do you expect God's mercy when you demanded justice be done against your enemies? Do you expect Him to forgive you when you did not forgive others? Do you expect Him to show mercy on you when you showed none on your fellows? Do you expect Him to defer His vengeance when you did not defer yours? Do you want Him to confess your aggressiveness when He told you that *the meek shall inherit the earth?* Do you want Him to confess your avarice and lust for the things of the earth and the system that supported them in spite of His repeated warnings to eschew such things? Shall He honor your claim for a share in the kingdom of heaven when you spent your life seeking a piece of the prosperity pie? Do you expect to validate your claim to the crown of life as a result of spending your life pursuing the things of the earth? We can begin to see that justice in the traditional sense is integral to Christianity after all: as we do unto ourselves, so will be done unto us.

The pagan and the non-believer will find such questions nonsensical, but we have aimed this work at the serious Christian who presumably does not. So long as earthly concerns motivate us—be they as lofty as democracy, equality, the sanctity of family, the brotherhood of man and so on, or as mundane as the consumption of consumer goods—we live as part of the earth and therefore keep ourselves separate from the kingdom of God. To reiterate a final time, although we cannot serve two masters neither can we avoid service to one or the other! If we don't *actively* serve the Truth, we serve His usurper by default, and that makes *complacency*, the lukewarmness we mentioned citing Revelations, one of the deadliest maladies facing humanity. The opposite holds equally true. So long as we keep ourselves focused on the things above, on spiritual and heavenly concerns, then the travails and tribulations of the world matter not, for we see them in their finite time-frame and know that they will pass. *Let patience have its perfect work*. It has taken me over eighteen years to write that sentence, and it was well worth the wait.

Although we've written this for the serious Christian, even if you lack God-given faith and perception, we urge you to carefully consider what you've read in these pages. If you feel you should challenge these ideas, by all means do so. We intend this as a book of questions, not as answers; we want it to provide the impetus for further discussion and inquiry, not as a destination. But, to that end, don't be afraid to humble yourself before the Lord—indeed, we should greatly fear *not* doing so, for that failure is what brings about His wrath. Avoid the hubris inherent in trying to fathom the mysteries of the ages by way of your own intellect: Christ's Truth is *divinely revealed*, not excogitated.

As for those who have read this primarily as a matter of curiosity, we'd like to leave you with one final question: *what if the Bible is true?* Although a number of premises must be taken on faith, we invite you to accept them any way just for the sake of argument. If you do that, we think you'll find the conclusions very consistent, quite logical, and very reasonable. Given the proper premise, you'll find that rather than contradicting each other, faith and reason can work in cooperation.

In the main however,
Christ Himself summarized why we've written this:
Mark 13:37:
"And what I say to you, I say to all: Watch"
God bless you.
-30-